JONATHAN NEALE is the author of two non-fiction books and one novel. He has had ten plays produced in Britain in the last fifteen years and has a Ph.D. in social history. He speaks some Nepali and a little Sherpa.

Also by Jonathan Neale

Memoirs of a Callous Picket

*The Cutlass and the Lash: Mutiny and
Discipline in Nelson's Navy*

The Laughter of Heroes

Mutineers

The American War: Vietnam, 1960–1975

Lost at Sea

Tigers of the Snow

by

Jonathan Neale

An *Abacus* Book

First published in the United States
of America in 2002 by Thomas Dunne Books
First published in Great Britain in 2002 by Little, Brown
This edition published by Abacus in 2003

A CIP catalogue record for this book is available from the British Library.

ISBN 0 349 11350 5

Typeset in Giovanni Book by
Palimpsest Book Production Limited,
Polmont, Stirlingshire

Printed and bound in Great Britain by Clays Ltd, St Ives plc

Abacus
An imprint of
Time Warner Books UK
Brettenham House
Lancaster Place
London WC2E 7EN

www.TimeWarnerBooks.co.uk

For my father,
Terry Neale,
with love

CONTENTS

Maps

INTRODUCTION

In 1965 I was a sixteen-year-old boy in India. My school, Colvin Taluqdar's College in Lucknow, chose three boys to go to the Himalayan Mountaineering Institute in Darjeeling. I was one of them, probably because I was the only foreigner in the school.

Most of the year the Mountaineering Institute ran climbing courses for adults, but in the winter they ran adventure courses around Darjeeling for schoolboys. We trekked, made camp, read maps, and took compulsory cold showers at six in the morning. I made friends with boys from all over India.

The instructors were Sherpas, and we were in awe of them. Nawang Gombu, a stocky bear of a man, had climbed Everest two years before with the Americans and would, on that spring's Indian expedition, become the first man to climb it twice. Tenzing Norgay, who had climbed Everest with Hillary in 1953, was director of the institute. He came back from vacation on the last day of our course. When three of us boys saw him standing in the entrance to the institute, we stared at him in admiration. He smiled diffidently at us, the closest I've ever been to greatness.

The Sherpa instructors on our course were young, and I had never met men like them. They were supremely confident physically, strong and easy as they stood. And yet they were gentle men, soft-spoken and kind. I'd grown up in Texas, playing high school football. I wanted, someday, to be a man like the Sherpas.

We practiced climbing on a big rock near the institute. On the trail side the rock was about fifty feet high. On the other side it dropped off a thousand sheer feet. The instructors knelt on top of the rock and held the rope as we inched out over the drop and climbed up to them.

I panicked, freezing, my fingers digging into the rock, my legs shaking. I tried to force my body into the rock, screaming quietly for help.

At the top of the rock Pemba Sherpa held my rope.[1] I couldn't see him. The rock was too steep. But I could hear him, speaking to me gently, reassuring me, telling me I could do it.

I couldn't. The fear and trembling was worse. Telling me it would be all right, Pemba began to haul me up hand over hand, encouraging me to climb. I was a dead weight. I remember his constant, low voice and the strength in his hands as he hauled me up smoothly.

At the top I was ready to be humiliated. That's what a football coach would have done. Pemba spoke quietly, just to me, and said everybody was afraid.

I never forgot Sherpa men, or the mountains.

Thirty years later I returned to the Himalayas. I trekked round Zanskar, Annapurna, and Sherpa country in Nepal and learned some Nepali and Sherpa. Because I was a writer, I scoured Kathmandu's bookshops, where I found hundreds of books on European mountaineers in the Himalayas and none on Sherpa climbers.[2] So I decided to write one.

Sherpas are always there in the mountaineering books, of course, carrying the loads, making the tea, smiling. We see them through the eyes of their employers, and they seem loyal, strong, helpful, brave, and laughing. They also seem short, superstitious, irrationally fearful, and not quite adults – a sort of Himalayan Hobbit.

I have tried to see Sherpas from their own point of view. This involved living in a Sherpa village for six months, learning some of the language, and watching people work with trekkers and tourists. I also interviewed old men and women, to find out both what happened and how they felt about it. And I went back to the old climbing books, trying to read between the lines and guess what the Sherpas were thinking.

In 1922 Himalayan climbers were British gentlemen, and their Sherpa and Tibetan porters were 'coolies,' unskilled and inexperienced casual laborers. By 1953 Sherpa Tenzing Norgay stood on the summit of Everest, and the coolies had become the 'Tigers of the Snow.' This book is about the decisive moment in that change: the German expedition to Nanga Parbat in 1934. That year there was a terrible tragedy high on the mountain. How the German climbers behaved then, and what the Sherpa and Tibetan porters had to do, who lived and who died, changed forever how the porters thought of themselves. This book is primarily about one mountain, and one climb, but that climb reveals much about all the expeditions between 1921 and 1953.

There are fourteen peaks on earth over eight thousand meters (26,247 feet). All of them are part of the great chains of the Himalaya and Karakoram, north of the plains of India. Nanga Parbat, at 26,660 feet, is the tenth-highest mountain on earth. It is on the far western end of the Himalayan chain, in what are now the Northern Territories of Pakistan, and in 1934 it was part of the British colony of India.

The Urdu name Nanga Parbat means 'naked mountain.' Nobody quite knows why, but there are two theories. One is that almost all the other peaks of the Karakoram and Himalaya seem to rise from a dense tangle of surrounding ridges and summits and so are hidden from many directions. K2, for instance, is tucked away in a vast range of peaks, and even Everest is hidden from the south, the summit just poking over the intervening wall of Nuptse. But Nanga Parbat seems to rise alone from the banks of the Indus.

The other theory is that it's naked because the walls are so steep that comparatively little snow sticks there, and the black rock shines through.

The first attempt to climb Nanga Parbat was made by a British expedition led by Frank Mummery in 1895. J. Norman Collie, one of the climbers, said that when they first caught sight of the mountain from the trail, 'instinctively we all took off our hats in order to show that we approached it in a proper spirit.'[3]

Frank Mummery was one of the great Alpine climbers of his age. When he started, most English climbers were gentlemen, and almost all climbed in Europe with the help of local Alpine villagers who hired out as professional guides. Mummery was the first man to popularize what was then called 'guideless climbing,' where the gentlemen found their own way.[4] But Mummery knew he would need help in the Himalaya.

He approached the British Gurkha regiments to see if they could find hillmen for high-altitude porters. The Gurkha rank and file and noncommissioned officers were Nepalis who had taken service in the Indian army under British officers. They came from the hills of mid-Nepal, not the high mountains. But they were regarded as brave, tough, and loyal soldiers. They might be very useful.

Charlie Bruce was a Gurkha officer who had done some climbing. He jumped at the chance to go along with the expedition and chose two Gurkhas to climb with Mummery. Raghabir Thapa, Bruce wrote later, was 'a first-rate rock-climber [and] had been with me in Chilas and Chitral. . . . He was a first-rate man in every way, and had once or twice been on a rope. The other boy [Gaman Singh] was new, though, of course, a born hillman and full of keenness.'[5]

Nanga Parbat proved too much for a small expedition with two high-altitude porters in the conditions of 1895. The sahibs and porters struggled manfully up to various passes and ridges, looking for a possible route, often exhausted and freezing. Charlie Bruce's leave came to an end and he had to go back to his regiment. A few days later Frank Mummery, Raghabir Thapa, and Gaman Singh set off to reach a pass on the ridge and were never seen again.

They were the first three climbers to die on Nanga Parbat. Raghabir Thapa and Gaman Singh were the first two Nepalis to die on a Himalayan expedition.

The local people around the mountain, the Astoris, were Muslims and followed the one God. But the tragedy confirmed an old belief that dangerous spirits were on Nanga Parbat. Over the years, they warned their sons and grandsons not to climb the mountain. For thirty-seven years, no climbers came to Nanga Parbat.

PART I

Sherpas and Sahibs

Chapter One

THE SHERPAS

About five hundred years ago there was fighting in Kham, in eastern Tibet, and many refugees fled. A few families went to the region north of Mount Everest, and then over the Nangpa La, the high pass east of Everest, down into the valleys of Khumbu in Nepal. Those families were the first Sherpas.

Khumbu was three parallel glacial valleys. In the western valley, below the Nangpa La, the Sherpas built the village of Thame. The central valley came down from Cho Oyu, the ninth-highest mountain in the world, and there they founded the village of Phortse on a sloping slab of a hanging valley. In the eastern valley, below Mount Everest, they built the village of Pangboche on the Dudh Khosi, the 'milk river', its water white from the melting glaciers. As the rivers flowed south, each valley narrowed to a deep gorge. High above the confluence of the three rivers they built the villages of Namche Bazaar, Khumjung, and Kunde.[1] These villages were all at between 11,000 and 12,500 feet. Even in Tibet nobody, except a few hermits, lived above 13,000 feet year-round. The Sherpas grew barley and buckwheat, the traditional high-altitude crops of Tibet. In summer they took their yaks and naks (the female) to the high pastures in the upper valleys.

Over the next four hundred years many Sherpa families moved

from Khumbu down through Pharak, the 'middle place,' to Solu in the south. At 6,500 to 10,000 feet, Solu is warmer and more fertile than Khumbu. The Sherpas in Solu could grow two crops a year and enjoy the luxury of wheat bread. Yaks and naks pined and died at this altitude, but cows and sheep thrived. Today there are about three thousand Sherpas in the north, in Khumbu, and seventeen thousand in the middle and the south. But the northerners in Khumbu are important for our story because so many of the early climbers came from there.

Khumbu was frontier territory. Sometimes the Sherpas effectively had independence, and sometimes they were controlled by Tibetan or Nepali government appointees. After the 1865 border war between Nepal and Tibet, Nepal became, and remained, the power in Khumbu.

There were never many people in Khumbu, perhaps fifteen hundred in 1900. The highest land was useless rock and ice. Below that was the glacial moraine, good pasture for yak in summer, but too high for any crops but hay. The terrain below the moraine was mostly made up of steep hillsides. But here and there, between 9,000 and 13,000 feet, the angle was flat enough that people could carve terraced fields out of the hillsides. Each field was like a step in a giant staircase. One stone wall at the bottom of the field held the earth in, and another wall at the top held in the field above. Flying low over the hills of Nepal you can see hundreds of miles of such terraces, spilling down the hills for three thousand or six thousand feet, monuments to human intelligence and labor. But steep Khumbu has few fields, and the landscape is not the intricate palette of lowland greens, but grays and browns and sparkling ice.

The Sherpas sold their yaks across the border to Tibet, to be slaughtered, and bought dried yak meat back from Tibetans. The Hindu Nepali government forbade cow slaughter. Buddhism also discouraged the killing of animals, though in Tibet even monks have always eaten meat. People could never live by farming grain alone on the high Tibetan plateau. Then, sometime around 1880 the potato arrived in Khumbu. A field with potatoes gave a yield, in calories, three or more times that of barley. Potatoes became the staple crop, and people grew richer.

Some families raised sterile crossbreeds, *zopkyoks*, with a yak father and a lowland cow as mother. They sold the *zopkyoks* to Tibet, where they were much in demand to pull plows, a job yaks refuse to do. In Khumbu itself almost everybody plowed with human labor until fifty years ago. Two men pulled the plow, one man drove it, and a woman walked behind sowing the seed.

In winter a Khumbu family stayed in a small, high stone house. There was a room downstairs for the animals, and a long room upstairs for people. The windows were narrow, with ornamental wooden frames and shutters. In spring some of the family stayed in the village to plant potatoes, while the others took the animals to the high pastures. There they stayed in small stone houses and huts. Sometimes, too, they had a few fields and a hut down by the river. From summer to fall people moved up and down the hills, with food and hay, treats and firewood, to make love and party, keeping the family together.

Always there was color. The houses were painted white or left bare stone, but the windows and roof were bright green or red or yellow. From the roof flew the five colors of the prayer flags. A family with a bit of money would have a small chapel upstairs, with gorgeous paintings of gods in black and red and orange. For everybody there were the paintings and statues in the small village monastery, and inside the covered gate that stood at the entrance to each village. In each house, on the wall opposite the fire were dozens of brass and copper bowls and plates, polished with love, the firelight playing on the uneven, beaten metal among the dark red and brown shadows. Always, there was beauty. But life remained hard, and they still needed an income beyond potatoes and yaks. For most people, that meant carrying loads.

Khansa Sherpa was a climber in the old days, with Tenzing and the British on Everest in 1953, and with the Americans in 1963. He is sixty-five now and owns the Gompa Lodge in Namche. It

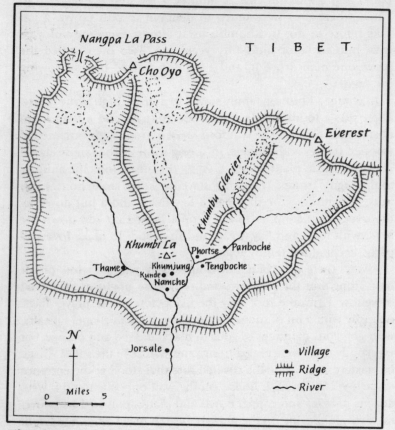

Khumbu

is on the west side, up the hill, below the village chapel – a small monastery without a resident monk. Western trekkers pass through Namche on their way to Everest Base Camp and occasionally stay in Khansa's lodge. But most are exhausted by the time they get to the top of the long Namche hill and stay somewhere lower down in the village.

Khansa is a religious man now, although he was not in his youth. You didn't think about that much, he says. When you're fifty, you realize you might die. Then you get religious.

Sherpa people follow the Buddhist religion. Sometimes writers say their religion is 'Tibetan Buddhism,' but that's like saying somebody's religion is 'American Lutheran' or 'Bulgarian Orthodox,' when they think of themselves as Christians. Devout Sherpas are proud of being part of one of the great world religions, and of sharing their faith with many Tamangs, Gurungs, and Newars in Nepal, and with Indians, Taiwanese, Japanese, Swiss, and Americans.

SHERPA NAMES

At birth all Sherpas are given the name of the day on which they were born. Nima means Sunday, Dawa is Monday, Mingma is Tuesday, Lhakpa is Wednesday, Phurbu is Thursday, Pasang is Friday, and Pemba is Saturday. This is the basic naming system. Then other names are added.

Ang means young. If there is already a Pasang in the family, the new baby will be called Ang Pasang. This remains his or her name for life.

Other names are often given as a child gets older, often religious names such as Ongdi (blessed), Tawa (junior monk), Dorjee (thunderbolt), Tenzing (pious), or Norbu (wealthy).

If an earlier child in the family died, the young person is often given an inauspicious name to distract the attention of malevolent forces. So a child may be called Pasang Ki (dog), Pasang Kikuli (puppy), or Pasang Kami. The Kamis are the traditionally low-status Nepali caste of blacksmiths. The child keeps this name for life, with no loss of status.

People are also given various nicknames. Pasang Bhutia, for instance, means Pasang the Tibetan. Pasang Picture worked as a photographer's assistant. Pasang Tawa means Pasang the Monk and could be used for a man who had been a monk but left the monastery. Other children, though, may be called Tawa or Lama because their parents liked the name.

Names also get shortened. Anu of Namche's full name was once Ang Nima Norbu, although hardly anyone but Anu himself now remembers that. Dawa is often shortened to Da, and Thundoop to Thundu.

There is no distinction between men and women in names. The two Ang Tserings I know best are a man of ninty-six in Darjeeling and a girl of three in Namche.

Tibetan names are similar to Sherpa ones, but not identical.

European climbers often spelled names in several ways, and so did many Sherpas using English. So Ang Tsering's name also turns up as Ang Tshering and Angtsering. Da Thundu is also Dawa Thundu and Dawa Thundoop.

Khansa walks a full circuit of Namche now, twice a day, morning and afternoon, turning his prayer wheel and praying quietly. The 120 houses of Namche and the surrounding fields sit in a horseshoe-shaped bowl, like a giant amphitheater. Khansa walks up past the gompa behind his house and across the ridge at the top of the village. Then he picks his way down the steep path on the east, the one that energetic teenagers race up on their way to school. That takes him down to the one-street bazaar, and the ceremonial arch where the path enters the village. Beside the arch is the chorten, a white pyramid decorated with the giant eyes of Buddha. The chorten is very old, dating from the time when there were only six houses in Namche and men went to fetch water together because they feared the bears. Namche people say they built the chorten then, and people from Thame claim they built it. Khansa walks clockwise around Namche, in the Buddhist fashion, and passes many places of great sanctity. Every time his prayer wheel turns, the prayer written on the paper inside goes to heaven. Khansa hopes his walks will prolong his life or help him in the next one. In any case, three hours exercise a day keeps him fit.

I sit with Lhakpa, Khansa's wife, on an unusually warm afternoon in winter. We are on the stone forecourt outside the Gompa Lodge, enjoying the sun, waiting for Khansa to come back from his walk. I tell her about my divorce, many years ago. She is fascinated and scandalized, and I am proud of my new ability to speak Sherpa badly. 'There's Khansa,' Lhakpa says. She points at a tiny figure far below, absorbed in his prayers as he walks. All the love in the world is in her voice.

He was not always pious and perfect, Khansa lets me know when he gets home. We speak English – he learned it climbing, and his English is much better than my Sherpa. Khansa has been at funerals the last two days. There were two deaths in Namche on the same day, of two people born in the same year, something that has never happened before. A man and a woman in their seventies; both had cancer and went to Kathmandu for treatment. When they knew there was no hope, both insisted on coming home to die.

At the funerals each body was sat up in his or her house, as a person would sit in life, and the neighbors paid their respects. A monk from the big monastery in Thyangboche, on the path to Everest, read to the corpse from a holy book that gave advice on how to find the way through the land of the dead. Other monks blew on their six-foot, thin, curved brass horns, and the deep tones reverberated across the village. Yesterday, on the last day of the funerals, they burned the dead on stone platforms, hidden away in the rocks above the village. Out walking, I saw one funeral pyre across the hill in the late-afternoon light. Four men stood, their shoulders slumped, their dark, bulky shapes outlined in front of the gray-white smoke, the five colors of the prayer flags whipping in the wind above their heads.

We talk about Everest in 1953, Khansa's first climbing job. He was eighteen. Thinking about it now reminds him that almost all the men he worked with then are dead. Drink killed most of them, he says. They got a little money, things got a little easier, and they spent the money on *rakshi* – homemade liquor. People had always drunk a lot of *chang*, the home-brewed beer. *Chang* keeps you warm, particularly when mixed with porridge on a bitter winter morning. *Rakshi* was stronger. Khansa himself could have gone that way, too, and nearly did. Then he stopped drinking. He's still alive and they're dead. Khansa misses them, and he's scared.

Several other men Khansa's age have stopped drinking, too. He belongs to a circle of friends who take turns holding parties in their houses after New Year. In the old days these parties were raucous, with heavy drinking. Happy and sloppy, men would sway together in one line and women in another, one person leading the singing and all stamping out the dance steps. Between songs, people would needle each other with sharp teasing until anger erupted into shouting fights. There was always anger beneath the surface, as in every village in the world. In Namche anger usually grew from grievances over land and sex. Perhaps two brothers had never really agreed how to divide their parents' fields, or one neighbor had encroached on another's field by a few inches every year. Perhaps long ago a man went away to work and on his return found his wife had been with another man. The other man paid compensation, and there was a party to make peace. Sherpas try to be forgiving people, and to be tolerant in sexual matters. But they feel jealousy, too, and thirty or forty years later bitterness can leak out of a drunken mouth. Now that Khansa and many of his friends don't drink, other people say their New Year parties are more civilized, but also more boring.

I asked Khansa how he came to climbing work.

When he was a child, he would gather wood for his father's house, then play, play, play. He had one particular friend, who lived just down the hill, in a poor family like Khansa's. He smiles at a memory. Khansa and his special friend would go off with their baskets to gather wood and spend a long day playing dice in secret. The stakes were lunch, each boy with a little pile of popcorn or bits of potato. Many times Khansa lost his whole lunch, and his friend would not give it back. Hours later they would return home and Papa would be furious: 'Where *were* you? What did you do?'

I asked Khansa if he was angry as a child.

It was a psychologist's question, and he gave me an economist's answer. Poverty made him angry. His clothes were thin, and he was cold. When he came home, there were only potatoes and turnips to eat. He grew to hate the diet. Khansa is a big man, and as he remembers, I can see the emotion fill his body and twist his face. But he contains it, keeping his voice low. I can see how the child contained his anger.

Who did you blame for the poverty? I ask.

'Nobody,' Khansa says. 'My father was poor, his father was poor, his grandfather was poor. They had no choices. I had no choice.'

In his teenage years, Khansa began carrying loads with his father. They carried eighty pounds each through Thame over the Nangpa La to Tibet. It usually took seven days for the round-trip. They went in groups, sometimes fifteen households together. All but the richest four houses in Namche had to do carrying work. They mostly carried Nepali paper, made in Solu, light but bulky. Sometimes they carried buffalo leather, which was thicker than yak hide and much prized in Tibet because it made better boots.

A rich man would pay them five rupees each for the four-day carry. The five rupees went to buy an eighty-pound load of Tibetan salt. Khansa carried that home to Namche. On the Nangpa La, 18,800 feet at the top, there was always snow and crevasses in the ice. In his kitchen, the old man stands up to show me how he would jump across a crevasse. Khansa pulls his arms in to his body, bends his knees, looks down fearfully, takes a deep breath, and jumps across the kitchen with an imaginary eighty pounds

JONATHAN NEALE

on his back. He says he always made it across the crevasses. On the Nangpa La they were deep, but not that wide.

To keep their feet warm on the Nangpa La, Khansa and his father lined their knee-high yak-hide boots with grass. The boots were soft, and back home in Namche they stopped to mend the holes. After that rest, Khansa carried the salt down through Pharak, the middle place, two or three days' walk to Jubing in Solu. On that trip he carried only forty pounds because in Jubing he traded the forty pounds of salt for one hundred pounds of corn (maize). He took the corn to a miller down there, then carried the flour home. Corn tasted strong, Khansa says.

One year young Khansa did the round-trip to Tibet and Solu thirteen times. He is not exaggerating when he says he carried eighty pounds over the Nangpa La as a boy. In those days the traders weighed loads in seers – one seer equaled two pounds. Today they weigh loads in kilos – one kilo is 2.2 pounds – and porters carry even heavier loads than in Khansa's time.

The hills of Nepal still have few roads. The paths are not wilderness routes, as in an American national park. They are regular thoroughfares, carefully maintained, and they have been trade routes for centuries. Today hundreds of porters walk to Namche every week from the end of the bus road. It takes them seven days. They are small men, thin, muscular, and mostly young. They typically carry fifty to sixty kilos (110 to 132 pounds) in baskets on their backs. Some, stronger than the rest, carry 150 pounds. The path is mostly steeply uphill or steeply down. Each basket has a strap – the tumpline – that comes across the forehead and takes the weight. It requires practice to carry that way, and strong neck muscles, but they say it's easier on the back. Each man has a short, thick walking stick, shaped like a T. The stick helps with balance, particularly downhill. More important, on the uphills a porter stops every few minutes and thrusts the stick under his basket to take the weight. Then he stands silently, recovering his breath.

There are women porters on the trail to Namche, too, laughing and flirting, traveling in groups with the men. At Jubing, two and a half days from Namche, they join with porters who have walked up from the plains of Nepal and Bihar, ten or twelve days away.

Porters carry everything in those baskets these days, mostly things for the tourists – Coca-Cola, Fanta, Tuborg, San Miguel, live chickens, rice, lentils, cheese and tomatoes for pizzas, onions, Mars bars and Snickers – but also school notebooks, prayer flags, and plastic shoes. They carry wooden roof beams up the Namche Hill – one man teetering under a twenty-foot tree trunk, stripped of its branches, weighing perhaps two hundred pounds.

Porters work for trekking expeditions, too. The pay is sometimes better, but they have to cope with higher altitudes and worse cold. On a trek round Annapurna in 1995, I met four Dutch hikers camping with forty porters. One of their porters carried a cast-iron woodstove for a whole three weeks, well over a hundred pounds. He took it over the Thorung La, at 17,800 feet, and the snow was deep that year.

There is a word that people use a lot in Khumbu – *dhukpaa*. *Dhukpaa* means hardship, but also suffering. It means work that is unfair, and too hard. It also means the oppression of employers who hire people for that work, and who treat them unfairly, who make the poor suffer. *Dhukpaa, dhukpaa*, they say, and sigh, meaning – There it is, what can you do about it, you have to put up with it, but this is not how things should be.

Dhukaa is the related Nepali word. A porter from the lowlands, working for a trekking company, walks down the main path in Namche, his load enormous and unwieldy. A child comments to him on his strength, and he says, in Nepali, *'Dhukaa, dhukaa'* – hardship, oppression – as he pivots, trying not to slip on the ice and smash his knees on the stone path.

Above Namche, going toward Everest Base Camp, porters work for trekking companies at elevations of up to eighteen thousand feet without shoes or in thin canvas sneakers. Helicopters evacuate sick trekkers, whose insurance companies pay $4,000 each time. There is no evacuation for porters with pneumonia or altitude sickness. In the great storm of November 1997, the snow trapped trekking parties all over Nepal. Many foreigners were taken out by helicopters. They left the porters behind because nobody would pay for their rescue. Several of them died. When they found one man dead of exposure, his pack was full of sleeping bags and down jackets for the trekkers.[2] For carrying this he would have made $3 a day, better money than the men who carry Coca-Cola into Namche.

People use *dhukaa* and *dhukpaa* most when they talk about carrying. When they recall the old days, men always remember two things exactly. How much weight they carried, to the pound, and how much they were paid for it, to the anna (one-sixteenth of the old rupee).

Khansa would not have starved if he had not carried loads. His family had potatoes. But for everything else – clothes, maize, oil, tea, roof beams, prayer flags, meat – he had to carry.

When Khansa was seventeen, in 1952, two Swiss expeditions came to Khumbu in the spring and fall to attempt Everest. Tenzing Norgay was the sardar, the foreman for the porters, on both expeditions. That winter Khansa ran away to Darjeeling with two friends. He wanted work on the British expedition the next spring. Darjeeling was in Bengal, in the foothills of the Himalayas, a three-week walk east from Khumbu. When Khansa arrived, he and his friends went straight to Tenzing Norgay's house. He knew Tenzing had already been appointed sardar for the British expedition.

They stood on the porch of Tenzing's house in the dark and called out. Tenzing came to the window and asked who they were.

Khansa, son of so-and-so of Namche.

I remember your father, Tenzing said. I climbed with him on Everest in the thirties. Come on in.

He didn't know the other boys' fathers and told them to go away. Khansa stayed four months in Tenzing's house, working hard, scrubbing pots, trying to make his mark. He would walk down the Darjeeling ridge with another boy to gather firewood and carry enormous loads back up, staggering. He hoped to impress Tenzing with his diligence and show the sardar his strength.

After four months, Tenzing said, all right, you can come to Everest.

That spring Khansa was on the Icefall on the south side of Everest, climbing for the first time in his life. Walking on the ice in crampons was the hardest bit, trying not to spike his legs or tear his trousers with the sharp points. And walking in mountain boots, clumping and clumsy. He shows me, staggering like a confused drunk. The boots didn't fit either, because the British were cheap and didn't bring enough pairs. In 1963, ten years later, Khansa worked on an American expedition that had boots in every size, and far more pairs than they needed. But in 1953 Khansa had to take what he was given and hobble.

The Icefall was the first part of the Everest climb, and the most dangerous. It's a tangled frozen river, always moving slowly across the underlying rock. You can lie in a tent at Base Camp and listen to the Icefall grind and moan all night. The whole weight of the glacier above pushes it down, so it's full of avalanches, and sudden convulsions in the ice can swallow the path and any men on it.

Khansa was afraid the entire time in the Icefall. He said constantly, inside himself so nobody could hear, 'Buddha save my life, Buddha save my life.' The older Darjeeling men were kind and taught him what to do. In a week he could walk properly in crampons.

In all that time, he says, no matter how scared he was, and he had never been so scared in his life before or since, he was happy. He was earning five rupees each day, instead of for four days on the Nangpa La. He could take his new clothes and sleeping bag home at the end of the climb, and there was a bonus of three hundred rupees if he made it up to the South Col at twenty-six thousand feet.

Never had he been so scared, he wants me to know, and never so happy at the same time.

Sherpas climbed for money.

To interview climbers in Khumbu, I drew up a list of questions.

The one that really worked was 'Why do foreigners climb mountains?' That was a hilarious question, partly because a foreigner was asking it. I used the usual Sherpa word for foreigner, which literally means 'white eyes' and is not very polite. (Sherpas feel about foreigners much as people do everywhere else when they work in the tourist industry.)

But mainly the question was funny because it was a mystery, and everybody's livelihood depended on this lunatic mystery. Some of the men I asked had been thinking about this question for close to fifty years, and they still hadn't come up with a satisfactory answer.

Obviously, foreigners did it for the money, and to be famous. Sherpas climbed for money. Some Sherpas, and not others, also said they wanted a 'big name.' Ming girpu – big name – is not quite the same as Western celebrity or fame. It means recognition in your own village, and maybe the other villages of Khumbu. I told one friend, an older Sherpa climber, that I had mentioned his name in several villages, and in every case the person I was talking to had heard of him. My friend was a reserved and taciturn man. But now he sat there silently, smiling to himself, reflecting on what I had said. It made a lifetime's work worthwhile.

Four men from the forty houses in the neighborhood of Lower Thame have climbed Mount Everest a combined total of twenty-nine times. Lhakpa Rita has been up five times, and his brother, Kami Rita, four times. Two men in their early forties, Appa and Ang Rita, have each climbed Everest ten times.[3] There is a bit of competition among them, but nobody comments on it much.

I sat eating dinner with a Sherpa friend in a cheap Tibetan restaurant in Kathmandu. We exchanged some pleasantries with a man at the next table – slightly built, fit, about forty, with a kind face. At the end of the meal my friend introduced us, saying this is Appa of Thame.

The Appa? I said. You're the man who climbed Everest ten times?

He nodded. I squeezed the hand I was shaking and gushed about how honored I was. His body twisted away from me, but his hand squeezed mine back and he turned his head so his eyes could smile at me. I saw that such open praise was rare for him, and he was pleased and made shy.

Reinhold Messner and Edmund Hillary deal with such adulation effortlessly. They're probably bored by it. If Appa and Ang Rita lived in America, they would be on the cover of *Newsweek* and *People*, bad-mouthing each other and making millions endorsing Nike and Pepsi. As it is, Appa is pleased to have a big name – the respect of a few thousand people.

It is extraordinary how little recognition most Sherpas get. Khansa Sherpa carried sixty-seven pounds of oxygen to the South Col of Everest in 1953. He had no photos of the climb or the team. In the summer of 2000, I gave him a paperback copy of Sir John Hunt's 1954 book, *The Ascent of Everest*. The book contains a group photograph, and Khansa is in the group. He turned the book in his hands, not knowing quite what to say. He showed the picture to his wife, to the servant girl, and to the neighbors. After forty-seven years, he had something to show.

Sometimes there is a photo on the wall of a small lodge of the man of the house, in goggles and down jacket, standing on top of Everest. A ceremonial silk scarf surrounds the picture, to show respect and pride. But usually when a Sherpa summits, nobody takes a picture, or nobody gives him one. Luckily, the Nepali government issues a certificate for climbing Everest, a simple form with a passport-size photograph attached. So Sherpa climbers can put that on the wall, along with the ceremonial scarf.

Kami Rita of Thame, the younger son of Mingma Chering, has climbed Everest four times. The best time was on a youth expedition organized and sponsored by the Nepali government as part of a year of celebrations that ended in a world youth congress in Havana. Kami Rita was one of the four young Nepalis who made the summit. That expedition was a relief, he says, because there were no foreigners. You could just make your tea in the morning and climb all day, without having to waste your time on carrying oxygen bottles and all that other stuff. Easy. And the government youth expedition gave him two commutative flags, the Nepali green and red, and the Cuban red and blue. He takes them out of a cupboard and holds first one, then the other, stretched out before him, standing in the window to catch the morning light, proud. Kami Rita is the only Sherpa I have met who says his main reason for climbing is a big name, not the money. That is what he has to show for climbing Everest four times. And he's lucky, because most people don't have a flag.

I ask Kami Rita and his father, Mingma Chering, why foreigners climb mountains, and they laugh like everybody else. Then they sit and think about it, on a spring day in the high pastures, all of us relaxing on a pile of soft, dark, dried leaves, fodder for the yaks. Finally Mingma Chering says it had to be for the big name.

Yes, says Kami Rita, who climbs for the big name himself and has two flags to show for it. But then he thinks some more and says, why would anybody who already has that much money still climb?

And we sit and mull that over, and nobody has an answer.

I ask Khansa Sherpa, in English, why foreigners climb mountains. He laughs and says to his wife, Lhakpa, in Sherpa, 'You know what he just asked me? Why do foreigners climb mountains?'

Lhakpa laughs, too.

Then Khansa tells me he's been reflecting on this matter since 1953. He's finally concluded that foreigners climb mountains because they like to. Unlikely as that seems, no other explanation makes sense.

Mountains kill.

There is nothing natural about climbing mountains. The people who lived in the Alps, the Andes, and the Himalayas never used to do it. The first great mountain to be climbed was Mont Blanc in the Alps, in 1786. In the nineteenth century, generations of British gentlemen pioneered Alpine routes with local villagers as guides. These gentlemen were the owners and heirs of the industrial revolution. They were the first class of men in human history who could imagine themselves as dominating nature, standing on top of her very peaks.

Sherpas and Tibetans went over the passes when they had to. As they neared the top of the pass, they were afraid, and with good reason. In Tibet, when you reach the top of a high pass on the road, you throw an offering of rice into the air to thank the gods and shout, 'Tse tso, tse tso' – long life, long life. The Sherpa language does not even have a word for the high point of a mountain. Older climbers, speaking Sherpa, use the English word *top*, as in 'top ki Chomolungma' – the top of Everest. Younger men speaking Sherpa use the English word *summit*, as in 'summit ki K2' – the top of K2.

My first Sherpa language teacher, Nwang Dhoka Sherpa, was the daughter of one of the great climbers of the sixties, Pasang Kami Sherpa. There was no textbook for Sherpa in 1995, so we were making up our own lessons. (Now there's the excellent *Sherpa Nepali English* by Ang Phinjo Sherpa.) I wanted words for mountaineering, so Nwang began our sample conversation: 'What is climbing Mount Everest like? Climbing Mount Everest is very dangerous.' And that was the end of the lesson about climbing.

Nwang had spent her childhood waiting to see if her father would come back. He always did. But between 1953 and 1983, 116 men from Solu and Khumbu died working in the mountains. Fourteen were from Nwang's village, Namche Bazaar.[4]

Her father is Pasang Kami – everybody now calls him by his English nickname, PK. His father died when PK was little, and his mother eked out a living sewing and weaving in other people's houses. When her employers fed her, she used to hide bits of food in her clothes to take home to her little boy.

PK didn't tell me that. The men who were boys with him in Namche did. They all look at PK now with wonder and envy. How come he got so rich, they want to know, when we started out ahead of him? And then, hurriedly, they say that he is a decent man. Unlike many rich men, they say, he treats everybody the same, invites a poor man in to sit and drink tea.

PK and his wife, Namdu, married for love, despite her family's opposition. But they've come round long since. There is an old picture, taken by a trekker over thirty years ago, on a postcard that still sells in Kathmandu. It shows a beautiful young Sherpa woman, in traditional dress, leaning out of a carved wooden window, smiling. That's Namdu.

When they married, PK was not an important man, but he was strong; and above all, he was smart. He knew how to make friends of Europeans, how to help them and get them to help him. He was Chris Bonington's sardar on the South Face of Annapurna in 1970, the first expedition to climb one of the great Himalayan walls. PK invested the money he earned and made friends with an American senator he met trekking, and with the owner of Northwest Airlines. In 1982 he guided Jimmy Carter to Everest Base Camp. He liked Carter, PK said, a nice man. Carter came with many Secret Service bodyguards, arrogant, burly men who dropped away on the trek, complaining about headaches, gasping for air, unable to keep up with old Jimmy. PK quietly enjoyed that.

He built one of the best tourist lodges in Namche, with a magnificent picture window looking out across the river to the south face of Kwangde. He is a partner in a trekking agency in Kathmandu and has traveled to America, New Zealand, and Europe. PK's daughter, Nwang Dhoka, trained as a dental therapist in Canada, and his son, Pemba, went to the best school in Bengal and to university in Australia. Tenacious, with no schooling, PK finally taught himself to read Nepali in his fifties. He died in his early sixties, in the winter of 2000.

Namdu is the emotional heart of the family and the manager of her family lodge. Her children are very nice people. Sitting in the dining room of her family lodge in the spring of 2000, I ask Namdu if she ever quarreled with PK over the climbing.

Yes, she says. A little.

I ask if they fought physically. I know some wives tore at their husband's arms, hung on, begging, trying to stop them from going to the mountains. The husband had to push past his wife to leave home.

No, Namdu says. Just words. But sometimes it was bad.

What about the money? I say, gesturing at the lodge, all the guests, the pictures of her and PK by the sea in New Zealand, her daughter graduating from college in mortarboard and gown, her husband with Edmund Hillary and Jimmy Carter.

Forget the money, Namdu says. I wanted him alive.

During another evening in a tourist lodge in 1997, three days' walk from Everest Base Camp, my partner Nancy and the two young boys of the house drew pictures for hours. The boys drew helicopters. When the other guests went to bed, our landlady finally got to sit down. She told us a story.

Her husband had been a climber for years. He'd been on twenty-eight expeditions and summited Everest twice. She was afraid all those years. But most expeditions paid $1,000 to $1,200 a season for work on Everest or Annapurna or the other big peaks. So her husband made $2,000 to $2,400 in an average year. They pay a bit better now, especially with the bonus for summiting Everest.

She kept telling her husband to quit. He said no, they needed to save a bit more, to build a tourist lodge, furnish it, and pay for the children's education in an English-medium school in Kathmandu, so the children would not have to scrabble for a living.

She said she'd rather have him alive. He said he had to work.

The last time her husband was on Everest, several expeditions were on the mountain at the same time. Three Sherpas from another expedition died in an accident. All three came from the village of Phortse. Looking out of our landlady's bedroom window, we could see Phortse, a hanging valley, some eighty houses and small fields.

The sardar on the expedition came down the valley to Phortse to tell the wives of the three men what had happened. It was his duty, and he was a decent man.

When he reached Phortse, the sardar was too upset to speak. The women of Phortse knew from his face that somebody had died. But they could not make the sardar say who. So the wives of the porters went down to cross the river and up to Thyangboche monastery on the hill. There the monks told them who had died.

Our landlady should have been relieved that her husband was all right, but actually she was suddenly frightened for him. She sent a message to him at Base Camp, saying that she was seriously ill, was being evacuated by helicopter to Kathmandu, and might die. It wasn't true. But she sent the message to get him off that mountain.

He got the message just as he was setting off up Everest from Base Camp. He turned around and ran for home. (She was proud as she told us – he made it home in five hours. His speed was a sign of his panic and love.)

Her husband came in, puffing, his chest heaving. 'What's wrong?' he said.

'Nothing,' she said happily.

He was enraged. She had made trouble with his job. And he had been so terrified for her.

'Now you know how I feel all the time,' she said.

His anger ended, just like that.

Now he works as a guide for trekkers in Nepal. He gets a lot of work. The trekkers are proud to be with a Sherpa who has climbed Everest twice.

Khansa Sherpa was not the only one to run away to Darjeeling. Sherpas had been doing it for over fifty years. Tenzing Sherpa (pronounced *Tensing*) was the most famous runaway.

Tenzing was born in Tibet in 1914, in the valley of Kharte, a little east of Everest, under Makalu.[5] He was the eleventh of thirteen children, only four of whom lived to adulthood. When he was quite young, Tenzing's family left Kharte with what they could carry on their backs, crossed the Nangpa La, and settled in Thame.

Poor Tibetans had been migrating to Sherpa country for four hundred years. The Sherpa language was different, but they could more or less understand it, rather like Spanish and Italian speakers, or Danes and Norwegians. The incoming Tibetans would begin by working for established Sherpas as yak herders or farmhands, then make fields of their own and maybe marry a local girl or boy. In later generations, people would remember that so-and-so's grandparents were Tibetan. But for most daily purposes they were Sherpas.

The Nepali governing class called them all Bhotias anyway, their word for all the people in Nepal who spoke Tibetan dialects and practiced Buddhism. The Sherpas did not like being called Bhotias, because they knew what the word meant to the Nepali elite. *Bhotia* implied dirty, poor, and stupid. There is a rueful Khumbu legend about a Sherpa who was tricked by a Nepali long ago. The Nepali climbed a tree and hid in the branches. When the Sherpa came down the path, he heard a sound, looked up, and saw the stranger in the tree. The Sherpa was so surprised his mouth fell open, and the quick-witted Nepali spat down into it. And that is why, to this day, many high-caste Nepali Hindus treat Sherpas as stupid and polluted.

Understandably, Sherpas preferred to be called Sherpas, which meant 'Easterners' in their language. Perhaps this referred to coming originally from the far east of Tibet, or perhaps it just meant a Bhotia in Nepal who lived east of Kathmandu.

But around 1920, when Tenzing's family arrived in Thame, there were no longer fields for the making. They had to work for other people. Tenzing says in his autobiography that even then he knew he was different. The other children played while he sat by himself and dreamed of adventures in Lhasa, the capital of Tibet, of leading men in war. As he grew older, he dreamed of Kathmandu, and India, but always of money and a big name.

There were two roads to wealth in Khumbu in 1920 – government official or trader. After the Nepali-Tibetan war of 1855, the Nepali government got a grip on affairs in Khumbu. They appointed tax farmers, called *pembu,* to collect taxes and remit part of the money or grain to the central government in Kathmandu. There were eight *pembu* in Khumbu, and each had supervision of many houses in several villages. This was because people moved, and the *pembu* controlled the man and the woman and their descendants, not the land. The *pembu* took 20 percent of the crop, and several times each year his taxpayers had to work on the *pembu's* land for free. More than the taxes, they resented having to labor for free.

The other route to wealth was trade. The Nepali government gave the merchants of Namche Bazaar the sole right to trade north with Tibet over the Nangpa La. Traders coming from the south had to sell their goods in Namche, and traders and porters from Tibet had to sell in Namche, too. There was not actually a bazaar in Namche – traders went from house to house hawking their goods, and there were only about fifty houses in 1940. Four of those houses got rich on the trade.

Most rich families had some combination of *pembu* rights and trade, and most of them also controlled large herds of yak and nak. Twenty head of cattle was, and is, a big herd for an ordinary family. But in the 1920s one *pembu* owned four hundred head. In the fall, when his yaks and naks left the high pastures, the noise that came down the main path in Pangboche was like thunder, and small boys ran alongside the herd in excitement, shouting. 'The *pembu* is coming. The *pembu* is coming.'

Yet Khumbu was still the frontier, and government writ was weak. There was seldom any armed force to back up an oppressive official. In 1920, for instance, one *pembu* in Namche killed a man who challenged his authority. Suddenly neither the *pembu* nor anybody else in Namche knew what to do. Nobody could remember a previous murder. The *pembu* stayed in his house, not daring to come out, paralyzed by the disapproval of his neighbors. Eventually he slipped out and went to Tibet and never came back. Downhill or over the pass, the Nepali or Tibetan government would have sent troops to back their official. But in Khumbu, a rougher democracy prevailed. And if the forced labor and 20 percent tax were resented, it was not the third or the half of the crop that people owed to landlords and aristocrats in much of Nepal and Tibet.

Ordinary people were polite to the rich, but they did not crawl. Most people had their own land and would not starve to death if they crossed the local landlords. That gave them a basic independence. Later, in 1950, a democratic movement overthrew the Ranas, the feudal lords who had ruled Nepal for 150 years. When the Ranas fell, the *pembus* of Khumbu lost their power, too. The old *pembu* families are poorer now, and the new rich have made money from climbing and tourism. But men over fifty in Namche still drop their voices when they speak of the old rich. Sitting with an older man on the open hillside, just him and me and nobody for two hundred yards around, his voice goes almost to a whisper. It is an ingrained caution in the shadow of power.

The boy Tenzing must have known that there was no possibility of wealth for him in Khumbu. Success meant leaving. When he was a child, he was sent to the monastery, as so many boys were. He was naughty, like most boy monks. An older monk slapped his head hard, Tenzing said, and he ran away home.

British mountaineering expeditions came to the Tibetan side of Everest in 1921, 1922, and 1924, when Tenzing was between seven and ten. Men from Thame crossed the pass to work for them, and Tenzing began to dream of Everest. He was already working for richer families, herding yaks, and in the high pastures he would look at Everest.

When he was twelve, he ran away over the Nangpa La, back to Kharte where he was born. From Kharte, on a roundabout route, he walked to Kathmandu in two weeks. There Tenzing found food and shelter with some Buddhist monks at the great stupa of Bodhinath. He wandered around the city, drinking it in through his eyes, the lights at night, the women in red and gold saris, the urban forest of small temples. After two weeks Tenzing was homesick – he was twelve – and so he walked home. His parents hugged him and then beat him.

Tenzing then worked as a debt servant for a rich man in Khumjung village, above Namche. He does not speak of this in his autobiography. By then, after all the success, Tenzing was probably ashamed of the poverty of his youth.

Many Sherpa and incoming Tibetan families hired their teenage children out in debt service. For example, a rich man would give a poor man fifty rupees ($12) for his son of fourteen. The son would work for the rich man for five years, or until his father repaid the debt, whichever was first. The boy would tend the yaks, do heavy carrying and plowing, and whatever else he was told. Herding, in particular, was lonely.

A contemporary of Tenzing's, who was also a debt servant, says Tenzing's father mortgaged him over and over again. Such work varied enormously depending on how kind the employer was; some were kind and some were not. In either case, the servant was the lowest person in a house where all the other children were loved.

There was a solution to debt service – run away without telling your parents. Tenzing was eighteen when he ran away to Darjeeling, in a party with eleven other boys and girls. They hid food in the rocks for weeks beforehand. Tenzing left his parents to sort out the debt. After a year away, he missed them and walked back. When he arrived, they were getting ready for his funeral ceremony. This time it was all hugging and no beating. Tenzing worked around the family home in Thame for some months, then returned to Darjeeling. He had seen the world and wanted it.

LANGUAGES

In 1934 most Sherpas in Darjeeling spoke several languages. Their mother tongue was Sherpa. Depending on your point of view, this is either a dialect of Tibetan or a language related to Tibetan. Sherpa is unwritten, so traditionally the education offered by the monks was in Tibetan, and many older men can read it. Most Darjeeling Sherpas also spoke it well enough.

Nepali is the national language of Nepal. In 1934 most Sherpas in Khumbu did not speak it, although now like most other Nepalis, they are usually fluent. Nepali was, and is, also the predominant language in the Darjeeling district of India. So Sherpas who went to Darjeeling had to learn it quickly. Now many younger Sherpas in Darjeeling speak Nepali but don't know Sherpa.

Nepâli is part of the Indo-European family of languages that stretches from Gaelic in Ireland to Bengali in eastern India. So Nepali is more closely related to English than to Sherpa. Nepali shares many words with Hindi.

Hindi and Urdu are one language, like Serbo-Croat. The name of the language depends on who's talking. Hindus tend to say they speak Hindi, and Muslims to say they speak Urdu. But in 1934 the spoken form of Hindi-Urdu was called Hindustani. The language is a mixture of words from Sanskrit and Persian. It can be written in two ways. If you use a modified version of the Persian and Arabic scripts, it is called Urdu. If you use a modified version of the Sanskrit script, it's Hindi. There is also a very educated version of Hindi that uses many Sanskrit words, and a literary Urdu that uses many old Persian words.

In 1934 few Sherpas in Darjeeling spoke much English at all, although now many do.

Girls went to Darjeeling, too.

Galtzen, for instance, is eighty-four now, the second-oldest man in Namche, and the richest. He worked as a climber in the 1950s, then made good money as a trader in Tibet. But until he was almost forty, Galtzen never made more than a rupee a day, and he carried many loads.

As a young man he was working in debt service for a rich man in Namche, a kind, fat man. Only the few rich people had any chance of getting fat, and some of them had much success.

Galtzen's girlfriend came to him and said, I'm pregnant, what are you going to do about it?

Galtzen said he didn't know.

We have to run to Darjeeling, she said.

I don't know, he said, stalling.

She was always the intelligent one. They're still happily married now, over sixty years later, and she's kept her razor wit, cracking dirty jokes at New Year parties.

We have to go, she said. My father will make you pay a fine when he finds out, and where will you get the money for that?

I don't know, Galtzen said, and she got her way. They went to Darjeeling for several years and returned with children. Her father had to accept them, and that was that.

It wasn't just pregnancy that made girls go. Some of them ran away with a boy their parents disapproved of. But many went on their own, with friends, driven by the same sense of adventure as their brothers.

Darjeeling was something then.[6] Mingma Chering arrived in 1954 and stayed with relatives. In 2000, speaking English, wearing a New York Yankees baseball cap, he tells me that when he first saw Darjeeling, he thought it was one of the great cities of the world. 'You know how stupid I felt,' he says, 'when I got to Calcutta and Bombay?'

The British East India Company annexed the Darjeeling district from Sikkim in 1835, hoping it would make a good place for a convalescent home for British soldiers. The sick soldiers grew lonely and depressed in the cold mists. One winter fourteen of them committed suicide, one after the other, and the invalid home was closed.

But tea and tourists built Darjeeling. In much of the world, nobody has heard of Darjeeling town but many have heard of Darjeeling tea. The hills below Darjeeling are wet, cool, and fertile. By 1900 many British tea plantations and peasant tea farms had cleared much of the forest. Most of the plantation workers and small farmers were immigrants from Nepal, and Nepali became the language of Darjeeling district.

The town of Darjeeling itself became a 'hill station,' a holiday resort. Under British rule, the provincial government of Bengal moved up there during the summer months to escape the un-English heat of the plains. The town was built along a high ridge. Below, the green, terraced fields of tea and the forests fall steeply away. And then, beyond the valleys, the massif of Kangchenjunga rises, the great peak and its outliers filling the northern horizon. At dawn, in the winter, Kangchenjunga seems to float above the clouds that fill the lowlands.

In his life, Tenzing saw Makalu, Cho Oyu, Nanda Devi, Nanga Parbat, Everest, the Rockies, Tibet, New Zealand, and the Alps. Of all the world's mountains, he said, Kangchenjunga was the most beautiful. When he grew rich in middle age, he built his new house so he could sit in the small chapel and watch Kangchenjunga out the window.

With the government in the summer months came more British tourists, up for two weeks, or if lucky, the wife and children could stay the whole summer. By 1923 there were cricket, hockey, gymnastics, polo, horse racing, golf, bioscope shows at the palace of varieties, dancing, an ice rink, flower shows, horse shows, dog shows, carnivals, and a visiting circus. The meetings of the Society for the Protection of Animals campaigned for maximum loads for donkeys.

In 1934, Darjeeling had a population of about thirty thousand, of whom several hundred were Sherpas. They lived mainly in Toong Soom Busti, a Tibetan and Sherpa shantytown, close to the mall and the tourist area, but on the back side of the ridge with no view of the mountains. The Sherpas lived and worked mixed in with the other 'Bhotias' from Tibet, Sikkim, and Bhutan. The Tibetans, and therefore the Sherpas, had difficulty in getting the better paid and easier jobs as house servants and hotel workers. Tibetans with enough money to buy a horse could offer pony rides to tourists on the Mall but few immigrants could start that way. They mostly specialized in the hard work of carrying loads and pulling rickshaws. According to a 1922 guidebook:

> On arrival at Darjeeling the men mount ponies, and the ladies and children get into dandies and rickshaws . . . which carry them away to the several hotels and boarding establishments, to be followed shortly after by female porters. . . . The dandy is a chair with a well in front, not unlike that of carriages

in the plains, which rises to the level of the seat, and is carried by four stalwart men, usually Bhutias, who place the horizontal cross-poles by which the dandy is supported on their shoulders and swing off with their fares up and down hill at a jog-trot, looking extremely well pleased if the occupants shew the slightest sign of nervousness.[7]

These were the men who got work as porters on the mountaineering expeditions.

Ang Tsering, the last man off Nanga Parbat alive in 1934, is ninety-six now. He lives in Toong Soom, which is still a Sherpa and Tibetan neighborhood, but no longer a shantytown. Ang Tsering has a neat wooden bungalow, bright blue, with a riot of geraniums and pansies outside. Three of his daughters, widows in their sixties, live with him, and so does one son, a retired army sergeant. They're all proud of their father, and tender. They bring out his photographs and medals and laugh fondly at his jokes. He talks in Nepali, and his son translates. Ang Tsering was born in Thame, but he has been in Darjeeling for seventy-six years. He has a medal from the Germans on his wall, for Nanga Parbat, and his 'Tiger of the Snow' badge from the Himalayan Club is also on display. He is still a big man, lumbering around the house, making sure somebody makes me tea, looking for his old photo album.

Between 1924 and 1934 Ang Tsering worked on wheeled rickshaws, not dandies. One man would pull the rickshaw uphill, and two would push from behind. Downhill, one man led and two men held back the weight. The money was not that good – he took home about fifteen rupees a month. But sometimes parties at Government House lasted until the early hours of the morning, and the rickshaw men would wait outside, talking to each other and enjoying the music floating through the windows. That was a good part of the job.

Pasang Phutar, another climber, is ninety now. He came from Namche to Darjeeling and worked the rickshaws in the twenties and thirties. We speak Sherpa. He says it wasn't so much the weight of the British in the rickshaw he minded, it was the rain. The passenger seat had a cover, but Pasang Phutar could not afford a raincoat. He just drew his shoulders in and huddled between the poles. It rains a lot in Darjeeling, and at eight thousand feet it's cold. Climbing was warmer work.

Is that why you took climbing jobs? I ask.

Partly, he says. And partly – he flashes a conspiratorial smile – nobody ever got a big name pulling rickshaws.

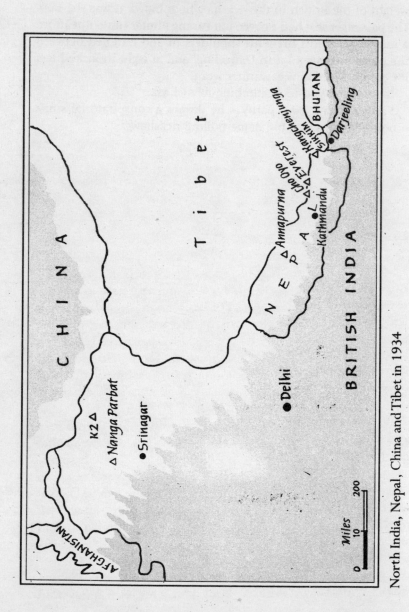

North India, Nepal, China and Tibet in 1934

Chapter Two

THE FIRST EXPEDITIONS

We turn now to the British climbers, and to Everest. There are two styles of writing running through this book. The two styles come from the two sorts of sources I have used.

One style is the historian's voice, based on the books and letters left by climbers. It is a measured voice, evaluating the evidence, pretending to rationality. This voice admits to passion, but avoids exploring the world of feeling. It gives the employers' view, because they left the records, and it ignores the Sherpas. This is the style that the British and German climbers used. It is also the style I use when writing their history.

The other style is from my interviews with older Sherpa men and women today. Here their voices, and mine, are chatty, colloquial, more direct and open to feeling. It is at times too simple a style, and this is my fault. I mostly spoke with people either in English, where their vocabulary was usually limited, or in Sherpa, where mine was even smaller. In both cases, my notes from conversations with complex and intelligent people tend to read simply on the page. So I have tried to use an English a bit closer to the complexity Sherpas used in talking to other Sherpas.

The problem, however, remains. There are two very different styles within the covers of one book, and some readers may find switching back and forth disconcerting. But the heart of this book is a contrast between very different views of the world, held by people whose places in the world were very different. This contrast cannot but be reflected in the style of the book. To make sense of what happened, we need both the historical record and the personal interview. We need both the climbers' point of view and the Sherpas'. This is the story of a relationship.

'Why do foreigners climb mountains?' I asked Sherpas, and they laughed.

The British climber George Mallory was on a lecture tour of the United States in 1923. In New York a journalist asked him why he climbed Everest. 'Because it is there,' Mallory replied.[1]

Generations of climbers have treasured Mallory's answer. It expresses their feelings about that question: Don't ask. I don't want to know. I don't want to tell you.

This is an important fact in itself. If you ask people why they fish, hunt, dance, or play football, you get reasonably clear responses. They are not always the same from one person to another, but they make sense. Football is not a mystery. When you ask Europeans why they climb in the Himalayas, the answer seems mysterious to them. Which, of course, is why it is a mystery to the Sherpas.

Something is being hidden here. Something that has to be hidden not just from other people, but from the climbers themselves.

Mallory, however, went on to explain to the journalist: 'Everest is the highest mountain in the world, and no man has reached its summit. Its existence is a challenge. The answer is instinctive, a part, I suppose, of man's desire to conquer the universe.'[2]

Mallory answered in words that were powerful for upper-class men in that time and place: *challenge, instinctive, man, desire, conquer*. They are the words of the first class of men in history who could imagine the universe as something to be conquered. But there is Darwin in those words, too, and Freud, and certainly the British Empire, which had conquered much of the world. There is also ambition, not quite stated, but shouting behind the words, and obvious to everybody who knew Mallory. His ambition led to the deaths of eleven men. We turn now to the story of Mallory on Everest, and how rickshaw men became climbers.

The Sherpas became climbers not because they grew up below Mount Everest, but because they were working as porters in Darjeeling. In 1921 a British reconnaissance expedition set out from Darjeeling to climb Mount Everest from the Tibetan side. Alexander Kellas, one of the climbers, had already mounted several small expeditions in the Himalayas using Darjeeling porters. He recommended them highly. The Everest expedition would probably have hired their porters in the Darjeeling bazaar anyway. That was where the porters were. They hired twenty men, mostly Tibetans from Sikkim and Tibet, but also some Sherpas.

The British had obtained permission to climb Everest in return for a substantial gift of armaments to the Tibetan government. Leading circles in Tibet were split about the wisdom of this move. The monks from the monasteries around the capital, Lhasa, and the leading monks in the government, were deeply suspicious of this British alliance. After all, a British army under Francis Younghusband had invaded Tibet in 1904 and briefly seized Lhasa. But a Chinese army had also briefly invaded in 1910, and for the moment the Dalai Lama and the Tibetan army were more worried about the possibility of another Chinese invasion. So they took the British arms and gave permission to explore Everest from their side.[3]

The villagers around Everest braced themselves, remembering the widespread looting by British officers on Younghusband's 1904 invasion – the officers were partial to Tibetan art. This time the villagers were pleasantly surprised when the climbers politely paid for everything they needed.[4]

In 1922 a second, full-scale expedition with many more porters left Darjeeling to climb Everest from Tibet. These Tibetan and Sherpa porters were not natural climbers. Many of them had crossed mountain passes, but in 1924 British climbers knew more about rock and ice than people from below Everest did.

* * *

The relationship between masters and men on these expeditions was paternalistic. There are two ways of looking at this paternalism.

Pasang Phutar, who said nobody ever got a big name pulling a rickshaw, remembers sitting on the benches around Chowrashtra in Darjeeling in the thirties, watching the pony rides. If a British climber came up to talk, the climber would sit down and Pasang Phutar had to get off the bench and squat at his feet. They were bad and evil men, he says, and working for them was *dhukpaa*, *dhukpaa* – oppression and hardship.

Ang Tsering, who started work in the twenties, remembers having to get off the benches, too. But he says the British were better than the Indian middle class who followed them. The British, Ang Tsering says, would hire a cook, a bearer, a watchman, a gardener, a sweeper, and a nanny. The Indians, with just as much money, tried to get by with one servant. From the servant's point of view, and Ang Tsering was a servant for a while, better a good paternalist than a cold employer.

There is a Sherpa word, *zhindak*. It means employer, but also a rich man who takes a young man under his wing, a patron. It is perfectly possible to have a bad *zhindak*; many people do. But it is better to have a bad *zhindak* than none at all. In the old days, a rich man would sometimes train a poor boy in the Tibet trade. Few poor boys got rich that way, but many heard stories of somebody who did. In Darjeeling, a British patron could change a workingman's life. So some of their Sherpa and Tibetan porters had an eye out for a possible British *zhindak*.

Many of the British climbers saw themselves as kindly fathers and (some of) their porters as loyal sons. Some other porters, of course, they found recalcitrant, lazy, weak, or bad. But with the ones they liked, the climbers felt they could share their vision of the mountains.

The climbers and porters called each other sahibs and coolies. The words ring strangely today. In Hindi, sahib originally meant 'master' or 'sir' and was a respectful term of address, particularly for an employer. But it came to be the term of address for all white people from all Indians who wanted to show respect – or had to. Memsahib was used for women. Burra sahib, literally 'great sahib,' meant a senior boss or the leader of an expedition. Sherpas used sahib as a synonym for white people. From the 1950s on, Sherpas in Nepal stopped using it to address white climbers, as they found it too colonial and subservient. Instead, they called the climbers by their first names, just as the climbers spoke to them.

In this book I have used the word *sahib* quite a lot, as I am uncomfortable writing *white boss*, which is what it means.

Coolie was, and is, Hindi and Nepali for 'porter' or 'unskilled laborer.' In Nepali it can be derogatory, as in 'Who's he?' – 'He's just a coolie.' It can also be neutral, as in 'What work are you doing these days?' – 'Coolie work.' British colonialists took the word to China, where they used it for Chinese workers. Now in English it sounds pejorative. I have largely avoided it here. However, when I quote sahibs using it, they are not being rude, just using the Hindi word for a porter.

The 1922 expedition was the first full-scale attempt to climb Everest. It reached Rongbuk Monastery, at the foot of the valley up to Base Camp. This massive monastery had hundreds of men and women meditating in its buildings or in caves farther up the valley. They were drawn to the grandeur and isolation of Everest, massive from the Tibetan side, and to the personality of the Rimpoche, the incarnate lama who had founded the monastery.

The Rimpoche later wrote his autobiography in Tibetan, parts of which have been translated. He seems to have sympathized with the monks in Lhasa and been against giving the British permission to climb Everest. In 1922 the local Tibetan government official urged the Rimpoche to meet the members of the British expedition. He didn't want to. The official said he at least had to meet the leader. The idea made the Rimpoche feel sick, but he told the official, 'If one meets one heretic, there is no point in keeping all the others back.'[5]

The next day the Rimpoche met the leader, Charlie Bruce, three other climbers and their interpreter, the Darjeeling Tibetan Karma Paul. Charlie Bruce was the Gurkha officer who had climbed with Mummery on Nanga Parbat in 1895. Now he was a general, fifty-six, big, fat, and fit, and had been climbing in the Himalayas for over thirty years. Bruce spoke fluent Nepali, relished fights with Punjabi professional wrestlers, and was an innovator in small-unit combat on the North-West Frontier. The Gurkhas who served under him said that Bruce had sex with the wife of every man in the regiment. The wives of the enlisted Gurkhas, of course, not those of his fellow officers.[6]

The Rimpoche asked Charlie Bruce why he had come to climb Everest. Bruce said it was to get closer to God, which is what he thought the Rimpoche wanted to hear. Karma Paul translated this into Tibetan as saying the British government would give Bruce a lot of money if they climbed Everest.

The Rimpoche told Bruce, 'As our country is bitterly cold and frosty, it is difficult for others than those who are devoted to religion not to come to harm. As the local spirits are furies, you must act with great firmness.'[7] He was trying to warn the British that Everest was dangerous.

The expedition Base Camp was in a high and empty valley. All around them were several hundred men and women meditating, each in his or her own cave or rock shelter. They were monks and nuns, local laypeople, and old people thinking of their fate. Some spent weeks alone, and some years. All had been drawn by the emptiness and the spiritual power of Everest towering above. Captain John Noel, one of the transport officers on the expedition, was impressed by

one tremendous reputed saint, who has been sealed up in a rock cell beneath Mount Everest, dwelling in darkness for fifteen years, meditating, sitting motionless, year after year. Once a day brother monks bring a cup of water and a handful of barley meal to this self-isolated priest. I myself watched, and saw through a hole in the wall of the hermit's cell a hand steal out and take in the water and the bread. Even then the hand was muffled, because not only must no one see him, not even the light of day may touch his skin.[8]

Thirteen ṣahibs, one hundred high- and low-altitude porters, and three hundred pack animals settled in among the hermits seeking peace and loneliness. It was forbidden to kill animals in the valley – General Bruce had to promise the Rimpoche he would not hunt. Every morning the climbers watched the wild mountain goats coming to the hermits' cells a hundred yards from the camp. Each hermit would feed the goats something, and they would go on to the next cave or rock shelter. All the animals were tame, and the rock pigeons and ravens fed from the climbers' hands.

Why did the British need so many porters?

They were using what was then called the Arctic Method and is now called laying siege to the mountain. Starting from Base Camp, the European climbers would find a route up, climbing on rock, breaking trail through deep snow, skirting potential avalanches, and putting fixed ropes and ladders in place for the men to follow. Then the porters, accompanied by other climbers, would carry the supplies up to Camp 1. Above them the lead climbers would be breaking trail to Camp 2.

Men moved up and down the mountain all the time. The European climbers took turns breaking trail and accompanying the porters. Exhausted porters went down to Base Camp, and rested men went back up. Some of the climbers might be breaking trail for Camp 6 while some porters were still carrying up to Camp 2.

Gradually, camp by camp, European climbers and Asian porters tried to work their way up until they established a camp just below the summit. From there two European climbers on one rope would go to the peak without any porters. They needed a pyramid of supplies to get two sleeping bags, two nights of food, some rope, and a groundsheet to the top camp. Getting those supplies to the top camp typically required ten European climbers, forty or fifty Asian high-altitude porters, and two or three hundred low-altitude porters to carry all the loads from the roadhead up to Base Camp.

In the Alps, two or four men might climb alone. But in the Himalayas, above seventeen thousand feet, camp-by-camp climbing was far safer. Anybody caught in a Himalayan storm could retreat down the mountain and soon find tents, warmth, food, and friends. If anybody was injured in a high camp, help could come quickly from the camp immediately below.

And Himalayan climbing was a sport invented by English gentlemen. On Everest the porters carried thirty-pound packs high on the mountain, and the British carried nothing – they were saving themselves for the summit. On the two weeks' walk to Everest Base Camp, the climbers rode horses and the porters walked, carrying packs. This seemed natural. The climbers had servants in England, and the British in India had even more servants. On a picnic by the river, or out hunting for tigers, the British expected somebody else to carry and serve. It was no different on the mountain.

Today some climbers do attempt Himalayan peaks in small 'Alpine' parties without porters. This seems more romantic, cleaner, to them. It is also cheaper, and they will not be responsible for the deaths of any porters. Indeed, today climbers try to do what has already been done in a more difficult or dangerous way, looking always for the chance to make the first solo winter ascent of the north face direct with no trousers on. But it is still, today, safer to climb the Himalayas by the siege method. And the British in 1922 were climbing at what was, then, the edge of human possibility.

Nobody attempted the faces of Everest until the 1970s. Instead they tried to climb up to the ridges and then along them. It was easier on the ridge, and they were safe from avalanches and rock-falls.

First the 1922 British expedition had to reach the ridge. They climbed straight up the side of the West Ridge to a saddle they called the North Col, at twenty-three thousand feet. It was the highest men had ever camped. From there four climbers tried for the summit and failed. Charlie Bruce, the leader and the most experienced Himalayan climber, and Wakefield, the expedition doctor, said it was time to go home. The monsoon had just begun, and the slopes were covered in new, soft snow – perfect avalanche conditions. George Mallory and Howard Somervell rebelled and insisted on going up for one last try.

Mallory was part of the British establishment, but not happy in it. A natural athlete, thin, muscular, and graceful, he had been the most beautiful man of his year at Cambridge. He was a life-long socialist, a campaigner for women's suffrage, and a noisy advocate of progressive education. Mallory was bisexual, published a book on Boswell, was working on a novel, and drew his friends from Bloomsbury's avant-garde of artists and writers. He enjoyed going up to London to pose nude for the artist Duncan Grant. In 1919, Mallory went to Ireland to see the war against Britain at first hand, from the point of view of his hosts there, the Irish Republican Army.

George Mallory existed on the margins of the British upper class. His wife, Ruth, had her own inherited income, and they employed five servants. Until he came to Everest, he had been a teacher at Charterhouse, one of the best-known 'public schools' – the British term for elite private schools. He disliked that job and quit to come to Everest in 1921. For the moment, he was dependent on his wife's income, and on giving lectures about Everest. Ruth had been persuaded to let him risk his life on the grounds that the cachet of doing well on Everest would change his prospects in life.

Mallory was intensely ambitious for the summit. On June 7, Mallory, Somervell, Ferdie Crawford, and fourteen porters were climbing above Camp 2 and had almost reached the North Col. These porters were all Darjeeling men. The expedition had hired Tibetan porters from around Rongbuk as well, both men and women, but they refused to climb above Camp 2. A goddess lived on the mountain, and they were afraid of the demons who guarded her.

The sahibs and porters were crossing a steep field of snow, the afternoon sun sparkling and refracted in the crystals. Avalanches are most likely in the afternoon when the sun has warmed and loosened the snow. But Mallory and Somervell were pushing hard for the top. Mallory heard 'an ominous sound, sharp, arresting, violent and yet somehow soft, like an explosion of untapped gunpowder.'[9] He had never heard that sound before, but knew immediately it was an avalanche. Within seconds he was covered in snow.

Mallory dug himself out of the snow. He had been roped to three other men – a porter, Somervell, and Crawford. The four men checked each other. They were all right. They looked down the slope. Below them, the four porters on the second rope were alive, too, sitting on the snow, pointing downward.

The avalanche had carried the nine porters on the third rope over the edge of an ice cliff.

Captain John Noel, the 'army crack shot', and Doctor Wakefield were watching from the camp below, following the black dots of the climbers struggling in soft snow. Noel and Wakefield looked away, and when they looked back, there were no black dots. Noel turned to the doctor:

'"What does it mean, man?" I cried.

'"Avalanche," he replied.'[10]

Noel had a look through the telescope and saw 'the whole surface of the cliff torn away. . . . [We] called to the porters, pointed to the cliff, and told them what had happened. They became terribly excited and started to talk among each other and cry. But we got them going.'

The sahibs and porters started up the mountain, carrying blankets and bottles of hot liquids, 'expecting that we might have to spend a night in the open. . . . Evening was already coming on. We did not know whether we would find anybody alive. With every available porter carrying the utmost he could in food and blankets, we struggled forward to reach the scene of the disaster.'

They found Mallory frantically digging in the snow. Above him, the surviving porters from the second rope sat on the edge of the ice cliff, where they had just stopped their fall. They did not dare to stand and walk, or even to crawl up the slope, for fear they would provoke another avalanche. For the next few hours those men sat there, motionless, watching the climbers below them dig for their dead companions. They waited for exhaustion and cold to make them slip over the edge to their own deaths. Noel, eyeing their position carefully, thought it would probably be impossible to save them.

The porters who had gone over the edge, Noel explains,

had been swept down with such force that some of the ropes between them had snapped like threads of cotton. The men lowest on the slope had been carried over the edge into the crevasse. Some had fallen into the jaw of the crevasse and were buried deep in the soft snow. Others had shot over the gaping jaw and had hit the hard lips of ice. They, we found afterwards, had been instantly killed, their heads and bones and bodies smashed.

We called upon the men we had brought out from the camp to aid us to find these fellows. These men were mostly blood relations, brothers and cousins of those who had vanished. But . . . demoralization seized them and they would not stir. 'What was the use?' they said. They must all be dead. The spirits had struck at them. Survivors would only be braving the spirits' wrath by going to help them.

[The sahibs dug.] Five were found dead, shattered on the hard ice. But nearby was a crevasse filled with soft snow. Two ropes, such as joined the men together, led to this crevasse and disappeared in the snow. We pulled, but could not budge the ropes. We dug into the fluffy stuff. Five feet down Mallory struck a boot, and digging farther, pulled a man out. He was unconscious, but although buried for over two hours, he regained consciousness and later completely recovered.

Another man was reached by digging along the strand of rope until the ice ax struck his boots. He had dived head-first into the snow. When dug out he was found to be stone dead. The rope around him went deeper into the snow. Mallory tugged at it. The other missing man was on the rope somewhere deeper down, but we could dig no more.

Lhakpa, Nurbu, Pasang, Pema, Sanga, Dorje, and Pemba were dead.

In 1916, Howard Somervell had been a surgeon at the Battle of the Somme. The surgeons had four operating tables in one tent, while several thousand men lay in row after row around the tent, dying on stretchers. On short breaks from the operating table, Somervell wandered among the rows of dying men, talking with them briefly. Not one of those men asked to be operated on ahead of the others. That day Somervell became a fierce and angry pacifist and remained one for the rest of his life.

Now, as he dug at the snow, he thought, 'Only Sherpas and Bhotias [Tibetans] killed – why, oh why could not one of us Britishers have shared their fate.'

'I would gladly at that moment have been lying there dead in the snow, if only to give those fine chaps who had survived the feeling that we shared their loss, as we had indeed shared the risk.'[11]

It had been Somervell and Mallory's insistence on climbing in such avalanche conditions that had killed the porters, and Somervell knew it. Two months later he gave up a promising career in London to become a doctor in an Indian mission hospital in Kerala and stayed there for the rest of his working life.

Finally, after hours, with night drawing in, Somervell and Mallory stopped digging and went back up to the men sitting on the edge of the cliff above them. 'The men had completely lost their nerve and were crying and shaking like babies,' wrote Noel, ever the tough soldier. 'Mallory and Somervell got them across and around the ice wall one by one. . . . It was pitiable to see their condition and their grief. They asked us where their brothers were, because some of the survivors had lost their brothers. They went to the crushed bodies and took their amulets and other religious family tokens from their necks.'[12]

The men who had sat motionless for hours were saved. Still, seven men were dead, and Mallory and Somervell had taken an unacceptable risk leading them over deep, soft snow in the afternoon. Down in camp George Mallory wrote to Ruth:

> The consequences of my mistake are so terrible; it seems almost impossible to believe that it has happened for ever and I can do nothing to make good. There is no obligation I have so much wanted as taking care of those men. They are children where mountain dangers are concerned, and they do so much for us, and now through my fault seven of them have been killed.[13]

It is the language of paternalism, of caring for men who are like children. But the anguish, and the guilt, are genuine.

That was the end of the expedition. General Bruce sent a messenger to the Rimpoche at Rongbuk Monastery, with money and the request for a ceremony. 'I was filled with great compassion for their lot who underwent such suffering on such unnecessary work,' the Rimpoche wrote. 'I organised a very important *bsngo-smon*.'[14]

On the way down, eight sahibs went to visit the Rimpoche. According to the Rimpoche, Bruce began by asking what had happened to the money he had sent and if the Rimpoche had performed the ceremony for the seven dead porters. The Rimpoche cut across his flow of words, asking Charlie Bruce:

> 'Are you not weary?'
> 'Me. I'm alright. A few men died,' he replied and was a little ashamed.
> I gave him a wooden tub-full of beads and a gold and

copper image of [the deity] Tara; I resolved to pray for his conversion to Buddhism in the future.[15]

Bruce wrote later that the Rimpoche had been 'intensely sympathetic and kind over the whole matter. It is very strange to have to deal with these curious people; they are an extraordinary mixture of superstition and nice feelings.'[16]

After Bruce left, the local villagers knew the British had left behind considerable stores of flour, rice, oil, and other luxuries. The upper valley was sacred land, but twenty young men from one village went up there without telling the monks. According to the Rimpoche, they passed by the monastery 'secretly at midnight and, at dawn, arrived at the base of the mountain. From a cleft in the nearby scree, seven bears came out. At first one man caught sight of them; after that they all saw them. Whatever their hope when they saw the supplies, in a great panic, they all ran away.'

The men, terrified, went to the monastery and admitted what they had done. They asked the Rimpoche, 'Is not this inauspicious sight terrible and will not our lives be harmed?'[17]

The Rimpoche assured them that the spirits were angry, but the monks would do the proper rituals and no harm would come.

The Rimpoche does not mention it, but it cannot have seemed accidental that seven men had died and seven bears were found in the food stores.

When Sir Francis Younghusband, the expedition organizer back in London, heard the news of the tragedy, he wrote to his wife: 'They have done so splendidly it is particularly bad luck. But thank goodness no European life was lost.'[18] Younghusband began planning another expedition to Everest.

Mallory returned to England. Three climbers from the expedition – Charlie Bruce, Strutt, and Longstaff – implied that Mallory and Somervell had, at the least, made errors of judgment that had led to the deaths of the seven porters in the avalanche. Mallory successfully defended himself to the Mount Everest Committee, a joint venture by the Alpine Club and the Royal Geographical Society, under Younghusband. By now Mallory seems to have persuaded himself that it was not his fault. Certainly his wife, Ruth, felt strongly that his guilt was self-destructive and that he should leave it behind. With recommendations from the Mount Everest Committee and eminent climbers, he found a job as an extension lecturer at Cambridge University, teaching evening classes for the Workers Educational Association. He loved the job.

The Mount Everest Committee eventually agreed to onetime payments of 250 rupees to the families of each of the seven dead porters. In Indian terms, this was almost a year's wages per man. In British money, it was £17.50. For comparison, Mallory made £500 a year in his job at Cambridge, and the Mount Everest Committee raised £2,474 more than they spent on the 1922 expedition.

Younghusband and the Mount Everest Committee organized another expedition, and in 1924 Mallory and Somervell were back on the mountain, with Charlie Bruce the leader again. His nephew Captain Geoffrey Bruce, another Gurkha officer, was in charge of hiring the porters. Geoffrey Bruce later wrote:

> Our experience proves that the light, well-proportioned, clean-bred man is the one to take. All carrying porters should be either Sherpas or Bhotias. The Civil Surgeon at Darjeeling will always help with medical examination of all prospective starters. Old hands should only be employed a second time if their record and conduct on the previous occasion were outstandingly good. A few old hands should be chosen for obvious reasons, but should be very carefully chosen. Otherwise new keen men are infinitely preferable, and less likely to play the 'old soldier.'[19]

It is easy to see why Captain Geoffrey Bruce wanted to avoid 'old soldiers' with memories of the disaster in 1922. New men would be easier to control and more likely to take risks. But maybe it wasn't quite like that. Captain Noel was there, too, and he said:

> We were greeted by all our old Sherpa porters, who wanted to join us again, despite the catastrophe of 1922. Many other men also offered their services. The general [Charlie Bruce] and Doctor Hingston held a careful inspection of them, but often, as one old favourite after another presented himself and saluted, the general would slap him on the back and pass him quickly by the doctor. 'Why, here is old Chemshar again! Fine! Of course he must come; and there is—'. So all the old men were collected again.[20]

General Charlie Bruce, after all, was an 'old soldier' himself, 58 in 1924. One of the old soldiers he chose was the man Mallory had dug out of the snow alive after the avalanche. In all, there were fifty Tibetan high-altitude porters from Darjeeling, and five Sherpas.

The prejudice against experienced Sherpas persisted among some sahibs for years. Frank Smythe was on the 1933 British expedition to Everest. There, he wrote, 'only young men were being chosen for our porter brigade, for "old soldiers" have a knack of grousing and imparting discontent to their fellows, whilst some of the men of past expeditions were still a prey to the superstitions woven about Everest.'[21]

What the superstitions around Everest boiled down to was the idea that the mountain was dangerous and climbers should be careful. Avoiding porters who had learned this lesson made it easier to climb the mountain, but also more dangerous. So Captain Bruce wanted to hire men without experience, because he had to control the porters, and General Bruce wanted to hire men with experience, because he needed them.

When the 1924 expedition reached Rongbuk Monastery, a monk approached John Noel:

An old man with a gnarled face and only two teeth in his head, shuffled over the courtyard wrapped in his maroon gown, and led me to the temple entrance, where on an inner wall, so dark that I could not at first distinguish it, he showed me a freshly executed painting. Looking at it carefully, I saw it was . . . [of a] speared white man lying below Mount Everest surrounded by guard dogs and Sukpas and horned demons. I got my interpreter Cheddup to explain it; and I took a photograph and tracings of it. It was a curious picture.[22]

The picture showed the feelings of the monks and nuns at Rongbuk, and their pleasure at the idea of dead British climbers. Although he did not spell it out for his British readers, Noel understood this. He also understood what fun the old monk was having showing him the picture.

The porters must have seen that picture, too.

This time the sahibs made sure the porters never climbed alone. If a porter died, there would be a sahib dead on the rope with him.

The 1924 expedition worked their way up to Camp 3, a day's carry below the North Col. As sahibs and porters stocked Camp 3, Mallory established a route up to Camp 4, on the North Col itself. He chose a route that passed slightly above the site of the avalanche two years before and hoped he had it right this time.

The porters at Camp 3 were in trouble. Two years before, Mallory had disdained the new oxygen apparatus the scientist George Finch was testing on Everest. By 1924, Mallory was planning on using oxygen and seemed convinced it would make the difference between success and failure. He was in charge of moving supplies up the mountain and decided to give oxygen cylinders priority over loads of food, clothes, and blankets. The British climbers wore good stout English boots, Kashmiri puttees, four pairs of socks, wool trousers, several cardigans, and sometimes an anorak. The porters wore much less and ate worse. The British climbers had meat, cheese, and sugar. The porters did not.

Now, with their rations cut further to facilitate moving the oxygen up, hunger helped the cold cut deeper, and the weather turned bad. On the ridges, the wind reached one hundred miles an hour and snow was blown a thousand feet into the air. Many of the porters complained of altitude sickness at Camp 3, and many got frostbite.

The sickest men were evacuated down the mountain to Base Camp. Shamsherpun, a Nepali Gurkha soldier, died just above Base Camp of frostbite and a brain hemorrhage. Man Bahadur, another Gurkha, was frostbitten so badly 'his legs went dead as far as his hips.'[23] At Base Camp his legs turned black and putrid, and slowly he rotted to death.

Shamsherpun and Man Bahadur died because of an error of judgment about supplies by George Mallory, an error caused by his will to succeed. He pushed on.

The climbers asked the Rimpoche at Rongbuk Monastery for a ceremony to put heart into their broken porters. The British interpreter, Karma Paul, later told Captain Noel that during the ceremony the Rimpoche had blessed the men and said of Chomolungma (Mount Everest): 'Great Chomolungma, the Goddess Mother, is guarded by the spirits of our ancient religion. I will intercede with the gods for you. Your turning back will bring pleasure to the demons. They have forced you back, and will force you back again.'[24]

One of the porters who listened to the Rimpoche was Sherpa Ang Tsering. He was twenty, he had only been in Darjeeling six months, and it was his first expedition job. Ten years later Ang Tsering would be the last man off Nanga Parbat alive. Now he listened as the Rimpoche warned the porters that the gods of the mountain were angry. The Rimpoche told the porters to do their job, that was what they had to do. But he warned them to dump their loads quickly at the highest camp, leave the British there, turn round, and come back down immediately. People were going to die up there, the Rimpoche said. Don't let it be you. Ang Tsering believed the Rimpoche and followed his advice.

*   *   *

Back up at Camp 3, Mallory had finished the route to the North Col. It was always going to be tricky taking the porters up the North Col for the first time. Toong Soom Busti was a small place. All the porters in 1924 must have heard about the avalanche from the survivors of 1922. Some of them had been there.

On May 21, 1924 Somervell, Irvine, and Hazard led the first twelve porters from Camp 3 up to Camp 4 on the North Col. Somervell didn't like the conditions: 'It was wild and stormy, with showers of light, powdery snow which obliterated all the tracks' (which Mallory had made earlier).[25]

On the hard pitches the sahibs had to cut steps in the snow for the porters. Mallory had fixed ladders up an ice chimney, and the porters went up them hand over hand. Just below the North Col they came to the difficult bit, a steep ice field two hundred feet wide they had to traverse. They did it without mishap.

Somervell and Irvine, their duty done, turned back down to Camp 3 for the night. They were feeling strong, and they didn't want to use up the supplies at Camp 4.

Hazard, the other sahib, and twelve porters climbed for a few more minutes up to Camp 4 at 22,700 feet. There they put up tents and settled in for the night.

Next day it snowed. Down at Camp 3 Somervell wrote in his diary: 'Awful day. The party we hoped to bring up the North Col to complete its equipment couldn't even start. [Camp] 3 was hell – I think the thirteen of them on the North Col are more comfortable than we are. But this snow is making the way up very dangerous. We hope to send another party up tomorrow, but it's not too safe on the slopes of the Col.'[26]

Somervell feared another avalanche.

Next morning Captain Geoffrey Bruce, Odell, and fourteen porters started up to the North Col with more supplies. But the fresh snow was so thick they had to dump their loads below the ice chimney and return to Camp 3.

Above them, Hazard Sahib and twelve porters were trapped in the tents on the North Col for thirty-six hours. They must have talked about many things in those tents, including the avalanche two years before. Now they started down. It was snowing, but if they stayed where they were on the North Col, the weather might well get worse.

Almost immediately below Camp 4 they came to the ice field they had crossed without mishap two days before. It had now been snowing for forty-eight hours. Fresh snow causes avalanches. Fresh snow lying above a sheet of ice is particularly dangerous. And they were just above the site of the 1922 avalanche. Four of the twelve porters refused to cross the ice field. Hazard and the other eight porters left them there and went on down to Camp 3.

Why did Hazard leave the four men behind? It is difficult to know what went through his mind. Somervell had earlier written to his brother from Base Camp: 'Hazard has built a psychological wall round himself, inside which he lives. Occasionally he bursts out of this with a "Egad, this is fine!" – for he enjoys (inside the wall) every minute of the Tibetan travel, and even hardship. Then the wall closes, to let nothing in.'[27]

Hazard was an experienced Alpine climber. During the war he had been an officer of sappers, digging tunnels under enemy lines, but he had not been to the Himalayas before. Of course, he did not make the decision alone. Eight other men went down with him. But Hazard was the leader. He was the only sahib and the only climber among them, and he was the employer. In that time and place Hazard's words would have counted for more. But the eight porters who came down with him were neither children nor moral imbeciles. It seems likely that they, and Hazard, thought that the four frightened men were choosing death, and they did not want to make the same choice.

From Camp 3 Somervell saw them coming down. Relieved, he wrote in his diary: 'Hazard seems to be coming down with his coolies – the best thing he could do, and a bit more snow would have been a proper mess-up.' But then: 'Later. Hazard arrived with only eight coolies – that means four of them are still up there – we all felt it a great mistake to leave anyone behind; either all or none should have come down.'[28]

Somervell was furious. It continued to snow.

Somervell and Mallory, the survivors of 1922, felt they had no choice but to rescue the four porters from the North Col the next morning. Edward Norton had taken over the leadership of the expedition after Bruce had fallen ill and returned to Darjeeling. Now Norton volunteered to go with Somervell and Mallory. Norton was a lieutenant colonel in the Gurkhas and spoke Nepali fluently. He knew the men up on the North Col were people. He felt

the only thing that mattered was to get the men down alive. Personally my one fixed determination had all along been that we must on no account have any casualties among our porters this year, and here we were, faced with the very real possibility of losing four men; for it must be admitted that our chances of rescuing the marooned porters did not appear rosy at this time. We were all distinctly the worse for wear; both Mallory and Somervell had very bad coughs and sore throats, which hampered them badly in climbing, the condition of the North Col slopes must make climbing exceedingly slow and laborious, and there was danger of avalanche. As we lay in our tent that night and listened to the soft pattering of snow on its walls, I know that neither Mallory nor I would have taken a bet of two to one against a successful issue to our undertaking the next day, although at the time we kept such pessimistic views to ourselves. About midnight the snow stopped falling and the moon came out.[29]

It was quite possible, of course, that the sahibs themselves would die in the attempt.

Above them, the four porters lay in their tent together, listening to the barking of the gods who were the guard dogs of the mountain. They had eaten the last of their food that morning, and they did not expect to be rescued. They lay in dread, waiting for the demons and death.[30]

Norton, Mallory, and Somervell left at eight in the morning

and climbed slowly. Only Norton had crampons. Somervell felt 'avalanches imminent almost everywhere.'[31] And it was difficult to move through deep snow at almost twenty-three thousand feet.

By six in the evening they reached the ice field just below the Col and saw one of the stranded porters on the other side waiting for them. They shouted at him to move.

'Up or down?' he said.

Norton suddenly thought that the porter did not recognize the extent of the danger if he did not see the importance of getting down immediately. Norton wondered if stupidity and inexperience had led the men to stay up.

'Down,' Norton shouted across the ice field, and the man disappeared. He returned a few minutes later with the other three.

The sahibs had brought a two-hundred-foot rope. Now Mallory and Norton buried their ice axes in the snow to provide a secure belay for Somervell. Somervell then walked across the ice to the waiting porters. He ran out of rope twenty feet from the porters – about eight paces away.

Somervell spoke a little Hindustani. So did the porters. He encouraged the porters to work their way up so that they were standing more or less above him, and then to walk down to him. He drove his ax into the ice, belayed himself, and caught the first two men. Those two men then worked their way along the rope to Mallory, Norton, and safety.

The two men left above the ice field watched in relief. They couldn't bear to wait any longer. Without working their way across above Somervell, they started straight into the ice field. One of them slipped and started a small avalanche. Somervell watched helplessly as both men slid toward the cliff and death. But they stopped just above the cliff. Somervell thanked God. He thought he could reach them: 'I chaffed them and said cheerio (as well as I could in their not too familiar tongue) to prevent wind-up and struggle which might lead to further disaster. I told them to remain perfectly still.'[32]

Somervell pulled his ax from the ice and drove it in closer to the two men. He untied the rope from his waist, wrapped it once around the head of the ax, and tied the rope around his right wrist. Mallory and Norton held their end of the rope out at arm's length.

Somervell walked carefully across the ice toward the two porters sitting motionless on the edge of the cliff. The rope on his right wrist stopped him just short of the two men. Somervell was a big man. He reached out his left hand as far as he could. Spread-eagled, he could just grab one porter by the scruff of the neck and haul him back to the rope.

Then Somervell went back and got the second man.

Down at Camp 3, Noel had been filming the rescue from a mile and a half away. (He was making the movie of the expedition.) Now he set off to meet Somervell and the others coming down.

We had toiled through the darkness for about one and a half hours when, in reply to our frequent call, we heard answering shouts. . . . When we met, the whole lot of them sank down in the snow. . . . The porters were like drunken men, not knowing what was happening. Norton, Somervell and Mallory hardly spoke. We got out our hot food to give them. One of the porters vomited as quickly as he took the stuff into his mouth and the other we had to prop up with our knees. . . . They were not fit for another stroke of work for the rest of the expedition. In fact, during the next few days there was a general exodus from Snowfield Camp of everybody who was not up to the mark.[33]

That was how paternalism was supposed to work, with the good fathers taking care of their men.

Ang Tsering was one of the men who stayed, who was 'up to the mark.' He had gone up, dumped his load, and got down fast, as the Rimpoche had advised.

Norton and Somervell went for the top first, without oxygen. Somervell had to stop. Norton, climbing alone without oxygen, got to within one thousand vertical feet of the top before he gave up.

Then Mallory got his chance, with oxygen. They had, he calculated, just enough. He had a choice of two companions. One was John Odell, an experienced climber who had been moving strongly the last few days. The other was Sandy Irvine, twenty-one, beautiful, broad-chested, and strong. But for the expedition, he would have rowed for Oxford against Cambridge that year. Irvine had been on one arctic expedition, but had little experience of climbing. It was a sign of the amateurism of the British climbing world, and their class confidence, that a chap could make it to the highest camp on Everest on the word of other Oxford men who found him a useful fellow.

Mallory chose Irvine over Odell as his companion for the summit attempt. It has been suggested and is possible that this was because Mallory was romantically drawn to Irvine. But it seems more likely that it was because Irvine was a strong, young engineering student who knew how to fix the oxygen apparatus.

When Mallory was married ten years before, he wanted to take his wife, Ruth, climbing in the Alps on his honeymoon. His old friend Geoffrey Young, who had taught him much on Alpine ridges, wrote to Mallory to warn him that he tended to take too many chances with inexperienced, young people. Mallory was hurt and still took Ruth climbing.

Now he took Irvine. Several hours later Odell saw them heading for the summit, and they were never seen again. Mallory's body was discovered high on the mountain in 1999, but to this day nobody knows if he and Irvine made the summit. Mallory's ambition had led to errors of judgment that killed Lhakpa, Nurbu, Pasang, Pema, Sanga, Dorje, Pemba, Shamsherpun, Man Bahadur, Sandy Irvine, and Mallory himself. That very ambition, his willingness to die to get to the top, to strive despite all obstacles, made him a hero and a legend for millions.

The total cost of the 1924 expedition to Everest was ten thousand pounds. Captain Noel had put up eight thousand pounds of that in return for the right to make a film of the expedition. Now he needed to make his money back. In Britain the film was hyped, in the words of the *Weekly Dispatch*, with 'Everest as leading lady,' a story of 'man's passionate struggle to conquer the dreadful virgin of the snows.'[34]

Captain Noel had persuaded five monks from the great monastery at Gyantse in Tibet to come to Britain with him. Buddhist monks in Tibet did long ritual dances at special ceremonies every year, reenacting the coming of Buddhism to Tibet and the driving out of malevolent demons by the clear light of religion. Now, on the stage of the Scala cinema, dressed in cheap masks, the monks did short reprises of what Noel called 'devil dances.' The headlines in the *Daily Sketch* read:

Bishop to Dance on Stage
High Dignitaries of Tibetan Church Reach London
Music from Skulls
Tom-Tom Ceremonies from the Himalayas[35]

Other Tibetans were living in England. Some were studying at the military academy, Sandhurst, some were in business, and one was married to a British diplomat. They sent the news of the Dancing Lamas home. In any case, the Dalai Lama subscribed to the London papers. He, and the Tibetan government, took offense. The opposed monks were finally able to win the argument against the British alliance. Tibet made a formal complaint to the British foreign office, and no British expeditions to Everest were allowed for the next nine years.

What did those Sherpas think as they waited motionless on the ice while Mallory dug in the snow beneath them? Captain Noel wrote as if the porters, in their fear of the mountain, were subject to a superstitious dread. By making their fear religious, he made it foolish. But we must be careful here. What the Rimpoche and the porters were saying was that Everest was dangerous. This was also what Charlie Bruce tried to tell Mallory, though he put it in secular language. Mallory and Somervell ignored them all, as many foreigners have ignored many Sherpas over the years.

In 2000, I interviewed an experienced Sherpa climber in Kunde, a careful man, polite and diplomatic. We talked for an hour without him saying anything critical about anybody.

I asked him what were the best and worst expeditions he had worked for.

All good, he said.

Who were the best and worst individual foreigners you worked for?

All good, he said.

Do foreign climbers understand about avalanches? I asked.

He looked at me, lost for words, unable to think of a diplomatic reply to such a stupid question.

Almost every experienced Sherpa climber I have talked to agrees that avalanches are the major danger on the Himalayan peaks, that foreigners do not understand avalanches, and that the main danger on expeditions arises when foreigners will not listen to warnings about avalanches.[36]

The more risks you take with avalanches, the likelier you are to reach the summit of a Himalayan peak. If you don't climb in the afternoon, there is less risk of avalanche, but it takes much longer to get up the mountain. Usually the steepest possible route is the safest from avalanches, and also the hardest and slowest. Major Himalayan expeditions work within small margins for success. The foreigners, for whom the summit is most important, accept risks. What matters to the Sherpas are their lives and families. They don't want to take those chances, but often have to do what their employers say.

For instance, Major H. P. S. Ahluwalia, who was on the 1965 Indian expedition to Everest, said that 'Camp III was established at 22,300, and although it was considered safe, it was very unpopular with the Sherpas.' This means that it was considered safe by the Indian climbers and unsafe by the Sherpas. Ahluwalia goes on:

In 1952, during the Swiss attempt, a Sherpa was killed in the area by an avalanche. Ever since then a superstition has developed that the ghost of the watchman wandered around that area. Sherpas avoided staying overnight at the camp if they could help it. They complained of being disturbed by a nocturnal visitor – the watchman knocking at their tents. One of our sherpas, Nawang Tshering, refused in 1960 to stay at Camp III in spite of very bad weather. Two years later, in 1962, with the second Indian expedition, he was hit by a rolling stone and died in the same area. This only helped to strengthen the superstition and the camp, although well stocked, remained 'haunted.'[37]

What Major Ahluwalia is saying here is that the Sherpas are superstitious because they believe it is foolish to pitch a tent in a place where an avalanche has previously killed somebody. But if there is any doubt about lightning striking twice in the same place, there is no doubt about avalanches. They happen in the same place, time after time after time, year after year after year. When Nawang Tshering refused to stay at Camp 3 in 1960, he was not being a superstitious primitive. He was trying to save his life by learning from what the Sherpas of 1952 had told him. Two years later another Indian expedition used the same site and Nawang Tshering died in a rockfall there. The same conditions that produce avalanches produce rockfalls. But even after two deaths the Indian climbers could not hear what the Sherpas were trying to tell them: that place is unsafe.

The same process was happening on Everest in 1922. The Sherpas and Tibetans on the mountain, and the monks at Rongbuk, were religious men. They thought in religious terms. But what they were saying, in these terms, was that the mountain was unsafe.

The British climbers treated this information as superstition.

I ask Khansa in Namche if Everest is safer now.

He says yes, and I ask why.

Because the climbers and Sherpas have better technique and better gear now. Moreover, there is less snow now than in 1953. And there used to be a very dangerous campsite for Camp 3, just under the Lhotse Wall where there were a lot of avalanches, but the Sherpas finally managed to persuade the foreigners to stop using it.

This was the same campsite Major Ahluwalia was talking about, where Nawang Tshering died in a rockfall in 1962.

I ask Khansa when Sherpas get angry with foreigners.

When trekkers are rude, he says. The Sherpa's face falls, he looks at the ground. Every day this happens.

And on the mountain? I ask.

Khansa says that climbers are more polite than trekkers, and Sherpas are seldom driven to anger on the mountain. But sometimes, in bad weather, a sahib says, 'You' – Khansa waves his arm imperiously upward – 'You carry a load up to Camp 3.'

The Sherpas know the weather is likely to precipitate an avalanche, but they can do nothing. They just sit there, angry inside themselves. (Khansa puts his hand on his chest under his shirt, showing me how it feels to hold your anger inside.) The Sherpas talk together, in little groups of four or six, to give each other courage. Then they sit down together and refuse to carry loads because they are angry.

Sometimes, however, they are not angry enough. On the 1963 Everest expedition, one of the American climbers ordered Khansa and the other Sherpas to carry up to Camp 4.

Khansa imitates a weak, whining Sherpa, speaking pidgin: 'Weather is too bad. Avalanche.'

He imitates a stern, deep-voiced American: 'No. You go.'

So they went in 1963, Khansa says, and just ten minutes after they set out, an avalanche caught them. It was all new snow, which saved their lives, because it was not packed hard. There were no cutting shards of ice. It was like riding on a bus, with everything trembling beneath you – Khansa bounces up and down on the seat by his kitchen fire, like a man on a bad country bus, smiling playfully, remembering being alive.

As the snow swept him along, he was caught up to his neck, but could turn his head and see his two friends on the rope falling with him. The fourth man was just outside the path of the avalanche and belayed them all with an ice ax.

The avalanche passed, and they dug themselves out. They left the oxygen bottles they were carrying in the snow. (Khansa smiles. That was a little revenge.)

They went back and told the American about the avalanche.

'I'm sorry,' the American said. (Khansa holds his hands to his face, imitating an agitated American, flapping his hands, helpless, feeling hassled.) 'I'm sorry. I'm sorry.'

Sometimes you are angry, Khansa says to me, his body trembling slightly with remembered anger at the American who did not want to know.

Are you angry when somebody dies? I ask.

No, Khansa says. You are sad.

Chapter Three

THE GERMANS

This book is about the German expedition to Nanga Parbat in 1934. Two years before that tragedy, in 1932, an earlier German attempt was made on Nanga Parbat. No Sherpas were on the 1932 expedition, but it is worth telling what happened then in some detail. The Germans had terrible trouble with their porters in 1932, and those troubles tell us a great deal about what the climbers expected of their employees and how they treated them. Although the story of 1932 tells us little about Sherpas directly, it does tell us what they had to deal with in 1934.

The German expeditions to Nanga Parbat grew out of a mountaineering rivalry with Britain. The Germans were not allowed a crack at Everest. The leader of German climbing was Paul Bauer, a Munich lawyer, a strong nationalist, and a very determined man. The British, unable to get Tibetan permission themselves, still controlled access to Tibet. They told Bauer the Tibetans would not let him in. Bauer suspected he was being kept out. In fact the Tibetan government would probably have given the Germans permission. They were trying to keep out the British and the Chinese, not all foreigners. When they did finally give the British permission three times in the 1930s, the British did not share it with other countries.

Bauer had to settle for Kangchenjunga, the third-highest mountain in the world, within sight of Darjeeling. Kangchenjunga, with its long, high, serrated ridges and steep faces, proved far more difficult than Everest. Three expeditions failed in quick succession: Bauer's German expedition in 1930, the Swiss climber Dyhrenfurth's international expedition in 1930, and another German one led by Bauer in 1931.

Back in Germany, Willy Merkl, a climber and railway engineer in Munich, decided to try Nanga Parbat. Nepal and Tibet were both closed to Germans. Of the Indian peaks, Kangchenjunga was proving too difficult, and K2 was known to be even harder, with long supply lines. That left Nanga Parbat, still higher than any other mountain yet climbed.

Photographs of Merkl on Nanga Parbat show a handsome, smiling man with a curly, blond beard and a feathered Bavarian hat. When the climbers played word games on the mountain, trying to guess the names of famous people, Merkl was the expert on engineers and factory owners. But he had difficulty raising money for Nanga Parbat. Germany was suffering through the Great Depression, and Merkl found little business sponsorship and no government support. The climbing clubs of Germany and Austria raised what they could in small donations from their members. Merkl added two Americans to the party to raise money.[1] Rand Herron was rich, tall, dark, wrote poetry in Italian, and climbed well on Nanga Parbat, but Merkl took him for his money. Elizabeth Knowlton was a Sarah Lawrence graduate, a climber, and a considerable fund-raiser. She was the expedition journalist, and the book she wrote afterward is the main source for this account of the climb.

Even with the two Americans, the expedition was still poor. None of the climbers had been to the Himalayas before. The German climbers with Himalayan experience, and the British climbers in India, all urged Willy Merkl to hire the Tibetan and Sherpa porters in Darjeeling. They had done great service for the British on Everest and the Germans on Kangchenjunga. Merkl said no, he could not afford them, and would try to hire cheaper local porters near Nanga Parbat. He was to regret this.

Between 1919 and 1932 the independence movement led by Mahatma Gandhi had transformed the relations between British rulers and Indian subjects. That, in turn, had changed the relationship between white climbers and Indian porters. This was to present Merkl with considerable problems.

The center of militancy closest to Nanga Parbat was in the North-West Frontier Province (the NWFP). NWFP, along the border between British India and Afghanistan, was Pathan (or Pushtan) country.[2] In the hills the Muslim Pathans had their own tribal organization and had fought local wars with the British on and off for eighty years. The British army would march into the Pathan hill valleys, shoot some people, burn their homes, and then retreat. In the more vulnerable plains, and in the provincial capital of Peshawar, the British authorities ruled over the Pathan peasantry as they did over the rest of British India.

In 1919, Mahatma Gandhi and his Indian National Congress began agitation for independence across India. The scale and enthusiasm of the demonstrations unnerved the British authorities. In Amritsar, the holy city of the Sikhs in the Punjab, Gurkha troops under British officers surrounded a crowd in a large square, the Jallianwallabagh. The soldiers blocked the roads out of the square and then opened fire on the unarmed crowd. The official estimate was 379 dead, but Indian estimates were much higher.

General Dyer, the officer in charge, told a commission of inquiry his aim was not simply to disperse the crowd. He had hopes of 'producing a moral effect.'[3] He did, but the moral effect was the opposite of what he'd expected. Faced with outrage and agitation across India, the imperial authorities disassociated themselves from Dyer and his massacre, but did not prosecute him.

In Muslim and Pathan Peshawar, the capital of the North-West Frontier Province, there were for the moment no demonstrations of protest at what had happened in Amritsar. But Ross-Keppel, the district commissioner, wrote to his superiors from Peshawar that Amritsar had 'united all in hatred of British rule.'[4]

India was only one of many countries seeking independence in

1919. For forty years Afghanistan had been only semi-independent, its arms imports and foreign policy controlled by British India. Now the new Amir of Afghanistan wanted full independence. In May he sent the Afghan army down the main road from Kabul to India, to the Khyber Pass on the border, with orders to attack British positions.

Demonstrations of solidarity with the Afghans now erupted in nearby Peshawar. Ross-Keppel wrote to his superiors 'the whole country is poisoned . . . Large numbers hate us with such bitterness that they would welcome even an invasion if they saw a chance of getting rid of us.'[5] The British, with mass unrest in India at their backs, used martial law to restore order in Peshawar, but quickly conceded full Afghan independence.

Abdul Ghaffar Khan then began the patient work of slowly building an Indian nationalist movement among Pathans on the North-West Frontier. The Pathan villages had long been controlled by 'khans,' large feudal landowners with gangs of armed servants to keep their sharecroppers in line. Now Abdul Ghaffar Khan called his new movement the Servants of God (*Khudai Khitmagar* in Pushtu, the Pathan language). The British called them the Red Shirts, from the long shirts their volunteers wore as a uniform.

The Servants of God were led by educated young men, many of whom came from rich families. Abdul Ghaffar Khan was himself the son of a landlord. But as they recruited more and more volunteers in the villages from among the poorer farmers and sharecroppers, the landlord khans began to seem weaker and weaker.

Then, in the spring of 1930, Gandhi and Congress launched another mass national agitation. The Servants of God joined in. The colonial police arrested two of their leaders in Peshawar; a crowd gathered outside the police station. Deputy Commissioner Metcalfe, the number two British official in Peshawar,[6] led a detachment of police and four armored cars out of the station to quiet the crowd. The crowd threw bricks and stones, one of which hit Metcalfe. The police opened fire and one of the armored cars drove through the crowd, crushing people. The police called in the army. The crowd still refused to disperse. For the next four hours soldiers and demonstrators confronted each other, with the soldiers intermittently bayoneting demonstrators who came too close.

The crowd remained determined and largely nonviolent, although some did throw stones. Many people in Peshawar, then as now, had guns. None of them were used. When it was all over, no policeman, soldier, or white person had been killed. But the official police estimate was thirty dead in the crowd. The Congress immediately sent Sardar Vallabhai Patel, a national leader and a Gujarati Hindu, to Peshawar to conduct an inquiry into the events. Patel's inquiry discovered the names of 125 known dead, but he said there were of course more whose names they did not know.

The courage of people willing to face bayonets for four hours had a considerable moral effect. Two nights later two platoons of the Royal Garwhali rifles, an Indian army regiment of hillmen from near the Nepali border, refused an order to patrol the city of Peshawar, saying they were not prepared to fire on other Indians.

The British feared that other army units in Peshawar might follow the example of the Garwhalis. That could lead to a general refusal to fire by native troops throughout the country, and that would mean the end of British rule. So the British withdrew all troops from Peshawar. For the next nine days, the Servants of God and the Congress controlled the city. The senior British administrator suffered a nervous breakdown and left town. By the middle of May the government was confident enough to send troops back into Peshawar and slowly restore some sort of order. But in the surrounding countryside something quite new was happening. For seventy years the British had fought the tribal Pathans – the Waziris, Afridis, Mohmands, Shinwaris, and the rest – in their mountain valleys. But now volunteer tribal armies – lashkars – were marching on Peshawar, the British redoubt, in support of an urban nationalist movement that united Hindus and Muslims against the British.

These tribal risings were eventually subdued, and by the fall of 1930 the British authorities had regained physical control of the North-West Frontier Province. But that fall the Servants of God turned to mass campaigns of noncooperation with the authorities. They organized refusal to pay the land tax, and by the next year tax collection was down to a third of normal. At the same time they undermined the rule of British law. They set up their own courts, parallel to the official machinery, and dispensed their own justice. Crowds confronted policemen attempting to arrest people for the British courts. Neighbors went at night to intimidate people who were thinking of being witnesses in British courts. The Servants of God organized crowds to invade British courtrooms and disrupt proceedings. This was not an attempt to overturn the law, but to take control of it from the British.

Within a year, in June 1931, the Intelligence Bureau reported that, in one rural area alone, 'Khattak country is going red with great rapidity. . . . The chief leaders . . . claim to have enlisted many thousands of volunteers' in the Red Shirts. Another British official worried that the Servants were 'in danger of assuming the character of a mass movement of the poorer and needier classes.'[7]

The movement peaked in September and October 1932, when Peshawar city alone saw twenty-seven large demonstrations, nine large public meetings, and one general strike. Six months earlier, the German-American 1932 expedition to Nanga Parbat had walked into the hills and begun to hire porters.

The 1932 expedition hired servants, cooks, porters, and pony men in Kashmir. They marched to Astor, a small town just to the east of Nanga Parbat. From there the climbers wanted to make their Base Camp on the other side of the mountain and climb it from the west. That meant carrying supplies over paths too steep and narrow for ponies. So they told the Kashmiri cooks and servants, who until then had not carried packs, that they would now have to carry loads like the porters.

The cooks and servants refused. They said they had not signed on for porter's work. Abdul Bhatt, the foreman of the servants, an experienced hunter, his face wrinkled and wise, his white beard dyed red with henna, gathered the servants and porters together. Elizabeth Knowlton said Abdul Bhatt

> made a dramatic speech, in which he showed by gesture just the way he would cut the throat of any one who should side with the sahibs, instead of upholding the natural rights of the Indian servant. . . . This was our first experience with native 'bolshevism,' a term which seemed to be loosely used for any lack of submission to the white man's traditional authority. We were told that it was spreading through the hills. For example, formerly any native seeing a white man approach on the road, would leap from his horse, and wait dismounted, as a sign of respect, while the sahib passed. Now, it was pointed out to us, many of the young men no longer do this, but ride brazenly by, like equals.[8]

The Kashmiris, and the hill people around Nanga Parbat, had all heard about the movement in the Pathan hills. The mountain valleys around Nanga Parbat – Chilas, Astor, and Hunza – had only been conquered in the last twenty to forty years. Middle-aged people could remember independence from the British, and now they could imagine it coming again. They weren't getting off their horses to bow to sahibs.

Willy Merkl did not know what to do about the striking Kashmiri servants. He turned to the liaison officer the British had provided, R. N. D. Frier, a lieutenant in the Gilgit Scouts. Gilgit was the British headquarters in these remote hills where India, China, and Afghanistan came together, and the Gilgit Scouts were a regiment of local men under the command of British officers. The British political agent in Gilgit had sent Frier to translate, help with the porters, and keep an eye on the Germans. Frier spoke Urdu and some of the local hill languages and thought he knew how to deal with natives. He fired the protesting Kashmiri servants and porters and began to look for new porters locally.

The Kashmiris had signed on because they needed the money. The new men were not quite such free labor. The British ruled much of India directly, but in these far northern hills they ruled indirectly. In some places near Nanga Parbat there were fully fledged local kingdoms with their own rulers, like the Mir of Hunza. In other places small lords such as the Nahim Tesseldar in Astor would rule a few neighboring valleys. Theoretically, these local rulers were largely free to manage their own affairs. In practice, the British political officer in Gilgit held real power over them. He had sent Frier to Astor, and now Frier asked the Nahim Tesseldar of Astor to find porters. The Nahim Tesseldar had to comply.

It was the custom in many parts of the hills of British India, Nepal, and Tibet for both the local lords and the government to summon corvée labor to work for free on portering, irrigation, and road building. Villagers were also summoned to work without pay on the fields of the local ruler or his officials. The 120 Astori men that the Nahim Tesseldar found for Frier in 1932 were, by contrast, promised and then paid wages. But they were not volunteers.

And they had not forgotten the expedition of 1895, and the deaths of Raghabir Thapa, Gaman Singh, and Frank Mummery. It was a long time ago, but Astor had been Mummery's base of operations. At the time many Astoris had felt the expedition was foolhardy. The Astoris were Muslims, and monotheists, but those who believed in the existence of dangerous demons on Nanga Parbat were proved right. They passed that information down to their grandchildren, who were now being assembled as porters.

These young Astori conscripts did not know what to do. Frier had told their lord to call for them, and they had come. They did not dare to refuse, but they did not dare climb Nanga Parbat either. So they refused to work on the grounds that the loads were too heavy. Frier, confused, told them that the Nahim Tesseldar had already agreed that they would carry fifty pounds each. The Astori men stood firm. Frier couldn't understand what was going on. Porters carried fifty pounds all the time. He told Knowlton that he hoped 'the consequences' for the porters 'would override their inexplicable obstinacy.'[9] The consequences he spoke of were what the Nahim Tesseldar would do to them if they stayed on strike.

The Nahim Tesseldar had also provided forty Balti porters for Frier. The Baltis were from the villages to the east, Muslims who spoke a language related to Tibetan. They had a traditional reputation for mild manners – their neighbors often intimidated them – and in this case they were willing to carry the loads the Astoris were refusing. So Lieutenant Frier organized the forty Baltis to carry loads in relays round the mountain to Base Camp. The next morning, the Astoris finally agreed to carry their loads, too. The Nahim Tesseldar had probably explained those 'consequences' to them. But there had also been some negotiation, and Frier had to accept the Astoris' insistence that they would not climb on the mountain itself.

At some point in the next few days, the forty Baltis made it clear that they, too, would not work on the mountain. They must have spoken with the Astoris.

The political officer in Gilgit had already asked his friend and client, the Mir of Hunza, for help. Hunza was a kingdom in the very north of the Karakoram, at the foot of the pass where the old dirt road from India crossed to Chinese Turkestan. Some said that people there routinely lived to a hundred, and others claimed it was the model for Hilton's novel about Shangri-la. It is a beautiful valley, a high desert with a few patches of irrigation, dirt-poor but famous for its apricots. The political officer in Gilgit had hopes that the Hunzas might turn out to be natural high-altitude porters. They were, after all, born hillmen like the Sherpas from Nepal. And their isolated homeland was much farther from the centers of nationalist agitation than Kashmir and Astor.

Thirty Hunza porters joined the expedition on the march round the Nanga Parbat massif, and Knowlton found it 'exhilarating to see [them] come strongly up the hillside, laughing and joking under their heavy loads. They were tall dark sinewy-looking men, of Aryan build and features' – like the sahibs. She was pleased they were 'cheerful, willing and ambitious.'[10] With them came their foreman, called a *jemadar*, the Urdu word for 'sergeant.' He was the Mir of Hunza's man, and in everything that followed he took the side of the sahibs.

A few days later they all reached Base Camp, in the flat place the Europeans called Fairy Meadow, where the local Chilasis pastured their sheep in summer. Above them was the long massif of Nanga Parbat, white ice and rock. The porters pitched the sahibs' tents, then made their own shelters of boughs, leaves, and grass a few hundred yards away. On the mountain the high-altitude porters would have tents like the sahibs. Here the Hunzas had to shift for themselves.

Lieutenant Frier and Willy Merkl agreed to pay off the 120 uncooperative Astori porters and send them home. They kept the forty Baltis, who were still refusing to climb the mountain, but who would be useful to ferry loads up to Base Camp. Some loads had been stolen on the march in, and Markl sent ten of the Hunzas and their foreman back to look for them.

That night, with their foreman gone, the Hunzas made trouble over food. They had been promised rations of a pound of wheat flour and eight ounces of lentils a day, about eighteen hundred calories in all. On the early part of the march they had lined up before one of the sahibs at dusk every day. Each man would step forward in turn, holding out his shawl before him, and the sahib would carefully pour a ration onto it. The man then nodded thank-you and went back to his place.

One thousand eight hundred calories is what people on diets eat. Three thousand calories is what people need for hard manual labor at sea level. Western climbers in the Himalayas today, eating more than three thousand calories a day, regularly lose twenty to forty pounds on an expedition. Exertion at altitude, even sleeping, strips fat and then muscle. The Hunzas were 'sinewy' men to start with.

The 1932 expedition was underfinanced, but they were not being cheap. British expeditions gave the same rations. The porters were also given tea, and a bit of salt and oil to cook the flour into flat chapati breads.. They received no meat, milk, cheese, vegetables, fruit, biscuits, candy, or sugar for their tea. The sahibs had all of these. This, too, was standard. Of course the Hunza porters were small men, and poor, and would not have eaten many more calories at home. But at home they would have had greens with their bread and would not been trying to climb the tenth-highest mountain in the world. Dorjee Lhatoo, the eminent Indian climber, says he thinks one reason so many porters at that time got sick at altitude was sheer malnutrition.

On the last part of the march around the mountain to Fairy Meadows, the promised rations had not been provided. The Hunzas had been issued rice instead. Rice is now a luxury food in those northern hills, much prized, and served at weddings. In 1932 rice was still a strange and foreign food. The Hunzas wanted their chapatis. So the first night at Fairy Meadow they reported for their rations, were offered rice, and refused it. Lieutenant Frier advised the sahibs to pay 'no attention to their strike. . . . Like naughty children, they would forget their stubbornness by morning.'[11] Early the next morning Lieutenant Frier took his gun and went off with one of the locals. Somebody had seen an ibex, the longhaired and beautiful mountain goat. With Frier and the foreman gone, the twenty remaining porters refused the rice again. They sat down in a semicircle in the middle of the sahibs' tents and began to make speeches to each other. When Knowlton later thought back on that summer, she remembered endless speeches and imagined that was what revolutionary Red Russia must have been like. She picked out 'one particularly active and talkative Hunza, whom we had already noticed as trying to stir up trouble on the way in. He was big, with a black mustache, and spoke in a loud, very emphatic voice. Another of the ringleaders, a little shifty-eyed man, was dressed appropriately enough, and conspicuously among the duns and grays, in a long faded red cloak.'[12]

The speeches went on and on, one man jumping up to speak his heart, then another. Finally Fritz Wiessner went and got the cook to translate for him.

Merkl was the leader, but Wiessner was taking charge. This was partly because Merkl was the only climber who spoke no English. But Wiessner was also an experienced climber, and a businessman with a chain of pharmacies in Germany and an import business in America. Back in Germany some people had said Wiessner should have been the leader, commenting on the good grace with which he took a backseat to Merkl.

Now the cook translated, and Wiessner stood there, trying to look relaxed and authoritative. Negotiations began. Quite quickly, Wiessner explained to the Hunzas that it had been the plan all along to double their ration of flour once they started climbing the mountain. It seems unlikely that this had been the plan. If it was, somebody would have told the Hunzas. But putting it that way allowed Wiessner to make a major concession without too obviously giving way. The Hunza porters were satisfied, stopped giving speeches, and took the rice.

Lieutenant Frier came back that afternoon with a dead ibex. That evening he explained to the porters that among the loads stolen on the march were the packs containing most of the high-altitude porters' gear: sweaters, gloves, boots, woolen hats, mufflers, goggles, ice axes, and crampons. There was only enough left for nine men. The sahibs had decided that the porters would take turns. Each man would take a full set as he went up the mountain, and when he came down to Base Camp to rest, he would pass it on to another man.

This time the porters did not make speeches. Quietly, they began packing to go home. Knowlton does not say why, but we can guess. High-altitude porters usually received their expedition clothing as a bonus at the end of the job. Such gear was worth a great deal more than their wages. In Khumbu, at that time, an expedition jacket, sleeping bag, and boots together could be sold for as much as a small house. The Hunza porters must have realized that few, if any, of them would be able to take their mountain clothing home. They must, by now, have talked to the local Astori porters about the 1895 tragedy and the god or demon who lived on the mountain. They were led by men who had never been to the Himalayas and couldn't organize boots or chapatis. It would not make sense to anyone to trust his life to such leadership.

The Hunza porters politely told Frier they were going, and all but three left. Standing, the sahibs watched silently until the Hunzas disappeared down around the corner of the path. Then the sahibs sat, despondent, in the suddenly silent camp. How could they climb with only three porters left?

One climber remembered that ten Hunza porters and their foreman were still down the valley looking for stolen loads. Perhaps, he said, they would meet the mutineers on the path and the foreman would recall them to their duty. Another climber said that the mutineers would probably persuade the others to go home to Hunza with them. 'I don't really think they'd do that,' Lieutenant Frier said with the easy confidence of a man who knew his power. He explained that the foreman was a friend of the Mir of Hunza and would 'certainly try his best to make them stay with us. And they know that I'll report what has happened, and they know, too, what the [Mir] can do to them if they leave us without good reason, like this. He has the power to take away one's land, and even to banish them completely from Hunza. Also, they don't have enough rations to get that far. Don't worry. They'll be back tomorrow, with their tails between their legs.'[13]

These were ugly threats Frier was making. A man who lost his land would become a sharecropper, getting between a fifth and third of the crop while the landlord took the rest. He would have difficulty finding wives for his sons, and in defending his wife or daughters from the unwanted attentions of richer men. He would regularly be humiliated in public situations and each year have to worry about finding enough food to feed his family.[14] Hunzas were feudal dependents, not free labor. Frier's warning to the Hunzas also suggests what 'consequences' he may earlier have held over the heads of the reluctant Astoris.

The mutineers did meet the foreman and his ten men on the path. They argued back and forth, and two of the foreman's men went on home with the mutineers. The foreman and the other eight returned to Fairy meadows that evening. They had found none of the missing kit. The sahibs decided that those eight Hunzas, plus the three who had not joined the mutiny, would give them eleven porters, and that would have to be enough.

The next morning three of the missing strikers walked back into camp, tense and silent, greeting nobody. They went straight to Frier and told him that almost all the others were in hiding just down the path, waiting, 'begging to be forgiven and taken back.' Frier let them sweat for an hour or two before he forgave them. Only 'three or four of the worst trouble-makers had not returned.'[15] The ones who came back to Fairy Meadows might be pressganged labor, but they had not lost their land at home.

From Fairy Meadows the climbers could see avalanches thunder down the mountain two or three times an hour, many falling between eight thousand and twelve thousand feet. The easiest routes to climb in the Himalayas, the relatively gentle slopes, are also usually the most likely to avalanche. The steep faces are harder to climb but less likely to avalanche because less snow sticks there. The ridges are safest of all because the climber is always on top, with the snow dropping away on either side. The ridges are also colder, swept by the full force of the wind. It takes longer to make altitude on a ridge because the climber has to go up and down, up and down, always following the vagaries of the ridge. So choosing a route in the Himalayas is always a trade-off between danger, difficulty, and time.

The climbers could see that the avalanches ruled out the easy route diagonally across the Northwest Face. The only safe route seemed to start well to the north of the summit. They would go straight up the face there, picking their way in and out of a jumble of ice and steep snowfields. Then they could reach the North Ridge, somewhat north of the low point of the ridge. From there they would have to walk down along the North Ridge, then back up it toward the summit. That would take days, perhaps weeks, of establishing camps on the ridge. All of it was over twenty-three thousand feet. It did, however, look a lot safer than the direct route.

It was; but only relatively safer. The climbing went slowly. A week after they started, they had only reached Camp 2, about a third of the way up the face to the North Ridge. One day Wiessner and Aschenbrenner led four porters and a cook up to Camp 1. That night the two sahibs shared one tent and the four porters and the cook the other. This was normal on expeditions – sahibs and coolies did not share tents. In the middle of the night all seven men woke suddenly, hearing the roar of an avalanche. The noise grew, they waited for the impact, and then it hit. Both tents buckled, their poles snapping. Wiessner and Aschenbrenner tried to push the canvas of their tent up a little off their bodies to create a pocket of air so as to breathe for a little longer.

Slowly, silence returned. All seven men found they could breathe and crawled out of their tents. They had camped just under the shelter of an ice wall, and the avalanche had gone over them. The great wind of the avalanche, a sort of bow wave in the air, had broken their tent poles, and whirling snow in the wind had covered their tents. But they were alive.

If they had camped a few feet away, where Herron and Kunigk had slept five nights before, they would not have been protected by the ice wall and the avalanche would have killed them. This cannot have increased the porters' confidence in the sahibs.

The porters were awake the rest of the night, praying. Knowlton says they prayed to Nanga Parbat, the god of the mountain, and maybe they did. But they were Muslims, and they must certainly have prayed to Allah as well.

At dawn the four Hunza porters refused to go on. They went down to Base Camp and told the others about the avalanche. They all decided, again, to go home. Then they hesitated, torn between two fears. If they stayed, they might end up in a grave in the ice. If they left, they faced the wrath of Frier and the loss of their land. So they came across from their makeshift shelters at Base Camp and sat in a clearing in the middle of the sahibs' tents, squatting on their haunches. For two days they argued with Frier and their foreman. The foreman was the bad cop, shouting at them. Frier was the good cop, although he was the one making the threats and holding the ultimate power. The porters made speeches and held their ground. Gradually Frier was forced to offer them more and more money. At the end of the two days he was proposing five rupees a day for work on the mountain, five times the usual rate. In 1932 it was more than a laborer would make in England, and about three-quarters of the federal minimum wage introduced in the USA in 1938. The Hunzas took it and went back to work on the mountain.

The sahibs and porters worked up to Camp 4, two-thirds of the way to the North Ridge. Knowlton went up with a rope of porters. At every rest stop they begged her for cigarettes, the only English word they knew. She gave each man one cigarette, and matches. One man would light his, pass it round the circle for each to take a puff, and the others would each put his carefully away for another day. In return they gave Knowlton the famous dried apricots of Hunza they had brought from home.

Climbers smoked like chimneys in those days. In his autobiography, Tenzing Norgay says that he never smoked above Base Camp. When I first read that, I was surprised he smoked at Base Camp. When I read more mountaineers' books, I realized Tenzing was boasting about his self-control. On Annapurna in 1950, Maurice Herzog, a bear of a climber, a man of extraordinary endurance, was always stopping for a refreshing smoke after a particularly difficult pitch.

The other thing the Hunza porters begged for high on the mountain was sugar for their tea.

It took the expedition three months and seven camps in all to reach the North Ridge at twenty-three thousand feet. The climbers on Everest in 1924 had reached the same height in six weeks with four camps. The Germans seem to have been going very slowly. Of course, they were working with a smaller number of porters, and apparently the sahibs didn't carry packs until virtually the end of the expedition. But even with those handicaps, one might expect them to climb more than six thousand feet in three months.

It is difficult to tell how fast they were going from the book

Knowlton wrote afterward. Most expedition books give quite precise, and often boring, lists of dates and camps and who went where. Knowlton does not. She was an experienced climber and a skilled writer. Probably she doesn't give precise dates because they would have revealed how slowly the climbers were going, and how many rest days they took.

Their bodies were learning, the hard way, what their minds had not yet grasped – just how difficult the great Himalayan peaks actually are. The face they were climbing was convoluted and steep. In places the snow was up to a man's waist, and in other places the ice was slick. They were at their limits and had to rest. So they did. Then they blamed the porters for their slow progress.

One day – Knowlton does not say what day – Wiessner, Bechtold, Merkl, and two Hunza porters were at Camp 6, just below the North Ridge. One of the porters, sick with altitude, lay groaning in his tent. The other porter refused to leave him, so the three sahibs decided to go on alone. They made the North Ridge and returned. But Camp 6 was 'not a cheerful place,' Knowlton wrote, with the sick porter moaning all the time.[16]

The sahibs knew the man had altitude sickness. In 1932 climbers knew that too little oxygen could make people sick. They did not yet understand that the only cure was to get the sick person down the mountain, and fast. Merkl, Bechtold, and Wiessner were anxious to establish Camp 7 on the ridge. They told themselves that from Camp 7 they could make the summit in two days. This was wildly optimistic, but it sprang from a deeper pessimism. They could feel that their bodies were not up to two weeks of climbing at this altitude. So they told themselves it would only take two days. They could believe this because they could easily make that kind of climb in the Alps. Their minds had yet to understand that their bodies could not do it at Himalayan altitudes, in Himalayan weather.

So they wanted to press on to stock Camp 7, not to take the sick porter down the mountain. But the next morning he was clearly so ill that they felt they couldn't leave him with only the other porter for company. This suggests that they were worried he might die. Wiessner, Bechtold, and Merkl drew straws to see who would stay with the sick man – Wiessner was 'the unlucky one'.[17] He waited, expecting Lieutenant Frier and several more porters in support.

That day Merkl and Bechtold established Camp 7 on the ridge and came down. No Frier, no porters, and 'the sick Hunza, who had now spent days in this fearful spot, groaned worse than ever. There was no hope in any load-carrying from him and his companion. Camp Six had been a dreary place for Wiessner, waiting there all day, with the coolie groaning.'[18]

That night the sky looked threatening. A snowfall would trap them all at Camp 6. Finally they decided to go down, taking the porter. Bechtold and Merkl climbed on one rope, and Wiessner took the two porters on the other. Wiessner was a safety-conscious climber all his life, and, it would seem, a more generous man than Bechtold and Merkl. The sick man, after at least four days at this altitude, could neither walk nor crawl. The healthy porter went first, Wiessner last, and the sick man between them, prone on the ice. Sometimes they dragged him, and sometimes they slid his body down the snow on a rope. They came to a steep snowfield, all jumbled with great seracs, and the healthy porter picked his way down the boulders of ice first. Below him the ice dropped away into crevasses, and to death if he slipped. The Hunza made it down to a safe stance, drove his ice ax into the snow, and wrapped the rope around it to belay Wiessner. Wiessner started down, lowering the sick man before him.

It went wrong as they reached the man on belay. Knowlton says that Wiessner 'lightly brushed' the healthy porter's shoulder and the man lost his balance. But in fact Wiessner must have fallen heavily, for the impact sent the porter flying hard enough to tear his ice ax from the snow. He slid down the mountain, pulling both the sick man and Wiessner after him. As they fell, Wiessner turned and managed to drive his own ax into the snow and hold on tight. Wiessner stopped the fall, but all three men knew his slip had nearly killed them.

In Camp 5 they found that Lieutenant Frier had just come up with more porters. The porters saw the sick man. The healthy porter must have told them about Wiessner's fall and that the sahibs had kept a seriously ill man up at Camp 6 for days. The porters all told the sahibs they were too sick to go on. Some of them certainly were. The rest were refusing to die. The sahibs had no choice but to give in, and they all went down to Camp 4. There the snow trapped them.

They stayed at Camp 4, day after day, waiting out the storms. (Knowlton, again, does not say how long this lasted.) The weather around Nanga Parbat is always a gamble for expeditions. The theory is that Nanga Parbat is a long way from the origins of the summer monsoon in the Bay of Bengal. It's in the 'rain shadow' of the Himalayas, so there is usually little rain or snow in the summer. Moreover, it's difficult to get there early, because the porters have to cross high passes that are still blocked by deep snow in the spring. So most expeditions go in the summer and hope. The problem is, sometimes this works, and sometimes it snows. During the summer of 1932 it snowed.

The sahibs found that they could get down from Camp 4 to Base Camp, and back up, but above Camp 4 the snow was now too deep. They argued back and forth among themselves. It was getting too late in the summer for their planned siege method, with careful support and well-stocked camps. Even if it had not been too late, they probably did not have the strength for it. They fell back on their experience in the Alps and decided to go for it in one last continuous push with eight handpicked porters.

The weather finally cleared and the sahibs told the eight men to get ready for the summit attempt, but those eight Hunzas told Frier they had nothing left to eat. While they'd waited out the weather in their tents, bored, cold, frightened, and hungry, they had eaten more of their chapatis than Frier had counted on.

Rand Herron, the American, had come up to Camp 4. Now he wanted to go for the summit with another climber and two porters. He said they still had enough chapatis left for that. Merkl and Wiessner told Herron they couldn't do it. With only two porters, the sahibs would have to carry packs and break trail at the same time. In the deep snow below the ridge, that would be beyond the capacity of the sahibs.

Most of the porters went down to Base Camp to get more chapatis. Some of them came right back up to say that there was no flour left in Base Camp either. They made it clear that they expected the sahibs to come down the mountain and go home.

The expedition went down to Base Camp, but Wiessner and Merkl refused to give up. They sent the porters down the valley to buy more flour, and on August 28 they finally had enough for chapatis. Merkl, Wiessner, Herron, and twelve Hunza porters set out from Base Camp for one last push. Knowlton's book doesn't say how the twelve men managed with clothes for only nine men. Maybe they borrowed some from the sahibs who stayed behind, and maybe they were cold.

They took ten and a half hours in slushy snow to reach Camp 2, instead of the usual four, with Herron and Wiessner taking turns breaking trail. They told Knowlton later:

> The coolies were getting steadily slower, and more sulky, and the sahibs were putting all of themselves into it. Morally as well as physically, they must drag the porters up the mountain, with the force of their unbreakable will and purpose. It was back-breaking work, for shoulders only a little less heavily loaded than the coolies', fighting and tramping a way up the rise, through the deep soft snow: but, worse than that, it was heart-breaking work. The physical energy was nothing to the nervous energy. Merkl's voice was pleasantly commanding; Herron spent himself in earnest friendliness; Wiessner went through prodigies of bluff good humor; all of them continually urging on those twelve flagging men.[19]

Note that the men who had taken three months to climb less than six thousand feet now had an unbreakable will. Note also that the men with the lighter packs are urging on the men with heavier packs. But note also that porters can resist, and in the end the sahibs have to persuade them.

Down at Base some porters were getting ready to carry up more chapatis for the Hunzas above. The sahibs were to get something much better, Knowlton said,

a sort of Christmas box for the climbers. The little white sheep must be condemned to die [and be] roasted by the interested and sympathetic old cook 'for the sahibs.'

'And bread for the sahibs?'

'Yes, bread. Bot (much) bread.' Atta scones were baked. And a few little delicacies they might be running out of . . . extra jam, and sugar. . . .

The cook brought me the food. . . . The Jemadar came with him, all interest, and helped me find a bristol-board 'bokkus' [box]. He was sure the one I had chosen was too small. Hunzas drifted up. . . . As I wrapped, the Jemadar put things in the 'bokkus,' while all the other coolies leaned over his shoulder and made suggestions as to the arrangement of parcels, and vied with one another in speaking of more things to send up to the sahibs.

'Chai? (Tea?)'

'Upar bot hai. (There is some above.)'

'Chini? (Sugar?)'

'Bot. Bot. (Much. Much.)'

'Cigarette?' . . .

Everything was finally packed to the complete satisfaction of everybody . . . and all was smiles . . . [but sometimes] coolies would approach me, demanding plaintively everything from shirts to shoestrings, talking on and on in incomprehensible Urdu, pulling their clothes open to exhibit their need. And generally I would not have what they wanted.[20]

The bokkus of treats went up the mountain. The three sahibs and twelve Hunzas had reached Camp 4, climbing up to their waists, and sometimes their chests, in snow. The next morning the new snow outside the tents reached their chins. Nine of the porters were sick, and the three who were left refused to go on.

The sahibs knew they could ask no more. All fifteen men went down. They paid off the Hunzas and went home.

The sahibs blamed the porters for the failure of the expedition. Knowlton said the Hunzas were 'capricious and temperamental, physically almost as sensitive to hardship as Europeans, no stronger than the sahibs in load-carrying, and much quicker to succumb to illness. Altogether, as mountain porters, they were . . . most unsatisfactory.'[21]

The porters were ordinary farmers from Hunza villages. The sahibs were among the strongest and toughest men in Germany, a country with fifteen hundred times the population of Hunza. The porters were tall for Indian peasants, but the sahibs were bigger – Herron and Kunigk were both over six feet tall. The sahibs ate meat on the expedition and the porters ate bread. When their bodies were formed as children, the Hunzas had sometimes been short of bread, and the Germans had belonged to a class whose members could eat all the meat they wanted. The Germans had warmer clothing. The sahibs had sleeping bags and the Hunzas only blankets. The Germans had waterproof coats; the Hunzas did not.

Yet Knowlton was disappointed that these ordinary farmers were almost as sensitive to hardship as the elite climbers. In other words, they were tougher than the sahibs, willing to endure more, but not tough enough. And she was disappointed that they were 'no stronger than the sahibs in load-carrying.'

Knowlton was making explicit here what most white climbers believed. A contradiction lay at the heart of their ambition. They usually talked as if the white men were the better men, and the conquest of the mountain was theirs. But deep down, like Knowlton, they did in fact expect the Indian porters, men who were given no names in mountaineering books, to be stronger and tougher than the white men who took the credit. If the porters were not stronger, the white men knew they could not climb the mountain and blamed the porters for their failure.

This contradiction in the thinking of white climbers was not on the surface of their minds. Consciously, they assumed white people were stronger athletes, more likely to climb the great mountains just as they were more likely to one day run a four-minute mile. This was a time when white Europeans and Americans were still surprised by a black boxer like Jack Johnson, a football player like Paul Robeson, or a runner like Jesse Owens. Many, in fact, were angered by the success of such men precisely because they laid bare the equality between the bodies of different races. While many others could see that such men were great athletes, small Asian men did not fit anybody's athletic stereotype.

But most climbers did assume the porters would be able to work harder. They rarely made this point explicit, precisely because it challenged their own feelings of superiority. This was not simply racism. These were very good, or great, climbers. They were competitive people, and competitive about climbing above all else. So they held in their minds two utterly contradictory ideas: the porters are stronger so they must carry the loads, but we are stronger so we will be the ones on the summit. The moments when reality forced these two ideas to collide could lead to anxiety, to anger, and sometimes to a realization of equality.

Many times on Nanga Parbat in 1932 the sahibs wished they had employed the Sherpa and Tibetan porters from Darjeeling, of whom they had heard so much. Two years later Merkl and Bechtold were back, with generous funding from Adolf Hitler's new government, and enough money to hire Darjeeling men. They blamed the Hunzas for their failure the first time. Now, with the Sherpas, they knew they could succeed.

PART II

The Climb

Chapter Four

CHITS AND KNIVES

In 1934 a hurricane-force storm trapped sixteen men on a long ridge high on Nanga Parbat. They slept out, night after night, without food or water, frostbitten, confused, and exhausted beyond imagining. As they struggled slowly down the ridge, nine of them died, one by one.

During the long retreat through the storm, different men acted from love, terror, faith, courage, and ruthless selfishness. What happened there changed forever how Sherpa climbers thought of themselves. The Nanga Parbat expedition is central to this book because it was a turning point in Sherpa history. Before 1934 the sahibs were paternalist leaders. They looked after the porters, well or badly. After 1934 the Sherpas knew that they were the decent and responsible people on the mountain. If things ever went wrong again in that way, the Sherpa sardar must take control. They could no longer afford the consequences of being treated as children.

On Nanga Parbat the leader of the expedition, Willy Merkl, tried to push up the mountain too fast, without first setting up enough support camps in case anything went wrong. Merkl made that mistake because he didn't understand altitude, and because of political pressure from home.

We will come back to the problems of altitude later. The

political pressure came from the new Nazi government. When Willy Merkl had left Nanga Parbat in 1932, it was not at all clear that he would be able to organize and fund another expedition. Then Hitler's Nazis came to power in Germany in January 1933. The new Reich sports leader, von Tschammer und Osten, enthusiastically provided everything Merkl needed. This support was welcome, but placed great expectations on Merkl's shoulders. This is a book about Sherpas, not German politics. But to make sense of what went wrong on the mountain, we have to understand what was going wrong in Germany, why the Nazis supported Merkl, and what that meant to him.

Germany in 1934 was a bitterly divided society.[1] The divisions stemmed from the way World War One had ended. In the fall of 1918 the German army was beginning to lose the war in the trenches. The navy was ordered to put to sea for one last desperate battle. The sailors refused, mutinied, and walked off their ships. On their way home, groups of sailors went from one army unit to another, agitating for mutiny.

Several years later Adolf Hitler, writing in prison, remembered those days. An army corporal, he had been gassed in the trenches by the British. Some sailors came to the military hospital where Hitler was recovering, and they asked the soldier patients to join what was fast becoming a revolution. Hitler loved the army and the war, the comradeship and sense of purpose. He felt the sailors were traitors. Most German soldiers, however, hated the war, and the sailors won Hitler's fellow patients to their side.

All over Germany the soldiers refused to fight. The German government had to beg the allies for an immediate peace, any peace, on any terms. The soldiers and the workers in the cities began electing revolutionary committees. A revolution removed the monarch, Kaiser Wilhelm, and turned Germany into a full-scale parliamentary republic. A government led by the Socialists of the Social Democratic Party took office.

The next five years saw mass strikes, local workers' uprisings, and considerable slaughter of workers by right-wing militias. At times it seemed as if the revolution might be pushed further. The example of the Russian revolution of 1917 was in everyone's mind. But for Adolf Hitler, and for millions of right-wing Germans, the real horror was still the end of the war. To them, Germany and the old order had been humiliated by the German people. Germany had not lost – it had been stabbed in the back.

After 1923 things settled down and the prospect of revolution receded. Hitler and his like had a very small audience until the Wall Street crash of 1929. In the world depression that followed, there was large-scale unemployment in Germany, and many small businesses failed. It was not an overwhelming disaster. Unemployment in the United States, for instance, was far higher. But in the USA, President Franklin D. Roosevelt and his New Deal were seen as mainstream champions of working people, and there was no mass communist movement to Roosevelt's left.

In Germany, by contrast, revolution was a real possibility – it had happened in 1918. After 1929 both the Communist Party and Hitler's Nazi Party grew quickly. The Nazis were a new sort of right-wing movement. Before the 1920s conservative parties in Europe were polite affairs, run by upper-class men, focused on parliament and the army. European conservatives could, and sometimes did, conduct military coups or send troops against the people. But they did not rely on mobs. Now Hitler, following Mussolini's example in Italy, organized a mass movement on the streets of the angry and anxious middle classes. His 'storm troopers,' the SA or brownshirts, marched in uniform and beat up Communists and Socialists.

The political and economic situation became increasingly unstable. Big businessmen and army officers were worried about the threat of mass strikes and Communist-led revolution. Most of these men did not trust Hitler, and they were not comfortable with mobs. But they began to feel it was a choice between a revolution of the left and a revolution of the right. In this situation, the majority of these men swung their support to the Nazis.

In the spring of 1932 Hitler's movement reached its height in the elections, taking about 33 percent of the vote. In the next election in the fall, support for the Nazis fell to 30 percent. The

Socialist and Communist vote combined was a little over 50 percent. Various smaller liberal and right-wing parties took the rest. At this point the general who had commanded the army in World War One, and now held the ceremonial office of president, invited Hitler to form a government. By the spring of 1933 the Nazis, with the support of the army and police, had turned this government into an out-and-out dictatorship.

Many supporters of the smaller right-wing parties rallied to the Nazis. A bit under half of the people now backed the dictatorship. Slightly over 50 percent of Germans still supported the Socialist and Communist opposition. This support split along class lines. By and large, and with many exceptions, businesspeople, professionals, white-collar workers, and farmers supported the Nazis. By and large, again with millions of individual exceptions, the workers and unemployed in the cities supported the Socialists or the Communists.

The Nazis had to prove their strength to the German people. There was a brutal side to this – the concentration camps began as prisons for Socialists, Communists, and local union organizers. There was also a propaganda side. As part of this, the Nazis poured money into sport to show the world, and ordinary Germans, that they could make Germans winners again. This was the political context in which the Nazis were eager to support Merkl's expedition.

Nanga Parbat, in its small way, also played a part in easing the memory of Germany's defeat in the war. The Himalayan rivalry between Britain and Germany had always had military resonances. Now they were even stronger. Paul Bauer, the Nazi head of German mountaineering, wrote in 1935 that after the 'great struggles' of World War One:

At the time when we had to lay down our weapons, the empty hand felt around for the ice axe. Apparently robbed forever of the last foundations of life, we were driven to search for a new grounding in nature, there where she is lonely, wild and untouched. There the fight with the mountains gave us back the proud consciousness of honour and the ability to defend oneself.[2]

Finally, the Nazi were racists, and their racism was connected to a particular ideal of manhood. Of course it was not just Germans or Nazis who associated manhood with mountain climbing. Ideas of masculinity were everywhere on the mountains, often hardly mentioned precisely because they were so dominant. In the early years of the century the American Fanny Workman Bullock had climbed with her husband on smaller Himalayan peaks, and women climbed with men in the Alps. But on major Himalayan expeditions the matter almost never came up – it was simply unthinkable.[3]

The only leader to make an exception was Willy Merkl, when he took Elizabeth Knowlton to Nanga Parbat in 1932.[4] For the rest, it was a man's world. Many of the words climbers used – *strength, courage, attack, siege, struggle, fight* – were for them saturated with masculine associations. Nazi ideology added a twist to this. They emphasized the racial and physical superiority of German ('Aryan') men over Jews, foreigners, homosexuals, and German women. Part of what would make Germany great again was the purity and strength of German manhood.

Of course racism and sexism were common in other European nations, too. But that racism usually emphasized the intellectual, not physical, superiority of white men. The usual justifications for British rule over Indians, for instance, were that Englishmen were smarter, better organized, and more able to control their emotions. Nazism was different. Bodies mattered more. That is why the Nazis cared so much about sports and were so proud of the Berlin Olympics in 1936. Himalayan climbing was a particularly dramatic way of proving the superiority of German manhood. For here men's bodies were pitted against the strongest forces of nature. They struggled at the very edge of human possibility. Courage was not a slogan, for men really died. In a phrase popular in Nazi propaganda, the mountains were a perfect setting for 'the triumph of the will.'

This Nazi support made Merkl's expedition possible. But it also carried a cost, and Merkl was supposed to deliver. He was under other pressures, too. Most German climbers in the Himalayas, like most British and American ones, were business or professional men from comfortable homes. Merkl was not of this class. He had been raised by a single mother, in a small house in the Bavarian town of Traustein. He had attended a state technical high school, the *Realschule*, not the more selective *Gymnasium*. When he was eighteen, he joined the army as a private, not an officer. Luckily, the war ended a few weeks after he joined. Merkl then got an apprenticeship as an electrician at a local factory, the Bayerischen Stickstoffwerke (Bavarian Nitrogen Works). After several years there, he took a two-year engineering course at the local technical college, not the university. From there he got his job as a white-collar engineer on the railways, where he got Sundays off and two weeks' vacation a year to climb.

Merkl had come a long way to get where he was and had already failed once on Nanga Parbat. This was not as critical as it would be now. After all, nobody had yet climbed a Himalayan giant. The British had failed four times on Everest and the Germans twice on Kangchenjunga. If Merkl failed a second time, however, this would probably be the last expedition he led. Even

---

THE SAHIBS ON NANGA PARBAT IN 1934

THE CLIMBERS

Willy Merkl, expedition leader, a Bavarian railway engineer

Willo Welzenbach, the deputy leader, a civil engineer with the city of Munich

Fritz Bechtold, another Bavarian and Merkl's childhood friend, also making a film of the climb. Had been on Nanga Parbat in 1932

Peter Aschenbrenner, an Austrian mountain guide, also a veteran of the 1932 expedition

Erwin Schneider, another Austrian, a geologist and often Aschenbrenner's climbing partner

Alfred Drexel, Merkl's colleague on the Bavarian railways

Peter Müllritter, the stills photographer

Uli Wieland, who had been on Kangchenjunga with Bauer

THE NONCLIMBERS

Willy Bernard, the doctor, an Austrian

Hanns Hieronimus, in charge of Base Camp

Emil Kahn, Base Camp assistant, a Swiss

Three scientists doing research at Base Camp:

Richard Finserwalder, cartographer

Walter Raechl, geographer

Peter Misch, geologist

Two British liaison officers:

Captain Sangster

Captain Frier

THE PORTERS CAUGHT IN THE 1934 STORM

These men were all Sherpas born in Nepal and living in Darjeeling.

THE FIRST ROPE DOWN

Pasang Picture, from Charma Digma in Solu, the assistant to the film cameraman

Nima Dorje, who had climbed higher than anybody else on the expedition

Pinzo Norbu, from Khumjung

THE SECOND ROPE DOWN

Nima Tashi, from Khumjung

Da Thundu, also from Khumjung, Pinzo Norbu's older brother

Kitar, from Thame, had been on Everest in 1921, 1922, and 1924, and Kangchenjunga in 1929, 1930, and 1931. Da Thundu's father-in-law

Pasang Kikuli, from near Jorsale in Pharak, on the path between Solu and Khumbu

LEFT IN THE HIGH BIVOUAC

Nima Norbu

Dakshi, from Thame

Ang Tsering, also from Thame, and still alive today

Gaylay, a thin man of about forty from Paphlu in Solu

THE OTHER DARJEELING PORTERS IN 1934

There were thirty-four porters and one sardar in all, roughly equal numbers of Tibetans and Sherpas. Most of the porters who were not chosen for the final assault were Tibetans. These are the names of those mentioned by Ang Tsering or in Bechtold's book.

Lewa, the sardar

Ang Nima, went to Camp 5

Ang Tenjing, went to Camp 5

Aiwaa

Pasang II

Lobsang

Nurbu, went to Camp 7

Wangdi Norbu

Palten, went to Camp 5

Sonam Topgay

Nurbu Sonam

Nima Thondup

Tundu, went to Camp 7

Ramona, cook

Nima Dorje, cook

Jigmey Ishering, interpreter

if he did not succeed, he had at least to try as hard as he damn well could. Before Willy Merkl left for Nanga Parbat he went to visit his mother and his seventeen-year-old half brother, Karl Herrligkoffer. His mother asked Willy what he expected on Nanga Parbat. Willy didn't reply, just sat there looking sadly out the window. Young Karl understood that Willy might die.[5]

Of the men who went to Nanga Parbat in 1934, Ang Tsering is the only one still alive. He was born in Thame in Khumbu in 1904. When I spoke to him in Darjeeling in May and December of 2000 he was ninety-five or ninety-six years old.[6]

Ang Tsering laments the effects of age. His hearing is not good, he says, or his sight. Until two years ago he used to walk to Chowrashtra every morning, six hundred yards from his house each way. In British days, Chowrashtra, on the ridge between the Mall and the Planters Club, was the center of Darjeeling. Then and now, Tibetan men and women stand at Chowrashtra with ponies ready to give tourists a ride. Ang Tsering was one of them for many years. There are benches all round the open space of Chowrashtra, where old Tibetans and Sherpas come every day to sit and chat. Ang

Tsering misses those friendships. But he also regrets what age has done – he was always a big man, strong, proud of his body.

Other people say he remembers less than he did a year ago, is less acute. To me he seems astonishing for his age. When I returned to Darjeeling in December, I walked to Ang Tsering's. He lives in Toong Soom Busti, in a brilliant blue, four-room bungalow. The hill falls steeply here, and stone steps lead down from the road to his house. I stopped at the top of the steps and looked out over the valley four thousand feet below and the ridge rising on the other side. Ang Tsering was sitting in the sunlight on a small stone patio that jutted out over the drop. He recognized me at fifty feet and waved. There can't be that much wrong with his memory or his eyesight.

I went down and we shook hands. He had been sitting whittling the handle for a large garden fork. 'Making,' he said proudly, 'making.'

'Still working,' I said to his oldest son, Dawa Thempa.

'Always working,' Dawa Thempa said.

Of course he can't work much now, but his memory is still astonishing. He remembers every evening campsite, in order, on the walk into Everest Base Camp in 1924. He remembers many names, where those men came from, and to whom they were related. Of equal importance for a historian, when Ang Tsering doesn't remember something, he says so instead of guessing.

I went to see him again and again. His memory of Nanga Parbat was detailed and consistent. He remembered each camp, what he thought and felt there, and where each man died. Ang Tsering has told the story many times. It was, after all, his time as a hero, his moment in history. The Japanese climber and writer Nebuka Makoto had also interviewed him four years before me. What Ang Tsering tells me now fits with what he said then.[7]

I couldn't persuade Ang Tsering to speak Sherpa. He's been in Darjeeling seventy-six years, and he talks to his children in Nepali, the local language. So his eldest son Dawa Thempa Sherpa translated for us.

Dawa Thempa had been a climber, then spent almost thirty years in the Indo-Tibetan Border Police, retiring as a sergeant. He argues a lot with his father as he translates. Sometimes Dawa Thempa thinks his father has not understood what I am really asking or is replying off the point. Other times he thinks Ang Tsering is plain wrong. Then Dawa Thempa talks louder, almost shouting the words, implying the old man can't hear. Ang Tsering leans forward on the sofa, looking belligerent. His chin juts out, he replies loudly in more detail, his right palm cleaving the air. After some argument, Dawa Thempa turns to me and explains that he thinks one thing and his father thinks another. Sometimes he admits his father was right. At other times he says Ang Tsering is clearly wrong, but won't budge.

Both are men of strong opinions, but Ang Tsering seems to enjoy these arguments more than his son. He certainly is not about to be condescended to as an old man.

Dawa Thempa tells me that he got his first mountaineering work on an expedition with Ang Tsering. What was that like? I ask. It's not easy working with your father, Dawa Thempa says.

Yet, as he translates, the room is full of love. Dawa Thempa is trying to get it right, digging at the truth, because he is proud of his father. He wants me to write an accurate history. He has read Bauer's old book on Nanga Parbat and says some things in there are not true. I know the passages he means, and why they would hurt Ang Tsering.

In May, Dawa Thempa asked me to bring him a copy of Fritz Bechtold's book about the expedition when I came back. He read it in December and said it was surprising how little the sahibs say about the Sherpas. Dawa Thempa is concerned about the record I will write.

Dawa Thempa is the oldest child. When his mother lay dying thirty years ago, she asked him to look after his father. The man has eight children, she said, he can't look after all of them on his own. So Dawa Thempa promised his mother he would do just that, never married, and has helped support the family ever since. Now he lives with his father and three of his divorced sisters, a close family of five, all over fifty. One married younger brother lives next door.

So can we rely on what Ang Tsering says now about 1934? Far more than with the great majority of people his age, I think. We have his earlier accounts to Nebuka as corroboration. There is also an important issue of historical method here.

In general there are strengths and weaknesses to both 'oral history' – what old people say – and written sources. Documentary history is fixed. What people wrote in 1934, after all, cannot be changed now in the light of modern prejudices. Documents can be hidden, and historians can distort or lie about them, but they cannot be changed as memory so easily can. Documents are also likely to be more reliable as to dates, names, and places. Memory holds more of what we felt and meant.

However, written documents are not necessarily more truthful than memories. People write for public consumption, and old people looking back are often willing to admit things they would have tried to conceal in their youth. For Nanga Parbat the main documentary source is Fritz Bechtold's book, written immediately after the tragedy. Bechtold had shameful things to conceal, and so his account both omits and distorts. Ang Tsering's memory is more truthful, because he does not have to be ashamed.

There is another general point about oral history. Written documents tend to give you the views of the literate and the powerful. Often the only way you can find out what things were like for those who followed orders is to go and ask them, if they're still alive.[8] Of course, if everybody is long dead you just have to do what you can with the documents. And there is no point in doing oral history *or* written history. You have to do both.

I went out to Nepal and India to research this book knowing I wanted to write about the 1934 expedition, but not expecting to find any survivors. I was lucky indeed to find Ang Tsering still alive and mentally all there. Without him, and the memories of other porters, this would be a book where the sahibs stood in the foreground and we tried to glimpse the Sherpas behind them. You can get a long way by reading the records of the rich and powerful backwards, looking between the lines, wondering how you would feel if a white man spoke to you like that. But there is a limit to how far you can go.

Finally, there is a political point here. Who gets to make sense of history? Who analyses and reshapes it? The historians with all their education, or the old people who lived it?

My answer, with some reservations, is the old people. When in doubt, I have taken Ang Tsering's version. He was there, he almost died, and this is his story.

Ang Tsering tells how he came to be on the 1934 expedition, and how it almost didn't happen to him – it's a bad-luck story.

He was on Everest in 1924, and then the Kangchenjunga expeditions in 1929, 1930, and 1931. In 1933 he found a job as a servant to the wife of Willington Sahib, the British representative in Sikkim, which is situated between Darjeeling and Tibet. Now Sikkim is a state in India. In 1933 it was an independent kingdom in principle, but in practice Willington Sahib told Sikkim's ruler, the Chogyal, what to do. Ang Tsering was a waiter at table and a personal servant for Mrs Willington.

By and large Sherpa men were not hired as servants, so this was a fortunate position for Ang Tsering.

Servant work was safe, warm, and secure. With the Willingtons, it was also exciting. During the winter of 1933 Mr Willington went to Lhasa on a diplomatic mission, accompanied by his wife, and so Ang Tsering went, too.

Ang Tsering says Willington offered to build a hospital in Lhasa, which would give treatment and medicine free. He offered the Tibetan government arms and ammunition in return for being allowed to build the hospital. Ang Tsering says the Tibetan people seemed pleased by this deal. The three great monasteries around Lhasa, however, were not. They said, why do we need British medicine? We have our own perfectly good remedies we've always used. More important, they said, if the British give medicine in the short run, in the long run all they really want is to capture our land. So the monks blocked the proposal.

For Ang Tsering the high point of the mission came when he was allowed to attend Willington's one-hour audience with the Dalai Lama. When they returned to Sikkim, they learned of the Dalai Lama's death.

Back in Sikkim, Ang Tsering ran into trouble. Mrs Willington had several other servants, all more established than him. When she gave them tips, they kept the money for themselves. Ang Tsering said they should pool the tips and share it. They didn't, of course, and he resigned in anger. He found himself without a job in the middle of winter and had to go back and ask the Willingtons for permission to work until spring. They gave it.

Ang Tsering told the Himalayan Club secretary, Mr Kitt, that he would go to Nanga Parbat with the Germans in the spring, but then a better job came along. Another political agent, Charles Bell, was going on a new mission to Lhasa and offered to take Ang Tsering as a servant. Ang Tsering was delighted, but Mr Kitt told Bell that Ang Tsering was already promised to the Germans. Bell accepted that, and Ang Tsering lost the Lhasa job. He'd be going to Nanga Parbat.

And that, Ang Tsering says, is the train of accidents by which he came to be on the unfortunate 1934 expedition.

Pasang Phutar of Darjeeling tells the opposite story. He had the chance of going to Nanga Parbat that year and sensibly went to an astrologer first. No, the astrologer said, don't go, and Pasang Phutar didn't. If I'd gone, he says now, I would have died.

And probably he would have.

Because Merkl was a railwayman, the national Railway Sports and Gymnasium Society asked every railway worker in the country to contribute ten pfennings, a tenth of a mark, to the expedition. Merkl took two of the veterans of 1932 back with him, his boyhood friend Fritz Bechtold and the Austrian guide Peter Aschenbrenner. One of the new climbers, Uli Wieland, was sent ahead to Darjeeling alone to begin hiring the porters. This was probably because Wieland, a schoolteacher, had been on

Kangchenjunga in 1929. He would know Darjeeling, some of the sahibs in the Himalayan Club, and many of the porters.

Wieland was authorized to hire a sardar and thirty-four porters. He would have had in mind the names of a few men he remembered from 1929. Bauer and other German Himalayan veterans would have recommended other men, and so would the local secretary of the Himalayan Club. The sardar, once selected, would suggest men. Other people would simply approach Wieland.

Every man with any experience brought out his chits to show Wieland. *Chit* is the Hindi word for a letter. When an Englishman hired an Indian servant, the prospective cook or gardener would bring out his chits. These were single sheets of paper, worn and often torn along the folds, but carefully preserved, each with a recommendation in English from a previous employer. The servant rarely read English, but would have had them read by somebody who did, just to check what they said. The Darjeeling porters, too, had chits and held on to them with care and pride, their passports to work.

Wieland selected the likely looking men and sent them to the Victoria Hospital in Darjeeling for medical examinations. Since many porters were chronically ill, this was not just a formality.

When the British climber Frank Smythe left London for the international expedition to Kangchenjunga in 1930, Charlie Bruce of Everest came to see him off at Victoria Station: 'General Bruce was emphatic on one thing in particular. "Don't forget to worm the porters," he had whispered in my ear.' In Darjeeling Smythe found that few of the porters in fact had worms. 'More prevalent was a species of scurvy, due most likely to undernourishment, that showed itself in the form of skin bruising, and boils. A number of porters were so badly affected by this that it was impossible to take them.'[9]

This means that many of the men who were chosen for Nanga Parbat were already thin and undernourished before they got to the mountain. After the medical examination, Wieland finally had thirty-five men, about fifteen Sherpas[10] and twenty Tibetans. Willy Merkl and Fritz Bechtold then arrived in

Darjeeling. Merkl, as the burra sahib or big boss, would make the formal decision.

When Bechtold came to write the book of the expedition, he described the hiring of the porters in almost Homeric terms:

> The 'tigers' presented themselves for inspection in a long line. . . . Nima Thondup, Smythe's factotum, who had taken part in every Himalayan expedition since 1921; Wongdi Norbu, and especially Pasang, one of the best of Bauer's 1929 guard. . . . The post of first sardar was given to Lewa, who had distinguished himself in all expeditions by his extraordinary strength of will. . . . Among the porters of the Everest expedition [who came to Nanga Parbat] were excellent men, all of whom had been to Camp IV (22,800 ft.), fifteen to Camp V (25,500 ft.), and Nima Dorje II to Camp VI (27,400 ft.).
>
> It was most interesting to note the reverence with which this corps d'elite showed their testimonials. Every famous name in Himalayan history appeared among the signatories: Bruce, Ruttledge, Norton, Bauer, Smythe, Birnie and Dyhrenfurh.
>
> They awaited the arrival of the Bara Sahib with great excitement. When . . . Merkl engaged all thirty-five men assembled, there was great rejoicing and wild delight. Hats flew into the air, and for some time all discipline vanished. Lewa addressed them again with stirring words, and the Himalayan 'tigers' vowed loyalty to their new Bara Sahib in our struggle for Nanga Parbat.[11]

These were happy men, poor people who now had steady, well-paid work. Ang Tsering says that he was averaging fifteen rupees a month doing rickshaw work, and even that was seasonal. The 1934 expedition paid one and a quarter rupees a day, or thirty-seven and a half rupees a month, plus what a porter could make afterward by selling his clothes and boots.

There was no question here of the sahibs avoiding 'old soldiers.'

They wanted experienced men, and in the last few years many of these had become career high-altitude porters. The chits ('testimonials') they showed were proof of this. They were also a form of discipline. A porter might conceal one bad chit, but sahibs would probably pass the word amongst themselves. On the 1932 expedition the Hunza porters reacted to their circumstances day by day. In 1934 the Darjeeling porters always had to think ahead. If a man decided he was never coming back to the mountains, he could forget the chit and do what he liked. But if not, he had his career to consider. That would make a man try harder, be braver, choke back anger, smile, try to find a friend among the climbers.

From the sahibs' point of view there were two great advantages to the pool of Darjeeling porters: these men were experienced, and they were disciplined.

In 2000, an old woman and a little boy in Darjeeling taught me something of the importance of those chits. I went to see Pasang Phuti (pronounced *Pasang Pootee*), the widow of Ang Tsering Phenzing, called Pansy by the British, a great climber of the 1930s. I presented a gift of a few cakes, a customary politeness, and she gave me tea. Pasang Phuti's daughter-in-law brought out the few medals and documents they had. They showed me Ang Tsering Phenzing's Tiger Badge, the medal presented to him in 1940 when the Himalayan Club honored the ten greatest surviving Darjeeling porters. They told me the badge had been made in Britain. On one side in relief is the head of a tiger. On the back is engraved 'Ang Tsering Pansy, H.C. no. 51, 1940.' The Himalayan Club (H.C.) gave each porter on their rolls a number because so many men had similar names.

Then I was shown his chit from the 1936 British expedition to Everest. The paper had turned a yellow-brown and was torn and spotted. The family had recently laminated the chit to preserve it.

Most of the form is typewritten. The name of the expedition is across the top, and the porter's name below it. Next comes a blank for wages – since he was just a mess boy, Ang Tsering

Phenzing made only three-quarters of a rupee a day. His allowance for rations was six annas a day. Below that is the space for his wife's name and address, presumably for compensation in case of death. Then it specifies an allowance of ten rupees a month – perhaps payable to his wife? On the bottom, below this, is a handwritten recommendation by Hugh Ruttledge, the expedition leader. He says that although Ang Tsering did duty as a mess boy, he was always eager to climb high, and Ruttledge would recommend him to any expedition. Below this, at the bottom, is Ruttledge's signature.

In the left-hand bottom corner a small photograph of Ang Tsering Phenzing is attached. This was presumably to prevent anybody else from using the chit as a reference. Now it provides his widow with a picture of her husband as a young man.

As we talk, her young grandson bounces around the room. He's five, a student in the upper kindergarten class, but it's school vacation. In Khumbu boys his age sit quietly on such formal family occasions, serious little men, occasionally offering tea to the guest. In Darjeeling the Sherpa boys are like the Indian boys of my childhood, noisy and full of themselves. His mother, half-exasperated, half-proud, says to me *budmaash*, a word I heard often as a child, used for monkeys, village thugs, and naughty boys.

The boy is fascinated by the tiger medal and the laminated chit. He can see how much they mean to his mother, grandmother, and to me. He keeps trying to hold them, and we keep taking them back. We get lost in conversation, and the boy sees his chance. He has the tiger medal and dances out the door onto the balcony. I see small panic on the faces of his mother and grandmother. Closest to the door, I leap out, grab the medal, and hand it back to his mother. She thanks me and puts the medal and the chit safely away.

The sardar chosen to lead the porters in 1934 was Lewa (pronounced *Laywaa*), a Tibetan in his midforties. He lived near the cantonment, the army quarters on the ridge uphill from

Darjeeling town. When not climbing he worked in the cantonment at jobs like waiter and cleaner. This gave Lewa a steady living,
and also much better English than most Tibetan or Sherpa porters
spoke. An experienced climber, he had first been made a sardar
on Dhyrenfurth's international expedition to Kangchenjunga
in 1930.

In 1931 Lewa was the sardar on the British expedition to Kamet.
The British climber Frank Smythe wrote a book about that climb.
It is worth quoting at some length to show who Lewa was, how
he did the sardar's job, and how the paternalism between masters
and men worked before the 1934 tragedy changed things.

Smythe was drawn to Lewa's 'vim and energy.'[12] He contrasted
Lewa with Alam Singh, the liaison officer sent by the local Hindu
ruler:

> Alam Singh is a Hindu, and Lewa a Sherpa Buddhist, and
> it is interesting to compare the two men. Lewa, the hard-
> visaged fighting man, abrupt, brutal in his diction, never
> giving an order which he was not prepared himself to carry
> out, a man of magnificent physique, tough, alert, wiry, loyal
> to the core, sparing neither himself nor his comrades in the
> service of his Sahibs. Alam Singh, willing yet weak, intelli-
> gent yet lacking initiative, shelving responsibility wherever
> possible, expecting the expedition machine to run of its own
> accord, helpless in the face of a small difficulty or danger,
> a passenger not a captain on stormy waters, leaving most
> things to chance and God, yet, withal, a likeable man, who
> faithfully did his best to help us, and one whose cheery
> smile will remain a pleasant memory.[13]

Smythe had taken on board the colonial stereotype of Hindus
– weak and unable to govern themselves properly. Luckily another
race of men had come from across the seas to do the job for
them. But Smythe was also nervously aware that most Indians
wanted independence. Once the Kamet expedition got into the
mountains, 'we were no longer in range of Gandhi's activities,

and after the insolent stares of the "Congress Wallahs" of the lower hills and plains, it was pleasant to be greeted with a respectful and friendly "Salaam, Sahib" or "Salaam, Huzoor" from the villagers we met on the path.'[14]

One reason Smythe liked a man such as Lewa was that he was strong and dignified, but still loyal. He was fit to lead but chose to follow. There were few Congress wallahs – members of Gandhi's Indian National Congress – among Darjeeling Sherpas. Though they did not necessarily like Englishmen, they made their living in the tourist trade, and a good job as a servant or porter depended on British patronage. Moreover, the British authorities had swiftly moved to crush Congress in their beloved Darjeeling.

Another part of Lewa's appeal was his sheer physicality. One hears in Smythe's words the admiration of one strong man for another. Pictures of Lewa show a remarkably beautiful man, and Smythe saw that as well.

On Kamet, Lewa was the strongest load carrier and a tough foreman. The expedition had only nine Darjeeling porters. They hired Bhotias, local Tibetan speakers from the Garwhal hills around Kamet, as additional high-altitude porters. 'At first we were perplexed by their sullen and suspicious demeanor,' Smythe said. The problem, it turned out, was Lewa: 'Not only was he anxious to demonstrate his own superiority, but he regarded the Garwhal Bhotias as being racially inferior to the Darjeeling Sherpas and Bhotias. Therefore he adopted a bullying, truculent, parade-ground attitude.... Not unnaturally [the Garwhal Bhotias] resented Lewa's attitude and their resentment caused them to shun their work. In the beginning Lewa would exclaim passionately, "These men are no good."'[15]

Smythe and the other sahibs told Lewa to let up on the Garwhal Bhotias, and things improved.

Nima Dorje (pronounced *Neema Dorjay*), by contrast, was simply good fun. He was another Darjeeling porter, a younger man originally from Khumjung in Khumbu. On the walk in, 'Nima Dorje was continually talkative as we tramped along the path after lunch. His knowledge of English was greater than I had imagined, and he chatted gaily about Everest and Kangchenjunga [both of which he had worked on]. Like Lewa, he was profoundly optimistic as to the eventual conquest of Everest.[16]

As they worked their way up Kamet to Camp 4, it became clear Lewa and Nima Dorje were the strongest climbers. The sahibs reached the top camp, Camp 5, and flopped down in the snow:

> At length [the porters] appeared, a struggling line of weary men. . . . [They] squatted apathetically on the snow, slipping their heavy loads from their backs and their sweat-soaked head-bands from their foreheads. They had done a splendid day's work, but they were too tired at the moment to realize it. We expressed an admiration for their conduct as well as we could in the limited language at our command. A few minutes' rest served to restore them. An atmosphere of languor was dispelled as usual by Nima Dorje's inevitable grin. They busily set about erecting tents and cooking some tea for themselves and for us. How good that tea was![17]

Nima Dorje and Lewa were the only porters to stay with the sahibs at Camp 5. The next morning three sahibs were fit enough for the summit attempt. As they were making a film, they took Lewa and Nima Dorje along to carry the heavy camera and equipment.

On June 21, Lewa, Nima Dorje, Holdsworth, Shipton, and Smythe stood on the summit of Kamet. It was 25,447 feet, the highest peak anyone had ever climbed. But coming down

> Lewa was moving very slowly and was obviously distressed. His face was greenish in hue, his eyes rigid and staring from exhaustion. He groaned out that he was in great pain, and pointed to his stomach. There was nothing we could do for him save to encourage him to continued effort and relieve him of his load. As I lifted the rucksack with 20 lbs or more

of film apparatus, I was forcibly reminded of the amount of energy Nima Dorje and Lewa had expended getting it to the summit.[18]

Down at Camp 5 they found the second summit party, ready to go up the next day. Nima Dorje had been terrified on the summit. Now he told the other porters a dangerous god was up there. The next morning the sahibs all decided to wait at Camp 5 another day because Lewa's 'feet were so frostbitten that the sooner he was sent down to Base Camp the better. Greene [the doctor] said he would not be answerable for the consequences if this was not done; in the denser air of lower altitudes and increased oxygenation of the blood lay the only chance of saving his feet.'[19]

Note that they were now worried about Lewa losing his feet, not just his toes. So they sent him down the mountain, but did not send any sahib with him or anybody to carry him. They were all excited by the second summit attempt the next day.

Lewa may have been frostbitten because his boots had a hole or did not fit. Climbers are quickly vulnerable, for instance, if they lose a glove out of doors. But it is more likely that Lewa had simply asked too much of himself. Frostbite at altitude is often a sign that the whole body is closing down.

In extremity, the human body reacts by reducing blood circulation. The internal organs and the brain still get blood. But the flow to the arms and legs is reduced, the feet and hands get little, and the fingers and toes none. This makes physiological sense. At altitude the body has less oxygen to circulate. And it takes energy to produce body heat. The fingers and toes are the parts of the body where the surface area is greatest in proportion to the flesh. If you hold your hand out in front of you now, you'll see there is more skin on the fingers than on the hand. By the same token, mittens are warmer than gloves with separate fingers.

So when the body's system has to choose between risking the

extremities and risking the whole body, it lets the fingers and toes go. The mechanism is simple – the small arteries and capillaries snap shut.

When serious frostbite strikes, the hands and feet go numb and white. It hurts terribly when the limbs are warmed up again. If they are not warmed up, the flesh cut off from the blood supply begins to die. Within hours or days the fingers or toes go black, and then the hands or feet. This black flesh will never come back to life. It must be cut off, or gangrene will spread up the limbs, turning all the flesh black, and blood poisoning will eventually kill the person.

A climber with numb hands and unusable fingers finds it harder to handle ropes or an ax, and harder to pack. Simply doing up your boots is impossible with frostbitten hands. Climbers with frostbitten feet find it difficult to walk. Their feet are numb, and their legs fold under them. Even with friends walking alongside, they slip and stumble. Climbing down ropes, which requires both hands and feet, is hardest of all.

While Lewa, in agony, limped down Kamet, the second summit party at Camp 5 had a problem. They were 'not burdened with cinematographic apparatus, but they decided to take a porter with them to carry their odds and ends, their clothes and food, etc. But a porter was not easy to obtain. Not a Darjeeling man would go. Nima Dorje had shaken them profoundly; Lewa's feet had demoralized them.'[20]

Kesar Singh, a local porter, did volunteer to go, and the second summit party was successful. Now the sahibs turned down and found Lewa at Camp 2, unable to continue.[21] They found Lewa's feet 'were a dreadful sight, and it was obvious that if they were to be saved he had to be got down to lower levels without delay. Lying helpless, with his fierce impetuous spirit chained to a disabled body, unable to give orders, and forced to watch the inefficiency of his fellows without being able to intervene, was gall and wormwood to him.'[22]

They had to carry him down. Beauman and Shipton supervised

while four local Bhotia porters did the actual carrying. At Camp 1 the Bhotias refused to carry Lewa any farther. Instead they went back up to Camp 2 to get the rest of their loads, which probably contained the clothing and gear they hoped to take home. In any case, they were fed up with the way Lewa had treated them earlier in the expedition. 'Driving-power, and not tact, was Lewa's strong suit,' Smythe says.

The sahibs did not pursue the four Bhotia porters. Perhaps Shipton and Beauman wanted to protect their dignity, or maybe they were simply too tired. Instead they sent the ever-positive Nima Dorje to 'expostulate' with the four porters 'and bring them back. There never had existed any particular love or sympathy between the local men and the Darjeeling men, and words had run high. Finally, Nima received somebody's fist in his eye. However, enough men were got together to carry Lewa down.'[23]

From Base Camp, Lewa rode a pony, 'bowed and huddled' on the animal. Smythe watched:

> The tears were streaming down his cheeks and he was sobbing bitterly, not, I believe, so much from the pain as from what he felt to be an undignified position and thoughts of the future. He was but a shadow of his former self, and we could not help but perceive in his moral breakdown and distress the essential difference between the European and the native. Had one of us been seriously frostbitten he would at least have *tried* to bear his misfortune with stoical calm and fortitude. But a native cannot control his feelings; he is a child.[24]

Lewa had reasons to cry. The French climber Maurice Herzog got frostbite in his hands and feet when he climbed Annapurna in 1950. As the expedition doctor treated Herzog with injections, the feeling flooded back into his arms and legs, and he screamed and shook and howled like a dog. When the porters carried Herzog down the mountain, they often could not avoid jerking him, and the pain was unbearable. Afterward he lay by the river in a fever: 'The job was finished, and my conscience was clear. Gathering together the last shreds of my energy, in one last long prayer I implored death to come and deliver me. . . . I was giving in – the ultimate humiliation for a man who, up till then, had always taken pride in himself. . . . I looked death straight in the face, and besought it with all my strength.'[25]

Maurice Herzog was a tough man indeed. Frostbite is painful. And it goes on hurting. Lewa could expect, if he was lucky, twelve months of pain in hospital, and he knew it. His climbing life was probably at an end if he lost his toes, and his working life was at an end if he lost his feet. He could expect little compensation from the Himalayan Club, and no pension. Smythe is probably right that he was crying more from fear of the future than from pain.

There was also the loneliness. In Lewa's hour of need the sahibs had left him to go down on his own, and the men who worked for him had refused to carry him. Only Nima Dorje had stood with him.

Faced with Lewa's pain and fear, Smythe had strong reasons to shut his eyes. Smythe had been one of the people who had kept the frostbitten Lewa in Camp 5 an extra day. He had sent Lewa down to Camp 2 alone. He would not be giving his faithful sardar a pension. All this meant that Smythe couldn't take on board the full human force of Lewa's tears. Instead Smythe took refuge in paternalism. In good times, paternalism means that the white man is the father, the servant a faithful son, and the father looks after the son. In bad times paternalism means that the European is a man, the native is a child, and the white man does not have to look after a whining child.

None of this is to imply that Smythe was a cold or unsympathetic man. Among climbers of his generation, he was notable for his fondness for Sherpas. His books are a good source on Sherpa history precisely because he noticed individual Sherpas, talked to them, and wrote about them. Because he was actually looking at Lewa, Smythe could see him crying. Because he almost felt what Lewa felt, he had to turn another man into a child.

Lewa lost his toes but kept his feet. He didn't get climbing work for the next three years. His friend in need, Nima Dorje, got work with the British expedition to Everest in 1933. That year he was one of the eight porters to carry to Camp 6, higher than the summit of Nanga Parbat. (The sahibs again failed to reach the summit, although 'Policey' reached a record height for a dog at twenty-two thousand feet on the North Col.)

A year later both Nima Dorje and Lewa were hired for the 1934 Nanga Parbat expedition. The Germans knew Lewa would be a hard taskmaster. They engaged him, Bechtold said, for 'his extraordinary strength of will, both as mountaineer and as leader.'[26] His amputated toes might be a problem high on the mountain. But sardars in those days were largely expected to work at Base Camp, managing the flow of porters and supplies up the mountain. For that Lewa's feet were irrelevant. And he was still the man who had climbed Kamet. Nima Dorje had been with him on that summit. Moreover, on Everest, Nima Dorje had climbed higher than anyone on the Nanga Parbat expedition, and higher than any German ever had.

After they were hired in 1934, the Darjeeling porters took the train south to Calcutta, where they all had their pictures taken. Then, changing train after train, they went to Kashmir. Ang Tsering was in charge of the money boxes on the trains. He felt awe: he was protecting ten lakhs, a million rupees.

The expedition hired six hundred porters in Kashmir for the first leg of the march to Base Camp. The Darjeeling men were responsible for overseeing the local porters. Lewa, the sardar, took his duties seriously. Bechtold says, 'If 600 Kashmiri hurl themselves yelling on a towering heap of baggage, with an Oriental eye for a bargain and the savagery of dervishes, there is bound to be a certain amount of noise. The "tigers" set to work on the transport of loads with immediate success, leaping upon the Kashmiri like cats, while Lewa . . . stood like a rock in the raging surf.'[27]

Alfred Drexel, like Merkl, worked on the railways. As they climbed towards the Tragbal Pass, Drexel noted in his diary:

The porters go in groups of thirty men each under the supervision of one of the participants, a porter foreman, and a Darjeeling porter. The well known Sherpa and Bhutia-porters, recruited in Darjeeling, during the approach march play for us the role of police. They stand in relation to the unreliable Kashmiris as masters to underlings. . . .

The last contingents only reach the rest hours late in the night. They carry tree branches as torches: a long snake of lights climbs through the dark high forest, and provides a fairy tale picture for those of us who have no load on our backs.[28]

The eleven expedition members found refuge in a government rest house. The conditions were 'unaccustomedly cramped,' Drexel wrote, but 'nevertheless one is sheltered, the fire burns up the chimney, and our cook Ramona brings warm tea. One is doubly thankful for this comfort when one thinks of the night camp of the porters: as they crouch in the open around their camp fires, whether it is raining or snowing, whether stars or storm clouds stand above them.'

Partway to Base Camp the Kashmiri porters were paid off, and new local porters were hired. According to Bechtold, 'beyond Gurais some of the men lately engaged ran off to their native villages to fetch provisions for themselves and bid good-bye to their wives. Here and there one could see a sahib galloping up to these farewell scenes and cursing roundly as he dismounted, in his anxiety for missing loads. Rich Bavarian oaths mingled with the wailing and tears of the womenfolk.'[29]

Before the Burzil Pass, Peter Aschenbrenner remembered it was his birthday. The climbers held a party. Drexel wrote in his diary: 'We celebrate quietly as the porters are outside in the snow and freezing.' They left that camp at two in the morning in the hope the night cold would keep the snow on the pass hard. Drexel wrote:

Many porters are now snow blind, and receive from our doctor alleviation of the terrible pain. . . . On the other side of the pass it goes downhill very steeply: for us on skis a joyful opportunity, for the porters a real grind. . . .

For the porters the crossing of the pass was an unusual achievement. The previous night they had almost no sleep, then climbed up to 13,860 feet with 50 pound packs on their backs. With rags and straw sandals on their feet, some of them with naked toes, they waded 16 hours through the snow.

The next morning, according to Bechtold:

When 314 porters begin their work daily with wild shouts and fighting over loads, one learns in time to bear it with Oriental calm; but on this occasion, in snow and darkness, it was pretty bad. Lewa stood sternly by, callously striking at backs and heads with his stout stick, till the place rang with his blows. One porter, who wanted to divide his load and appoint himself second-in-command, was seized by Lewa with both hands and flung head-first over the verandah out into the snow. . . . [As we] set out in the starry night at the head of the column, we could still hear for some time the shouts of quarreling porters and the sound of Lewa's baton.[30]

The expedition soon met old friends. Frier was their liaison officer again, as he had been in 1932. He had recently been promoted to captain, and this time he was accompanied by Captain A. N. K. Sangster, also of the Gilgit Scouts.

As before, Frier and Merkl negotiated with the Tasseldar of Astor for local porters. This time they had far more gear, so they had to find 570 Astoris to carry it all round the mountain to the Fairy Meadows at the foot of the Northwest Face.

A Balti contingent again joined them to work as high-altitude porters. They had the same headman as last time, and some of the others must have been veterans of 1932. This time, though, the Baltis were only supposed to help the Sherpas and carry up to the first few camps. Before they were finished, however, many Baltis had carried thirty loads each up to Camp 4.

Now the expedition had to choose their route up the mountain. Any Himalayan climb is a trade-off among speed, danger, and ease of climbing. Looking directly up from the Fairy Meadows to Nanga Parbat, the most direct route would be straight up toward the East Peak and then to the summit. Avalanches ruled this out. They could see the breaks in the snow where giant walls of snow had already broken loose and could hear and see smaller ones falling constantly. So they could not go the direct way.

Instead, they decided to work their way up the face of the North Ridge, steadily veering to the left, away from the summit. This route was comparatively safe, and somewhat less steep. But from Camp 1 to Camp 3 they still had to climb slowly up an icefall.

An icefall is a complex phenomenon. Basically, it's a glacier sitting on the slope of a mountain. This glacier is made from snow that has been packed hard into ice over many years. Because the icefall is sitting on a slope, it moves slowly down the mountain. At the same time, new snow falls on top of the glacier and increases the weight bearing down. So the glacier, a giant wall of ice, inches down the mountain under enormous pressure. At any one moment it is probably not moving, but as the pressure continues to build, it lurches forward and downward a little bit. This is an icefall – great weights of ice slowly falling down the mountain.

Inside the icefall enormous pressures twist and bend the ice. The ice moves at different paces on the top and below. Great cracks – crevasses – are constantly opening in the ice. Some of these are three feet wide and five feet deep. Some are ten feet wide and a hundred feet deep, and some are great canyons in the ice.

In places climbers find a bridge of snow over a crevasse. They cross the bridge gingerly, roped to one another and their belays. In other places snow falls over the top of a crevasse and hides it, and often the weight of a person can send them unexpectedly

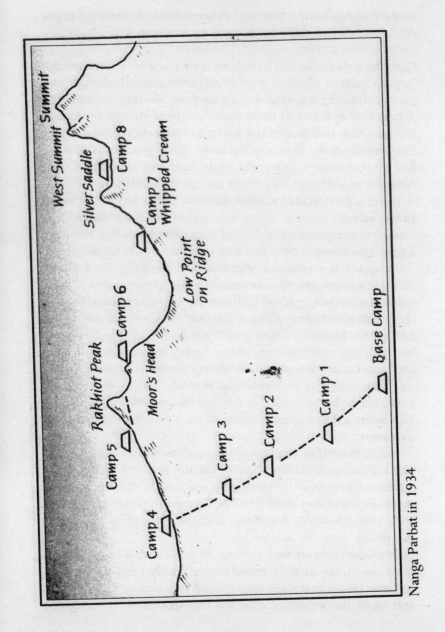

Nanga Parbat in 1934

crashing through the snow into the crevasse. Climbers cross an ice field carefully, with three or more men on a rope, so that if one falls into a crevasse unexpectedly, the rest can hold him.

When climbers can't find a snow bridge over a large crevasse, they put ladders across it. Those ladders have to be carried up the mountain. On Nanga Parbat they took up tree trunks from the forest below and laid them across the crevasses to make ladders.

In addition to the crevasses there are seracs, great boulders of ice that have split off from the glacier and lie on the surface of the icefall. As the ice moves beneath, it dislodges the seracs and sends them crashing down the mountainside. They can be one hundred or two hundred or three hundred feet high, and on Nanga Parbat they were that and more. Sometimes seracs stand straight up, blocking the path. Some lie crazily on their sides.

The ice is always moving. So the first party of climbers finds their way across an icefall, fixing ropes and cutting steps, looking for snow bridges over the crevasses. But then, day by day, the ice moves under their route. The pressure closes up old crevasses and tears open new ones along the route. Snow bridges that were once secure become fragile. Ladders and tree trunks across crevasses slip and are lost. New seracs fall across the path. So the route once made does not stay made. Each day the porters restocking the higher camps face new, unexpected dangers. The climbers must continually remake the old routes and find new detours. Sometimes they wind along the bottom of a crevasse, sometimes beneath a crevasse. Nineteen years later, in 1953, Hermann Buhl described climbing in the Nanga Parbat icefall 'through a labyrinth of clumps, towers, and caverns of ice so dense as to make one lose one's bearings. It was like being in a maze of streets in a strange city whose house-walls met overhead.'[31]

In 1934 the Sherpas and Germans picked their way through that icefall. From the bottom of a great crevasse they could look up and see their comrades, three dark, little figures a hundred yards above, picking their way carefully along the lip of the crevasse. Up there the sun burned on the packed snow, the light pulsing off. Sheets of hanging icicles flashed in the sun. At the rim the shadows played, and the canyon walls were shaded, cool, rough, knobbly like a limestone cave, buckling inward halfway up. But beneath the surface you could see great veins of trapped pure blue ice, in places almost green. It was never quiet. Always the ice moaned, or something distant snapped.

Merkl's people pitched Base Camp a day's carry above Fairy Meadow. Camp 1 was a day's carry higher on the snow at the foot of the icefall. Camp 2 was at the top of the icefall. But if they climbed directly up from there, they again faced a field of potential avalanches. So they detoured and traversed left, across and then up another icefall, veering back to the right, to Camp 3. From Camp 3 onward they were out of the icefall. They veered right again, walking up at an angle to Camp 4, where they were finally on the long North Ridge of Nanga Parbat.

From Camp 3, at the top of the icefall, they set out to establish Camp 4, actually on the ridge. Below the advance party, other climbers led teams of porters with fifty-pound loads up through the icefall, from camp to camp. The Balti porters, supervised by Darjeeling men, carried up to Camp 2. For the moment, only the Darjeeling men took loads above Camp 2. Bechtold was impressed by how much better the Sherpas moved on the ropes than the Baltis, as if the Sherpas had been doing it all their lives.

The Balti porters soon went on strike. They said that the Darjeeling men were being paid five rupees a day and they wanted the same. In fact the Sherpas were only making a rupee and a quarter a day. But in 1932 the Hunza high-altitude porters had been paid five rupees a day. The Baltis must have remembered this and believed the Sherpas would get the same. Captain Sangster, one of the liaison officers, negotiated with the striking Baltis but got nowhere. Lewa, the sardar, was made of sterner stuff. According to Bechtold:

> At the correct moment Lewa intervened. Knowing their kidney, he promptly removed their equipment, and left them standing in the snow with nothing more on than a loin-cloth. Then

he marked out an impossibly large stretch of snow with four poles, which would have to be shoveled away before they might depart. That did the trick. Twelve men declared themselves again willing to carry for the Bara Sahib, and the others were discharged that evening.[32]

Lewa was in a stronger position than Frier in 1932, who had to retain the loyalty of at least some of the Balti and Hunza porters. Lewa, with thirty-four Darjeeling men, could risk alienating all the locals.

At some point in the expedition, probably at Base Camp, the Darjeeling porters searched each other for knives.

They had done this on every expedition since 1931. That year three men, Tsin Norbu (pronounced *Teen Norboo*),[33] Pasang, and Hermann Schaller, were climbing a ridge on Kangchenjunga. Pasang and Schaller slipped and fell. Tsin Norbu managed to belay them and hold on. Pasang and Schaller dangled down the cliff on the rope, unable to climb back up. Tsin Norbu wasn't strong enough to pull them up, but held on. Then, exhausted and weakening, he knew that their weight would soon pull him off the mountain, too. Tsin Norbu took out his knife and cut the rope. Pasang and Schaller dropped to their deaths. Tsin Norbu survived.

Other climbers on other mountains have found themselves in the same situation.[34] Most experienced mountaineers have asked themselves what they would do in that situation, and it's not an easy question to answer. Why should two men die instead of one? But climbers rely on each other. Sooner or later almost all serious climbers fall, and as the rope pulls tight, another man or woman saves the climber's life. On difficult stretches, one always leads the climb, finding the route, while the other stands below, paying out the rope, braced, ready to hold. The dependence between two or three climbers is in the rope – their fates are literally tied to each other. On steep rock, when they can't see the other climber, they can feel the climbers on the rope. The pull, the slack, the tremble, the tension, a sharp jerk as an agreed message – all tell their story.

Climbers pay a lot of attention to knots.

More than anything else, the rope is trust. Old Sherpas say, quietly, without naming names, that they would rather not be on a rope with some men. Others you want there, know you can rely on. Climbing is not a team sport. Even on the massive expeditions, the individual competition is obvious. Yet the new sport of solo climbing feels wrong for most. The rope is safety, life, but it is also friendship.

To cut the rope may be necessary. But it is also to slice trust, to saw through love.

The Tibetan and Sherpa porters on Kangchenjunga understood what Tsin Norbu had done. They knew they themselves would probably have done the same. Yet they did not want to do it. So they resolved among themselves that none of them would carry knives.

It was not that simple, of course. They knew people might be tempted to cheat. So on every expedition for the next several years, including this one to Nanga Parbat, the Darjeeling porters formally searched each other for knives. They did not tell the sahibs.[35]

Chapter Five

IRON DETERMINATION

Ten people died on Nanga Parbat in 1934 because Willy Merkl led too many men up too quickly. We have seen one of the root causes of that mistake – politics. Now we turn to the other – the climbers did not understand altitude. We begin with what altitude did to one climber, Alfred Drexel, and how his comrades reacted.

Drexel was a manager in the same part of the railways as Willy Merkl, and they had often climbed together. On June 6, Drexel, three other climbers, and several Darjeeling porters were at Camp 3. The two Austrians, the guide Peter Aschenbrenner and the geologist Erwin Schneider, were looking around above Camp 3 for a new campsite that would be safer from avalanches. They used the skis they kept strapped to their backs as they broke trail up the mountain. Below them Willo Welzenbach, a municipal engineer from Munich, and Alfred Drexel were leading porters carrying loads up from Camp 2.

A snowstorm began, worse than anything Aschenbrenner had seen on Nanga Parbat two years before. He made it back down through the driving snow with Schneider to Camp 3. Below them, Welzenbach was on one rope with some porters and Drexel on another rope. Realizing he had lost touch with Drexel,

Welzenbach went back and found that Drexel and his porters had lost the path. Welzenbach got them back on the proper route and forged on. Drexel was the last man into Camp 3 that afternoon, exhausted. He said he had 'severe pains in his head; despite his fatigue he did not get a moment's sleep all night.'[1]

Drexel had altitude sickness.[2] The higher one goes, the lower the air pressure. Low air pressure means less air per cubic foot and therefore less oxygen in each breath. The natural thing when you need more oxygen is to increase the rate of breathing. This is why people pant after running or breathe fast while walking up a mountain. So at high altitude messages come from all over the body to tell the lungs to speed up and circulate more oxygen. There's a problem however. When the lungs breathe faster at altitude, the total oxygen intake is the same as the normal amount at sea level. But one breathes out more carbon dioxide, because the lungs expel the same amount of carbon dioxide as they would at sea level. So when you breathe faster at altitude, you lose more and more carbon dioxide from the body. That in turn lowers the pH in the bloodstream, the balance between acid and alkaline substances. This spells trouble.

The human body can only function within a narrow band of pH. If the body is too alkaline or too acidic, the mechanisms of the body do all they can to return to a normal pH. There is disagreement about why – one theory is that the digestive enzymes in the stomach can only work at a particular pH. Whatever the reason, the consequences are severe at altitude. The body will do anything to keep the pH in balance, including kill itself. So parts of the body cry out for oxygen and breathe more quickly. Then the mechanisms that protect pH send messages to breathe more slowly and preserve carbon dioxide.

When awake, one tries to breathe faster and succeeds for a while. Then suddenly you can't, and you're gasping. A climber or trekker sleeping at altitude breathes quickly for a time and then stops breathing completely. At that point the person wakes up, regains conscious control, and immediately starts breathing normally. If this happens, you don't know what woke you up, but you do know that you are afraid. Then you go back to sleep, and the process repeats. Soon you're awake again, gasping, disoriented, and anxious. All night long you wake up again and again.

Much of the time you're waking from the middle of a dream. People normally rise out of sleep slowly. But when they stop breathing, they wake up instantly, and the last image of the dream is before their eyes even as they're awake. It makes the dreams seem vivid. In a long night, they awaken many, many times, and the dreams grow increasingly anxious. In the morning most people believe it was the dreams that disturbed their sleep.

This is normal at altitude. Nowadays at Namche Bazaar in Khumbu, at eleven thousand feet, a considerable proportion of trekkers have headaches, sleepless nights, and vivid dreams. At some point on the walk through Namche to Everest Base Camp, about half of trekkers have ordinary altitude sickness. The most common symptoms are headache, loss of appetite, disturbed sleep, and a general lethargy. People also often get irritable and a bit confused. At eleven thousand feet you wait a day or two, and if it doesn't get better, you go downhill to the last altitude at which you were well.

People with ordinary altitude sickness who sit and wait at eleven thousand feet usually get better because their kidneys adjust to the altitude. The body loses carbon dioxide in two ways – through the lungs and in urine. After a few days at a particular altitude, the kidneys usually start sending less carbon dioxide to the bladder. Then the lungs can lose more carbon dioxide and so breathe faster.

Even at eleven thousand feet this does not always work. Alfred Drexler was at seventeen thousand feet and his ordinary altitude sickness was turning into acute mountain sickness. This can affect either the lungs, where it is called high altitude pulmonary edema, or the head, in which case it's high altitude cerebral edema.

High altitude pulmonary edema is a swelling in the tissues of the lungs. Two things seem to happen. One is that parts of the surface tissue of the lungs receive almost no oxygen, so they close down. Now a smaller proportion of surface tissue has to try to process thinner air, and breathing seems harder and harder. You begin to suffocate.

The other thing that occurs is that the balance of pressure between the blood and the air in the lungs is off-kilter. The pressure in the air has fallen, but the pressure in the body has not. So liquid may begin to leak out through the walls of the lung into the cavity, in effect pulled out by the low pressure in the lungs. This liquid builds up in the lungs, which try to cough it up and out. But if the liquid reaches a critical point, the person drowns. And you can drown from only half a pint of liquid in the lungs.

High altitude cerebral edema is a swelling in the head. Here the process is slightly different, and not quite so well understood. But basically, something seems to go wrong with what is called the blood-brain barrier. Your brain sits in the cerebral fluid, a sort of liquid cushion. The blood-brain barrier is a way of referring to all the membranes and processes that protect that fluid from the blood. They block infectious material and foreign bodies that may be carried in the blood, and they stop rising blood pressure from increasing the pressure of the fluid around the brain. In high altitude cerebral edema, that barrier stops working and the pressure builds in the cerebral fluid.

This is what happens on a small scale with the headaches many people get at altitude. It's similar to the headaches many women get who take the birth control pill, which also increases the pressure in the cerebral fluid. In both cases, you feel as if a hand is squeezing your brain, and that is roughly what's happening.

High altitude cerebral edema, as it squeezes the brain, can lead to ataxia, which means the brain and limbs are no longer coordinated. A person lurches, arms and legs flopping, and in time cannot walk. Sometimes two people can hold the sick person's arms and frog-march them downhill, and sometimes they have to be carried.

With both pulmonary edema and cerebral edema, the heart is

also doing dangerous overtime. Because there is not enough oxygen in the blood, the heart tries to circulate the blood round faster and faster. In ordinary altitude sickness, even while lying down, you're still trying to breathe quickly and your pulse is racing. In acute sickness, the pressure on the heart is worse, and often the heart breaks down before the lungs suffocate or the brain stops working. Or the arteries in the head may burst with the increased pressure, producing a stroke.

Pulmonary edema is much more common in the mountains than cerebral edema. Alfred Drexel may have had both. Today experienced climbers who see either set of symptoms in a companion know they have to get the person down the mountain, fast. If he can walk, good. If not, grab an arm and help him down. Lower him down on ropes if possible. Carry him on your back if you have to. And don't wait for morning. Get him down immediately, in the dark if need be. Often a small drop in altitude, sometimes as little as three hundred or six hundred feet, will restore a sick person to health.

The night of the snowstorm Alfred Drexel was delirious. The next morning the storm was over. The other climbers told Drexel to go down the mountain. He refused and they didn't insist. Drexel was dying, but they couldn't see it and so behaved as normal. Schneider and Aschenbrenner, the two strongest climbers, went back up to extend the route along the ridge toward Camp 4. When they came down in the afternoon, Drexel, now realizing how ill he was, agreed to go down the mountain with his orderly, Ang Tenjing. The others let him go down with no sahib to accompany him. They had their eyes on the prize. Drexel picked his way down the mountain, 'painfully supported on two ski-sticks.'[3]

Ang Tenjing helped Drexel until they were almost down to Camp 2, and then raced ahead for help. Bechtold, who was there, said that Ang Tenjing arrived 'in a state of agitation,' saying Drexel was seriously ill.[4] Pasang Picture and Müllritter immediately went up and came down with Drexel ten minutes later. Bechtold could see that Drexel 'was somewhat blue in the face, and breathing heavily,' but didn't think there was any real cause for worry. Bechtold wasn't listening to what Ang Tenjing was saying.

At Camp 2 they had only one tent and one sleeping bag for the sahibs. The sahibs often shared a sleeping bag to keep warm. Müllritter immediately volunteered to go down to Camp 1. That way Drexel would have a place to sleep, and Müllritter could tell the doctor to come back up the next morning.

Drexel was sick and not breathing properly, but they still planned to bring the doctor *up to him*.

Bechtold and Drexel presumably shared a sleeping bag that night. Drexel had 'a fearful cough, which lasted half the night.' In the middle of the night he went to sleep, but woke continually with 'confused feverish dreams.' Bechtold lay close to him, and it was a 'long, anxious night.' At eight Drexel woke up and seemed much better, as is often the case with acute mountain sickness. Bechtold told Drexel that they would now go downhill.

Suddenly Drexel was much worse. Bechtold felt 'there could be no more question of our setting out.' Bechtold, working from a model of illness at low altitudes, thought it more important to rest the patient than get him down. But he was worried.

Bechtold sent Pasang Picture with a note up to Camp 3, asking Willo Welzenbach to bring down another tent and a sleeping bag. That way they could be ready for the doctor. At the same time he sent Ang Tenjing, Drexel's worried orderly, and Ang Nima down to Camp 1. They carried another message, saying that Drexel was very sick, and when Dr. Bernard reached Camp 1 he must come up to Camp 2 immediately, even if he had to climb in the dark. The note ended: 'Not a moment to lose.'[5]

When Pasang Picture reached Camp 3, looking for the extra tent and sleeping bag, he found nobody. The sahibs and the porters had gone up to establish Camp 4. Pasang Picture did not have the confidence simply to take a sleeping bag. Worried, he raced back down to Camp 2. It took him three hours, round-trip. He got down to discover that Drexel was now unconscious.

Down in Camp 1, Merkl didn't send anybody up all day. There

was a 'heavy hailstorm'[6] and he was probably worried about the safety of anybody he sent up. Up in Camp 2, Bechtold could now see that Drexel was dying: 'From hour to hour he was visibly sinking.'[7] Frantic, Bechtold sent Pasang Picture out into the hailstorm down to Camp 1 to fetch the doctor. At five-thirty Pasang was back up with Müllritter and Dr. Bernard. Ang Tenjing, Drexel's orderly, returned with them. The doctor refused tea and went to his patient at once.

Bernard diagnosed pneumonia. The doctor, like the climbers, didn't know what he was facing. But he was very worried and said that Drexel needed oxygen immediately.

Again, climbers today would carry the sick man down to the oxygen. Bernard and Bechtold sent a message down to Camp 1 asking Merkl to send oxygen up. Pasang Picture and Palten went back out into the storm and down as fast as they could. Pasang Picture arrived in Camp 1 exhausted at about 7 P.M. just as it was getting dark. During the day he had now been up to Camp 3 and back down to Camp 2, down to Camp 1 and back up to 2, and now down to 1 again. The note he carried for Merkl from Bechtold said only: 'Send up more oxygen today, it's a question of Balbo's life.' Balbo was Drexel's nickname.[8]

Merkl had no oxygen in Camp 1. The expedition was not using oxygen to climb and had only a few sets for medical emergencies. Merkl sent Pasang Kikuli and Jigmey down to Base Camp to fetch an oxygen set.

The others waited in Camp 1. Wieland volunteered to go back up with the oxygen when it came. Pasang Picture and Palten would go with him. But for the moment, exhausted, they rested.

Up in Camp 2, Müllritter and Dr. Bernard did what they could for Drexel. Bechtold, who had not slept the night before, was lost in exhaustion and distress and unable to help. The storm rose again. Snow blew hard against the tent, and there was thunder and lightning in the darkness.

Far below, the porters Gaylay and Dakshi set out from Base Camp just after 8 P.M. with the oxygen for Drexel. They moved quickly up through the icefall in the darkness, one of them carrying a kerosene lantern. At ten twenty-five they reached Merkl's tent at Camp 1. Merkl gave them tea and a cigarette each, for which they were grateful, and went to wake Pasang Picture, Palten, and Wieland. By midnight all three men were off into the darkness carrying the oxygen up to Camp 2.

Drexel was already dead. At 9:20 P.M., a little over eleven hours after losing consciousness, he died in his sleep, a smile on his face. Dr. Bernard and the other climbers still did not understand what had killed him. The frantic energy with which the Sherpas had run up and down the mountain is evidence that they may have recognized the threat to Drexel's life.

When Bernard realized Drexel was dead, he threw himself across the body and wept. Then Bernard, Müllritter, and Bechtold knelt in the snow outside, crying and saying the Lord's Prayer. Drexel's orderly Ang Tenjing and the other porters stood round the sahibs and 'wept without restraint.'[9]

The three surviving sahibs left Drexel dead in their tent and moved into another. There they wept, then spoke of Drexel's parents back in Germany. After a time, they began to talk to Drexel's father and mother as if they were in the tent. Outside they could hear the porters lamenting, hour after hour. The climbers still didn't understand why Drexel had died.

Altitude kills some people, but it weakens everybody. The reduced oxygen makes climbers clumsy, slow, and stupid. Their words and thoughts get garbled, and so do their feet. People who are not mortally ill may still wake up all night at twenty-three thousand feet, constantly dreaming they are drowning. Climbers also constantly feel exhausted and drained.

The German climbers in 1934 didn't grasp this. The route they took later in the climb put them on a long ridge at high altitude for many days. Merkl and his companions then made decisions that would have made sense in the Alps but killed people in the Himalayas. There were two reasons for this. One was simple ignorance. The other was a refusal to learn.

We'll take the ignorance first. Some people had known about

altitude sickness for a long time. The first reports in written history come from ancient China, where government ambassadors and Buddhist pilgrims reported that, on the far southwestern borders, people could die on the tops of passes in the Big and Little Headache Mountains. By 1934 doctors in the Andes knew and had published a good deal about altitude sickness. Their work, though, was in Spanish, and European and North American doctors did not begin reading it until the end of the 1930s. Sherpas also knew of something they called 'pass sickness,' but nobody was asking them for advice.

European doctors and climbers did realize that altitude made climbing harder, but didn't understand edema. They did know that it was best to get somebody with a 'headache' or 'pneumonia' down the mountain, but didn't understand the urgency. And while they knew that it took people time to acclimatize to altitude, they constantly underestimated the difficulty. In memoirs and expedition accounts, one experienced Himalayan mountaineer after another emphasized the importance of acclimatization. Each said it anew, an indication that when climbers had first come to the Himalayas, they had read the point in other people's books but had not fully absorbed the fact.

One way to understand why it was hard for climbers then to accept the facts of altitude is to look at the reasons trekkers still die of altitude sickness today.

We now know that above about ten thousand feet, an average person should ascend no more than a thousand feet a day. They can climb higher than that, but should sleep no more than a thousand feet higher than the day before. Of course on most mountains, camps are more than a thousand feet apart in height. So if you go up to a camp two thousand feet above, you need to spend an extra day resting there to acclimatize. Or you can sleep one night at the higher camp, come down for a second night at a lower camp, and then go back up.

But even today many climbers and trekkers have difficulty accepting these limits. In Khumbu during the 1990s at least one trekker died every spring season and another in the fall. With the numbers of trekkers increasing, even more are dying now. The reasons are masculinity and time.

After living in Namche for three months in 1995, I was climbing the hill to Tengboche monastery and cheerily caught up with two Austrian climbers. They were on their way to Ama Dablam, a beautiful and challenging mountain of ice and rock. We stopped to chat. They wore beards and shorts, with blond hair on their enormous leg muscles. They were panting, and I asked them how quickly they'd come up in the last few days. They told me. I said they had to stop and rest a couple of days because they were moving much too fast. They looked at me and saw a man thirty years older and clearly overweight. What made it worse was that I was passing them carrying a heavier pack. So they paid no attention to what I said.

These two were strong men, and like most climbers proud of that strength. That's one of the points of competitive climbing, after all. It's difficult to grasp that acclimatization has nothing to do with strength or fitness and is only an adjustment in the amount of carbon dioxide the kidney passes in urine. What leads to acclimatization is time at altitude, not effort. Three days spent lying down in a tourist lodge reading Stephen King is every bit as good as three days of heavy load carrying. Moreover, people adjust to altitude at different rates. These differences have nothing to do with the differences between strong, fit people and weak couch potatoes. By and large, fatter and older trekkers have less difficulty at altitude. We tend to go up more slowly, taking more rest days.

But climbers, and many trekkers, are superb athletes. They've developed a habit of fitness training that they apply to altitude. In fitness, up to a certain limit, the more you push yourself, the more you gain. Any serious climber, faced with an obstacle in life, is likely to try harder, but trying harder is the wrong thing to do with altitude. It can kill you.

The secret is to stop, turn around, walk away from your objective, and lie down for a couple of days. It's hard for climbers to understand that what appears to be weakness leads to strength.

1 Darjeeling, 2000: Ang Tsering Sherpa on his patio, holding the handle of a rake he has been whittling.

2 Ang Tsering Sherpa's medals. His Himalayan Club Tiger medal is in the top center, his medal from Nanga Parbat in the lower left.

3 Darjeeling, 2000: The first page of Da Thundu's Himalayan Club log book, kept as a memento by his family.

4 Lhamoo Iti Sherpa, widow of Da Thundu, holding the medal he was awarded by the German Mountaineering Club for his heroism on Nanga Parbat.

5 Namche, 2000:
A family photograph
of Khansa Sherpa of
Namche as a young
man in the 1950s.
Khansa climbed to
the South Col with
the 1953 expedition
to Everest.

6 Khansa and his
wife Lhakpa Sherpa
at home.

7 Darjeeling, 2000:
Pasang Phutar, a
Sherpa climber in
the 1930s.

8 Namche, 2000: Namdu Sherpa in her hotel, Khumbu Lodge.

9 Anu Sherpa, climber and sardar, in his kitchen.

10 A porter just above Namche on the trail to Everest Base Camp, 2000.

11 Darjeeling, early twentieth century: Tibetan rickshawmen playing cards.

12 Tibetan rickshawmen and tourist rickshaw.

13 An old family photograph of Pasang Dıkı Sherpa, the widow of Nima Dorje. She later married Ang Tsering, and they had eight children.

13a Nanga Parbat, 1934: Nima Dorje reading a German sporting newspaper.

14 Lewa, the sardar in 1934.

14a Loads for the expedition in 1934.

15 Porters setting out from one of the lower camps at sunrise on Nanga Parbat.

In Khumbu today climbers and trekkers from the Alps, like those Austrians on the path, face another difficulty. They've already experienced altitude sickness, and it wasn't a problem. The Alps are much lower than the Himalayas. The summit of Mont Blanc, at a little less than sixteen thousand feet, is lower than Everest Base Camp. So Alpine climbers suffer mild altitude sickness and recover quickly. 'I had a headache when I climbed Mont Blanc,' they say, 'and it went away when I came down.' From this they conclude, 'I'll be all right.'

The Germans and Austrians on Nanga Parbat in 1934 were Alpine climbers. And they faced the other difficulty, besides toughness, that exposes trekkers and climbers to danger – the pressure of time.

Acclimatizing to altitude is slow. Climbers and trekkers are under economic pressures to ascend in a hurry. People have jobs they must get back to. In the 1930s many climbers in the Himalayas were independently wealthy. But on every expedition there were people who worked as doctors or teachers or engineers. Even more important was the sheer cost of all those porters and all their food on a big expedition.

The economic pressure is even stronger on commercial climbing and trekking expeditions today. Take the example of a group of trekkers in Nepal going to Everest Base Camp. The group members pay an agency for the trek, and the agency provides a sardar, tents, cooks, and porters. The more quickly they get to Base Camp and back, the greater the profit for the agency. Most treks go up at a pace that fits the average ability to acclimatize. In the nature of things, every trekking group of twelve people will include one or two people who are below average. But the trekking group does not have enough staff to split into two groups. So the trekkers who are acclimatizing more slowly are under pressure to keep up with the rest.

Then a certain kind of masculinity can kick in, particularly for middle-aged men who are often trekking to prove to themselves that they haven't really grown old. They feel under pressure to keep up with the group. They have paid a lot of money for the holiday of a lifetime. They don't want to go home and say they didn't make it to Everest Base Camp. They have an itinerary, and at the end of it there's a plane to catch and a job to go home to. So they struggle on.

People walking alone, or with a friend, simply stop and rest when their bodies warn of danger. Foreigners walking alone in Nepal almost never die. Instead, it's usually the slowest person in a group, the one who drags himself the last few hundred feet up the hill, then angrily says, 'I'm fine.' The slowest person is a woman as often as a man. But women seem more likely to admit they are ill. Some men find it more difficult to show their weakness in a mixed group, particularly in front of women they want to impress. The person who dies is usually somebody who tried to conceal his illness.

The Sherpas and other Nepalis who lead treks are constantly on the lookout for such people. They know what can happen, and they don't want to see it. The local lodge owners watch carefully, too. But European trekkers are by and large unwilling to listen to Nepalis.

All of the pressures that bear on trekkers today were stronger for the Germans on Nanga Parbat. They were superb athletes with experience of altitude in the Alps. The Germans were proud of their strength and used to overcoming obstacles. They were in a hurry and needed to succeed. They didn't listen to the Sherpas. They didn't understand altitude, and they found it hard to learn.

We need to know one more thing about altitude to fully grasp what happened on Nanga Parbat. Once they were trapped high on the ridge, the Sherpa porters were just as vulnerable as the European climbers.

Most Darjeeling porters on most expeditions had trouble at altitude. Of the fifty-five porters on Everest in 1924, for instance, only six reached the highest camp. This was not unusual. It was partly because porters were badly nourished, but it was also because the altitude made most of them ill.

The Sherpas and Tibetans were not and had never been adapted to life at extremely high altitudes. The majority of Sherpas in Nepal live well south of Everest, in villages between seven thousand and ten thousand feet. Tibetans, and Sherpas in Khumbu, mostly live between ten thousand and twelve thousand five hundred feet. Tibetan and Sherpa herders will take their animals to almost seventeen thousand feet in the summer pastures. But even then nobody sleeps much above sixteen thousand feet – and it is the altitude you sleep at that most affects you. Sherpas who move to lower altitudes in Kathmandu and New York have to acclimatize like anybody else when they return home. The Darjeeling men were living at seven thousand five hundred feet.

There is a qualitative break in human adaptation at about the altitude of Everest Base Camp, roughly sixteen thousand five hundred feet. There is a more important one somewhere between twenty thousand and twenty three thousand feet. From that point on, the human body steadily deteriorates. This applies to Tibetans, Sherpas, and Europeans. Most people can adapt, given time, to living at up to seventeen thousand feet. The important point, though, is that most Sherpas and most Europeans have trouble with really high altitudes. Up to the altitude of the highest pastures most Sherpas and Europeans can adapt. Beyond that, we are all human, although some of us are exceptional.

They brought Alfred Drexel's body down to Base Camp. All the climbers and porters came off the mountain for the funeral. The porters gathered flowers and Aschenbrenner 'carved a simple wooden cross.' They dug the grave, and all was ready. Six sahibs carried Drexel's body, covered with the swastika flag, to the grave on a stretcher.[10] There was a pause for Müllritter to take a photograph of the men carrying the body. And then, according to Bechtold:

> Late in the afternoon . . . the long procession of men moved up towards the hillock. Willy Merkl and Kapp in front,

behind them our beloved Alfred, borne by his friends, and shrouded with the flags of his native land. Then came the British transport officers [Frier and Sangster] and the long column of brave porters, thirty Darjeeling men and thirty Baltis.

Willy Merkl spoke at the graveside. In a few words, he sketched out the high purpose for which Alfred Drexel had died, saying how great was the gap thus made in our circle. He led our thoughts homeward to the stricken parents, and again back to Nanga Parbat, there gladly to continue the struggle with the iron determination of our close friend. Thus he bore our hearts to higher regions, and gave the stern spirit of a soldier's to this last journey.

Merkl had worked with Drexel in the same department of the railway and must have known his parents. Their fellow workers in the railway had all contributed small amounts of money to the expedition and had thrown a farewell party for all the climbers before they left Germany.

Kapp, the German consul in Bombay, spoke next. As India was a British colony, there was no ambassador and Kapp was the senior German diplomat. He came on the expedition partly as a translator who knew the country and could help with arrangements. Kapp was also, of course, the voice and eyes of the government that was funding the expedition. He spoke by the grave, Bechtold said, 'as a friend and as the representative of Germany. His speech ended with the Lord's Prayer. The national emblem [a swastika flag] and the tricolour flag fluttered down into the grave, wherein we cast earth, flowers and evergreen juniper. Hoarse throats sang the mountaineers' song; and then in the clear evening light from the snows a silent procession moved down towards our tent settlement.'[11]

The swastika, 'iron determination,' 'struggle,' 'stern spirit,' 'soldier's' burial – these were not neutral symbols and words in Germany in 1934. They spoke of militarism, the right wing, and the Nazis.

With the exception of the guide Peter Aschenbrenner, the climbers who went to Nanga Parbat were all professional or white-collar workers. That is, they were drawn from the part of German society that tended to support the Nazis. Willo Welzenbach was an officer in the SA, Hitler's paramilitary street fighters and marching troops before he took power. But he did not join them until 1933, after Hitler took power. Welzenbach's family later said he only joined the SA to protect his job as a civil engineer and surveyor of works for the Munich city government. In fact, until the Nazi seizure of power Welzenbach had been active in the Bavarian People's Party, a right-wing organization that competed with the Nazis.[12] In any case, Welzenbach was on the expedition not because of his politics but because he was one of the most brilliant climbers in Germany. When the going got rough on the mountain, he behaved more generously and decently than any of his less political fellow climbers.

The important thing was not the personal politics of the climbers, but the political pressures or personal ambitions driving them. A British example may make this clearer. On Everest in 1922 there was a bitter dispute among the climbers after the failure of their first attempt. Mallory and Somervell wanted to have another go. General Bruce was against it because the weather had turned bad and they were likely to lose lives. Mallory and Somervell got their way, and as we have seen, the second attempt cost the lives of seven porters.

Mallory and Somervell are far more appealing to a person of my political sympathies. Bruce was an imperialist of the old school. He spent many years repressing Pathan rebels on the Indian frontier, where he was a pioneer in leading night missions to assassinate rebels. Howard Somervell, on the other hand, was a lifelong pacifist who spent most of his years as a medical missionary in India. George Mallory was a socialist, vocal in his support of women's rights and the Irish rebellion against Britain. But Bruce, the right-winger, was also a Gurkha officer centrally concerned for the lives of the porters he led. Somervell and Mallory wanted, above all else, to climb the mountain.

On Nanga Parbat, too, that was what would matter – how badly did they need to reach the top?

The German press followed their progress closely. From the time they left Munich, Fritz Bechtold was filming his fellow climbers, day after day in Base Camp and on the mountain. They could feel the eyes of Germany on them through Bechtold's lens. The climbers knew the movie would be shown to large audiences in Germany – massive audiences if they reached the summit. Up until then they had largely been ordinary men, famous if at all only to a few other climbers. Now they could become heroes, representatives of a once humiliated and now proud nation.

Merkl soon had other worries as well. The next day Willo Welzenbach wrote home to his family from Base Camp. According to Welzenbach's biographer, Eric Roberts:

> In an extra note marked 'confidential,' Welzenbach reported a deplorable clash between Merkl and Schneider. Schneider had faulted Merkl for 'irreverent behaviour' in ordering publicity photographs of Drexel's body being transported down the mountain and of the actual burial. In Welzenbach's view 'he merely said what most of us were thinking.' This open disapproval infuriated Merkl so much that he wanted to 'banish Schneider from the expedition' because 'he considered that all criticism undermined his authority. . . . Merkl is increasingly trying to act like a dictator who tolerates no comments. He really seems to believe that a stern and uncompromising attitude serves to establish his authority and to suppress the inferiority complex which he obviously feels as an upstart. . . . In Balbo we lost an effective mainstay in the battle against Willy's delusions of grandeur and persecution mania.'[13]

Welzenbach had been Merkl's friend and had climbed with him in the Alps. But Welzenbach was a much more distinguished climber. He was also a civil engineer with a doctorate, while Merkl was a former manual worker with a diploma from a technical college. But there is another reason Welzenbach thought Merkl an 'upstart.' Nanga Parbat had been Welzenbach's idea, and his dream, before it had been Merkl's. Welzenbach had taken a backseat this time because Merkl had already led one expedition and been able to organize another. Now he was furious at Merkl's incompetent leadership.

The day after Drexel's funeral, the sardar Lewa, the consul Kapp, and the British liaison officer Frier took twenty Balti porters back onto the mountain to begin ferrying loads up to Camp 4. The rest stayed below to work on the grave. They built a burial mound of large rocks, spread earth on top, and planted flowers over the top. Then they waited to see how Lewa and the Baltis were doing.

It's unclear why they waited. As two years before, there seems to have been no sense of urgency. A few days later Lewa came down the mountain with the Balti porters. He said that the wind from the sides of the avalanches on the face had blown down the tents at Camp 1. This may have frightened the Balti porters. In any case, seven of the ten chosen to carry loads up to Camp 4 had said they were too sick and dizzy to go. The other three couldn't make it beyond Camp 3.

Dr. Bernard examined the Baltis and said they looked healthy to him. So Lewa fired eight of them, demanded they return their precious high-altitude gear, and sent them home.

A message came from Frier at Camp 2 that Pasang II, one of the Darjeeling men, was very ill with 'bronchial catarrh and rheumatism.'[14] (There were three Pasangs on Nanga Parbat – Pasang Kikuli, Pasang Picture, and this man called Pasang II by the sahibs so they could keep them straight.)

Again Dr. Bernard raced up to Camp 2 rather than bring the sick man down. But when he saw Pasang's condition, Bernard got him down immediately. Pasang II survived.

At Base Camp, Merkl had just discovered that they were out of tsampa. Tsampa is roasted barley flour, a traditional Tibetan staple and the mountain ration for Darjeeling porters on this expedition. It's an excellent high-altitude food. Like rice and wheat flour, tsampa contains a lot of calories for its weight. Unlike rice and wheat flour, it's easy to prepare at altitude. Simply mix it with hot water and you have a thick, tasty porridge that lines the stomach. It's still the breakfast food of choice in Khumbu on the coldest winter days.

But they didn't have any at Base Camp. Willo Welzenbach was furious about this, too. He also felt that even without tsampa they had enough other food to make an immediate try for the summit.

Merkl did not. The sahibs sat at Base Camp for days, waiting for the tsampa to be carried in from Kashmir. Finally it came. On June 22, eleven days after Drexel's funeral, they got ready to set out. Just before he went up the mountain, Welzenbach wrote home to his family:

The attack should proceed in two groups – first group: Merkl, Welzenbach, Schneider, Aschenbrenner, Müllritter. Second group: Wieland, Bernard, Kuhn, Sangster. The departure of the first group was originally planned for today. However, Merkl and Bechtold can't drag themselves away from Base Camp and won't follow us until tomorrow. Thus our advance will of course be delayed yet again. I believe that Merkl has still neither realized what is at stake nor that the success of the whole undertaking depends on taking very active measures. Otherwise we shall return home without reaching the summit and it is inevitable that Merkl will be called upon to account for what was achieved with the 175,000 or 200,000 Reichsmarks (the undertaking will cost that much). For the present letter-writing at Base Camp seems to be more important to him than the advance towards the summit. He likes it here in the role of pasha which he will probably have to give up when it is either do or die higher up. . . .

You will be wondering why I am telling you all this. Well, because I don't want to entrust it to my diary. You never know whose hands diaries will fall into. For example, Merkl seized Balbo's diaries immediately.[15]

His letter finished, Welzenbach, Schneider, Aschenbrenner, Müllritter, and eleven porters set off from Base Camp. Hanns Hieronimus was along on the expedition as camp commandant. As the climbers set off, Hieronimus played marching songs on the gramophone for them. The music followed them far up the mountain in the clear air, and their happy yodels drifted back down. Schneider knew that this time 'when we returned it would only be as beaten men or victors. We hoped as victors.'[16]

Almost all the ingredients of the tragedy that would follow were now in place. Merkl was under personal pressure and leading a divided expedition. He had chosen the politics of iron determination. And the route to a summit would mean many days on a long ridge at an altitude whose effects Merkl and his companions did not understand.

After four days climbing, the first party of sahibs and porters were at Camp 4. There they faced the Rakhiot Peak. Because they had taken a relatively safe route up to the ridge, they were on the wrong side of this peak, which now stuck up in the middle of the ridge between them and Nanga Parbat. They had to find a way to traverse around and below the peak. On June 26 four sahibs and five porters set out to find that route. That day they failed. The next day the porters went down to Camp 3 to fetch more loads, while the sahibs waited for them, and Merkl and Bechtold caught up.

On June 28 the porters came back up. With them came the second assault party, who had set out a few days behind – Wieland, the British captain Sangster, and several porters. They had left the climber Kuhn behind at Camp 3 feeling a bit unwell. The next morning a porter came up to say that Kuhn looked quite ill. Dr. Bernard skied swiftly down from Camp 4 and organized two Balti porters to take Kuhn down to Base Camp. Then Bernard went back up to Camp 4. He had seen Drexel die under his care, and Pasang II and Kuhn close to death. Bernard had now been up to Camp 4, and witnessed what the thin air did to bodies. When he came to India he hadn't, and couldn't have, understood altitude. Now he did, and he was worried.

In the morning, five days after reaching Camp 4, all the sahibs and porters were ready for the attempt to traverse below the Rakhiot Peak. Dr. Bernard made a formal speech to all the climbers. He impressed on them, for all he was worth, the dangers of altitude. Then he said – I want each of you to promise me something. When you get to the place where you know that if you go farther, you cannot get back down without help, you will stop. Promise me that. One by one, the sahibs formally promised the doctor. Then a porter stepped forward and placed a ceremonial silk scarf around Merkl's neck. A second porter sank to his knees in the snow and kissed Merkl's feet, a gesture of respect. They set off. That afternoon they made Camp 5 at 21,950 feet, just below the Rakhiot Peak. In the northern distance they could see the Karakoram mountains, including K2 and the Mustagh Tower.

For the next two days the German climbers took turns forcing the route up and across the steepest part of the ice wall below the Rakhiot Peak. With pitons, crampons, and ice axes, and without loads, they could have climbed across the face easily enough. But they had to make it safe for the porters to follow with fifty-pound loads, and without crampons to grip the ice. For much of the route, a slip would mean a fall of several hundred feet and death. So the sahibs cut steps in the ice for the porters to stand on. On the steepest part, just above Camp 5, they put fixed ropes in place. The porters could hang on to these ropes for safety and haul themselves up if they had to.

They fixed three two-hundred-foot ropes in all, a total of six hundred feet. Nowadays that sounds like nothing. On Everest, modern commercial expeditions take turns fixing thousands of feet of rope, all the way through the Khumbu Icefall and up the Lhotse Face to the South Col. Both porters and climbers simply clip on and trundle safely upward. But in 1934 it seemed to Fritz Bechtold both heroic and extreme to set so much rope.

On July 4 the sahibs and porters set off from Camp 5 and up the fixed ropes. Bechtold was a bit nervous about how the porters would take it. This, he thought, was the crucial test of the Darjeeling men. But 'whenever I looked back during a halt for breath, I caught sight of smiling, enthusiastic faces directly below.'[17]

They made it to Camp 6 on the other side of the traverse. As they set up the tents, the clouds lifted from the summit. Porters and sahibs alike stopped work on the tents and stood together, looking silently at Nanga Parbat.

The ridge stretched before them to the south. At first it was a broad whaleback of white snow, sloping downward to a low point, then rising slightly more steeply for about the same distance. At the top of that rise there were two black rock peaks, like sharp ears, on either side of a flat snowy pass they called the Silver Saddle. Beyond the Saddle they would have to go down again some ways, then turn sharply left onto the final summit ridge. They couldn't see that bit from where they stood – it was hidden by the Silver Saddle. But they could see, to the left of the Saddle, the final ridge rising first to one summit, and beyond that to the final summit.

What fascinated them all was the great rock and ice cliff that fell almost vertically over ten thousand feet from the summit to the grass and trees below. But they wouldn't have to climb that, or anything like it. Their way looked clear. The difficult climbing was over.

Ang Tsering says Everest was a difficult mountain, and Kangchenjunga was harder. Nanga Parbat was hardest of all because of the climb up to and round the Rakhiot Peak.

That night Bechtold shared a tent with Merkl, Welzenbach, and Wieland, the only three nonsmokers. They complained about his cigarette smoke so much he went off to share a tent with Schneider and Aschenbrenner. The three puffed happily together.

Willy Merkl had already decided that the next day they would push on toward the summit with everyone who was fit. He had made that decision back at Base Camp, and he was sticking to it.

In Ang Tsering's opinion this was the crucial mistake that caused the tragedy that followed. Ang Tsering was already an experienced Himalayan mountaineer in 1934, with five major expeditions behind him. His opinion carries weight and fits the facts.

Ang Tsering says that then, and still largely today, the customary way of tackling a Himalayan giant was to set up a string of camps and ferry loads up to them. One party in front would make trail and establish camps until they got tired, then come down while a second party went up. When the second party needed a rest, a third party would go up. The climbers and porters would leapfrog up the mountain.

The great advantage of this system was safety. If anything went wrong, the climbers in front could retreat one camp down, where they would find friends, food, and water. If they reached that camp sick or injured, there was somebody more rested to help them down to Base Camp. If they couldn't get down even one camp, they could wait for help to come up.

The leader's job, Ang Tsering says, was to lead from behind. He stayed down at Base Camp, or near there, and made sure the supplies got up and the system of ferrying loads worked. (Ang Tsering uses the English word *ferry* to explain this in Nepali.)

From Camp 4 onward, Merkl abandoned this system. He pushed on, with everyone going together. Instead of staying back to organize the loads, he continued with the other climbers. From Camp 6, just below the Rakhiot Peak, they would walk down the ridge, then back up to the Silver Saddle, then down a bit and along to the first summit and then the final summit. It should take three days from Camp 6. If they had to retreat, there would be tents to retreat to. But there would be no food or water in those tents, no fuel or friends or sleeping bags or blankets. The entire summit party would carry those supplies. If anything went wrong, they would be stranded on a long, high ridge.

Ang Tsering, a careful man, says he can't know for sure why Merkl decided this, so he won't speculate. But we can guess.

For one thing, they were behind. Drexel's death, the Baltis' illness, and the shortage of tsampa had set them back three weeks. The monsoon is not predictable at Nanga Parbat and may not come at all. But then again, it might. Merkl was also under political and personal pressure. Throwing everything he had at the mountain was the most likely way to get to the top. And Willy Merkl may have wanted to go to the top himself. He had been dreaming about Nanga Parbat a long time. Clearly, he was now one of the weaker climbers. Aschenbrenner and Schneider had done much of the route-finding and rope-fixing around the Rakhiot Peak. Willo Welzenbach was going strong, too: 'indefatigable,' Bechtold said of Welzenbach, 'whenever there was dirty work he was eager to be at hand.'[18] If a small party went ahead to the summit, it would consist of two of these three men.

If somebody had to stop and man a support camp, it would be Merkl. If he decided to go on himself and leave an obviously fitter man in support, there would be a bitter argument. So if Merkl wanted to go to the summit, he had to take everybody else with him.

Finally, I think, Merkl didn't understand the scale of problems posed by altitude. From his point of view, the hard climbing was over. What he saw before him was something that he could do in a day and a half, at most perhaps two days, in the Alps.

On the morning of the fifth of July the climbers calculated they were three days' climb from the summit. Three of the sixteen remaining porters were sick – Ang Tenjing, Palten, and Nima. (This was another Nima. The ever-cheerful Nima Dorje, who had climbed so high on Everest, was still doing well.) The three porters asked permission to go back down and were allowed to do so. The other six sahibs and thirteen porters set off. They walked a little down the ridge, then up a wide whaleback of deep snow that rose gently. Beneath the whaleback, on the other side, they found a single dark rock fifty feet high, with ledges and protrusions that looked like the face of a man. They called it the Moor's Head, from the old word for a dark-skinned North African, and marked it well. The large dark face in the white expanse of snow would be their guide home when the clouds came in.

Below the Moor's Head there was a steep downhill with a thin layer of snow on the ice, until it leveled out four hundred feet below. The lead climbers cut steps into the snow and ice, and the porters made their way carefully down. Now they walked downhill along a gentle ridge covered in deep, hard-packed snow. The slopes below them were in cloud. It was snowing down there, but up on the ridge it was a sunny day. They reached the low point of the ridge and looked up toward the Silver Saddle.

It's not easy to describe what they saw. You can look at the photographs they took (see plates 17 and 20). It's difficult, always, to find words for the Himalayas. In the photographs the rocks seem black because the contrast with the shining snow is so strong. Even if you stare at the cliffs from the valley, then turn away, your eye's memory holds black rock. But look carefully from the valley and imagine what paints you would use in a picture, or get closer, and you see the cliffs are every shade of brown and gray. The steepest places seem the darkest, where the snow cannot stick or hold. And yet even here there are little veins of white snow, running across where there must be ledges, and sometimes a patch of white like a small bandage.

On the slightly less steep places the snow lies deep, in great slabs, piled on top of each other. Constantly there are fault lines, where tens and hundreds of tons of snow have broken loose and avalanched, and now there is a cliff of ice, clean, sharp, and curved.

The perspective tricks your eyes. From the bottom, every cliff and every mountain looks possible. The air is thin and clean and brings everything closer. But the scale is such that the eye cannot credit what it sees. Then, as you climb, suddenly the below you have just left seems to fall far, far away. So always, you see that you have climbed a great distance, and the top is almost there.

As the climbers looked up, to the left of the ridge they were following was the Rupal Face, falling seven thousand feet, fluted ribs of angry rock. Farther on, the face swept up and off to the left, the rock chunkier here, streams of ice running down rivers in the rock. At the top of this face the deep snow billowed into cornices that overhung the cliffs. Far off, up and to the left, at the top of the face was the final summit.

Directly in front of them the first stretch up was a crooked ridge of snow, broad enough for safety. Then the ridge swept up steeply and broadened out into a face of thick, jumbled snow. At the top of that face the Silver Saddle shone against the blue sky and whirling clouds. The Saddle, covered in deep snow, was flat and long, a place you could imagine resting. When you got there, you could see your way left to the summit. On either side of the snow of the Saddle there were dark peaks, the pommel and back of the saddle. The peak on the left, the back of the saddle, was solid and rounded. The pommel on the right stuck into the air like a jagged thumb.

They began climbing. The clouds came up from the slopes below and covered them. They stopped often to breathe. Finally they came to a broad, flat place, like a terrace in the snow, about halfway between the low point on the ridge and the top of the Silver Saddle. There they pitched Camp 7, at 23,570 feet. All around them the snow had piled up in billowing dunes, so they called the campsite Whipped Cream.

As it was getting dark, the clouds and mist lifted, and they could see the summit again. Bechtold thought, 'Tomorrow or the day following, after our unspeakable labors, the great peak might fall to us.'[19] They were in bed before dark.

This was their third night at 22,000 feet or above (to be strictly accurate, 21,950 feet or above). The Silver Saddle was only 876 feet above, and the summit only 3,090 feet away – two hours climb at sea level for these men.

The next morning, as they were all ready to leave, Tundu and Nurbu said they were sick from the altitude. The sahibs could tell by looking at them that they were telling the truth. Aschenbrenner, Schneider, Wieland, and Welzenbach were all feeling strong and possible summiteers. Merkl was the leader. Bechtold, the sixth sahib, was selected to take Tundu and Nurbu down to safety.

He was unhappy to be going down, but thought he would be coming right back up with more supplies to support the summit team. Bechtold shook hands with the other sahibs and started down. He kept stopping to look back. He saw Aschenbrenner, Schneider, and Welzenbach, in the lead, near the top of the Silver Saddle, 'three small dark shadows in the spotless blue of a radiant morning.'

The two men with Bechtold were soon in serious trouble. 'Every minute the sick porters sat down in the snow, and I had great difficulty in getting them up again and again.'[20] The four-hundred-foot drop from the Moor's Head had seemed easy on the way down. Now Bechtold saw how difficult it could be for men with altitude sickness to climb. They took hours getting up to the Moor's Head. Then they traversed the steep ice wall below the Rakhiot Peak. Coming down the fixed ropes, Bechtold was in front, Nurbu in the middle, and Tundu last. Tundu, exhausted, slipped and fell. Nurbu held him. 'But it was a long time before they could gather sufficient strength to continue the descent,' Bechtold said. 'All my powers of persuasion and constant succour were needed to bring the poor fellows down the rope.'[21]

The three men made it down to Camp 5, where they found deep snow around the tents. Bechtold realized there must have been several days of heavy snow down here while they had been happy in the sun on the ridge. Trudging down to Camp 4,

we were suddenly enveloped in dense driving snow. The old track was snowed over. We kept constantly losing track in the blurred landscape, making many errors. Sometimes I had to be sharp with the porters, who wanted to sit down and sleep in the snow. The driving snow developed into a blizzard, and the approach of night grew threatening. . . . Now that our lives were at stake, my own fatigue vanished, giving place to a feeling of combat. The sick men were at the end of their tether.

Bechtold saw that Tundu and Nurbu would not survive a night out. The best way to save them, he decided, was to leave them behind and hurry down for help. He knew Camp 4 was somewhere nearby. He went on alone, as swiftly as he could, shouting for help. Finally he heard answering voices. The wind parted the clouds for a moment and Bechtold saw Bernard and Müllritter approaching.

He took them back up to the porters, and by dark Tundu and Nurbu had collapsed in the tents at Camp 4. Nurbu slept for two days, not even waking or reacting when Bernard came in and gave him injections.

Müllritter and Bernard asked Bechtold what he thought was happening above them.

'Tomorrow the peak falls,' Bechtold said.

It had been snowing heavily for four days at Camp 4, while the weather had been clear above. Now they didn't know what the weather was like higher up. Bernard and Müllritter wanted to carry supplies up to support the summit team. But the few porters at Camp 4 were all sick or done in. Only Ang Tenjing, who had come down ill two days before, was willing to go back up. Lewa volunteered to carry a load with him. It wasn't his job as sardar, but somebody had to do it. Lewa, with his toes cut off after frostbite three years before, was putting his feet in danger. But he was a hard man, and a responsible one. At this point the sahibs were not worried about the men above them, but Lewa almost certainly was.

That night it snowed heavily again. Ang Tenjing, Lewa, Bernard, and Müllritter set off early for Camp 5. They got nowhere, floundering and falling in deep new snow and were back in Camp 4 two hours later. They told each other they would try to get to Camp 5 without loads the next day, so there would at least be somebody to help the men coming down. All night the wind blew hard and the snow fell, and in the morning there was no possibility of going up. The men above them were now cut off from help.

Chapter Six

THE STORM

After Bechtold left to help Tundu and Nurbu down the mountain, five sahibs and eleven porters were at the Whipped Cream, Camp 7. The expedition had set out with thirty-four porters, roughly fifteen Sherpas and nineteen Tibetans. The two men who had just gone down sick may have been Tibetans or Sherpas – it's hard to tell from their names. But the remaining eleven porters on the final push were all Sherpas. Four of them came originally from the village of Thame, on the way to the Nangpa La pass into Tibet: Ang Tsering, Kitar, Dakshi, and Nima Norbu. Three of them were from the village of Khumjung: Da Thundu, Pinzo Norbu, and Nima Tashi. Gaylay came from Solu, in the lowland part of Sherpa territory.

Willy Merkl had chosen them over the Tibetans. Ang Tsering says the Tibetans were older men, many of them veterans of Everest in 1924. He thinks one reason Merkl selected the Sherpas was that they were younger. But Merkl had already been impressed by the way they climbed.

Merkl was following a general trend among the British climbers. General Bruce had begun with Gurkha porters, Nepalis from the middle hills, but found they would only climb so high. By 1921 Bruce hired mostly Tibetans. In the 1930s and 1940s the British began favoring the Sherpas over the Tibetans, and by the 1950s few Tibetans were hired for mountain work.

The British in India, like other upper-class people there, tended to see the world in terms of caste. To them, some castes were naturally suited to some jobs and not others. The British were particularly interested in soldiers for their army. They developed their own theory of caste, saying that some types of Indians were natural soldiers or 'martial races.'[1] The British officers thought that tall, light-skinned men would make better martial races. So they recruited northerners, particularly Pathans, Punjabis, and Nepalis. Following the same reasoning, they avoided recruiting both dalits ('untouchables') and Brahmins, whom they saw as both uppity and effete.

Tibetans were ruled out as a martial race and not recruited. The trouble was that they were too warlike. They didn't accept disrespect, and they didn't obey orders. The popular image in the West now is of Tibetans as a calm, nonviolent people. This reflects the personality and values of the current Dalai Lama. Some Tibetans have always been like him. Most have not. Traditional Tibet was a lightly governed and sparsely populated country. Many people were herders, and all over the world pastoralists steal each other's animals. Bandits were common. The great monasteries made war on each other, and each had its own regiment of warrior monks.

You can see the difference in Khumbu today. The Nangpa La pass into Tibet is open for ordinary Tibetans and Nepalis, although not for tourists or asylum seekers. Tibetan villagers come over the pass to trade in Namche. The men are charming, witty, and often beautiful. But something about them says: Be careful.

Khumbu Sherpas say the Tibetan men carry two knives. The one in the sock they use to draw fast and cut upward into your stomach. The one at the waist is for when they embrace you. They draw it, swing it up and out, then stab you in the back.

Sherpas laugh as they say this, and whether Tibetan men knife people much now is in doubt. That they carry two knives is not.

Dorjee Lhatoo, the eminent Indian climber, was born in Tibet to a Sherpa mother. When Dorjee was a boy in Darjeeling, Tenzing

Norgay used to visit his family. Tenzing was a snappy dresser, a good-looking man, and he had two knives. The boys would watch admiringly while Tenzing sat and chatted, sharpening a knife on a whetstone held on his thigh. 'He was a role model for us,' Dorjee Lhatoo says, and smiles.

The Tibetan porters in Darjeeling often got in trouble with the British. They were unwilling to put up with what they saw as unfair or stingy treatment. The big expeditions to Everest and the like were run on military lines, with many Europeans. No Tibetan would dare make trouble there. But it was different on the more modest climbs and treks. When Dorjee Lhatoo first started climbing in the 1960s, the older men told many stories around the campfire of how Tibetans had stood up to the British on smaller expeditions.

Tibetans would hassle the British for better pay or even intimidate them. One of the campfire stories was about a British trekker who beat his porters with a bamboo stick every morning to get them going. The porters stood it for many days. Then one morning a Tibetan porter grabbed the stick out of the bully's hand, broke it into small pieces, and threw the bits in his face.

This was by no means the only time a Tibetan hit a sahib. After such incidents, the Tibetan rarely ran away. They didn't understand the fundamental rule of colonial society – never hit a white man. The sahibs would say nothing and bide their time. When they all got back to Darjeeling, the British would send for the police to take the Tibetan away. A lot of Tibetans ended up in jail that way.

Such incidents gradually convinced the British to hire Sherpas. They climbed as high as the Tibetans, Dorjee Lhatoo says, but they were more timid and subservient, and the British liked that.

That's one way of distinguishing them. There are others. I asked Anu Sherpa of Namche why there had been no murders in Khumbu for eighty years, but many across the border in Tibet. Anu said Khumbu had always been a blessed land. Even in the ancient days of Guru Rimpoche, holy men had come there on retreats because the valleys were full of peace.

Lhakpa Diki Sherpa explains it slightly differently. She came to Darjeeling from Pare, near Thame, in the 1930s and immediately found a job as a porter on a trek. She liked the work and did it for years. She says the British favored Sherpa porters because they could trust them. If other porters were late coming into camp at the end of the day, the British worried they had stolen the loads. When a Sherpa was late, the sahibs didn't worry even if the Sherpa never came that night. They knew he or she had been delayed, would sleep on the trail with the load, and could be relied on to turn up the next morning without having stolen anything.

In a way, Dorjee Lhatoo, Anu, and Lhakpa Diki are all talking about the same thing. From one point of view, the Sherpas were subservient and the Tibetans independent. From another point of view, the Sherpas were honest and kind, while the Tibetans were thugs. But everyone is agreed that the Sherpas were more acceptable to the British.

When the British began to choose the Sherpas over the Tibetans, they rationalized the decision in caste and racial terms. The Sherpas, they said, were particularly suited to high-altitude work because their homeland was at the foot of Mount Everest. This was scientific nonsense. Khumbu is no higher than the Tibetan plateau. The first Sherpas came over the pass from Tibet five hundred years ago. This is nothing like enough time in human evolution for physical differences to develop. And Tenzing Norgay, the greatest Sherpa of all, was born in Tibet.

Sherpa porters, however, didn't contradict the British theories. You don't look a gift horse in the mouth, and when a man offers you a job, you don't tell him he is under a misapprehension. Today Sherpas have been mountain specialists for sixty years, and many younger men now do believe that they are genetically suited to such work.

Like so many of the British, Merkl liked and admired Sherpas. His decision to take all the Sherpa porters up Nanga Parbat with him was a turning point – the moment when they ceased to be 'Sherpa and Bhotia' porters and became 'the Sherpas.'

*   *   *

Schneider and Aschenbrenner took the lead up to the Silver Saddle. The last seven hundred feet of the climb were steep, and the two Austrians stopped to cut steps in the snow for the porters to follow. A cold, hard wind was blowing as they reached the top of the Silver Saddle. Two black peaks stuck up like donkey's ears on either side of the Silver Saddle. The two climbers hunkered down in the shelter of the eastern peak and had a smoke. The route beyond the Silver Saddle looked easy. 'From here to the lower summit,' Aschenbrenner wrote in his diary, 'the snowy plateau reaches smooth and unbroken. New strength and joy of victory filled us at this sight.'[2]

They finished their cigarettes and walked forward along the flat plateau. The old snow was deep here, and in many places the wind had blown it into dunes. It was like a desert, or the pock-marked surface of the moon, but the light off the snow was harsh and crystalline. As always in the Himalayas, the perspective from below was faulty – in the clear air the lower summit looked close. Welzenbach, following them, reached the top of the Silver Saddle. Schneider and Aschenbrenner, children of the Alps, yodeled to him, and Welzenbach yodeled back.

Schneider and Aschenbrenner were across the plateau now, climbing up toward the first of Nanga Parbat's two summits. They reckoned they were at 25,300 feet, about 1,300 feet below the higher, final, summit. At about three in the afternoon they looked back down and saw the porters making camp on the flat plateau seven hundred feet below. Schneider went back down to persuade Merkl and the porters to climb the extra seven hundred feet, so they would be closer for the final attempt in the morning. Aschenbrenner waited for Schneider to bring them back up.

The wind on the plateau had been rising all afternoon. After a very cold hour and a half Aschenbrenner figured the others had insisted on staying at the lower camp, and he went down to join them.

Camp 8 was at 24,450 feet. It was their fourth night at 22,000 feet or above. As night drew on, the wind turned into a gale, though the sky was still clear blue. They made some soup and went to their tents.

That night, according to Aschenbrenner's diary, 'the gale increased from hour to hour and became a roaring hurricane.' The gusts of wind blew down one tent, and in the others the snow dust came through every chink. (These tents were tied at the front, not zipped.) The walls of the tents snapped and thundered in the wind.

The monsoon had arrived on Nanga Parbat. The hurricane lasted all night. Schneider and Aschenbrenner had packed a small rucksack for the summit attempt the next morning, with a flag, a camera, and a bit of food. But in the morning 'the blizzard was raging with such violence' they couldn't leave the camp.

There are two ways to tell what happened next. One is to follow the sahibs' version, given in Bechtold's book. But this is far from the Sherpas' experience. The alternative is to use Bechtold's account to reconstruct what happened from the point of view of one Sherpa, Pasang Picture. This involves some guesswork and empathy. But it's worth trying.

Pasang Picture was from Charma Digma in Solu. He had been on Everest once and Kangchenjunga twice. The other porters had given him the English name Picture on Kangchenjunga, where he'd been the photographer's assistant, as he was Bechtold's on Nanga Parbat. Pasang liked the name – he was proud of his work.

All day they lay in their tents on the bare plateau. Outside the wind blew the snow, sometimes horizontally, sometimes in mad whirlwinds, a hundred miles an hour. The snow was so thick it cut off the sun, and it was still dark at noon. The sides of Pasang Picture's tent rattled in the wind and now and then cracked like a gunshot.

It was the Sherpas' duty to cook. But the tent was shaking so badly they could barely heat water. Pasang Picture would light the stove, and the wind would hammer through the entrance and blow it out. All day they tried and managed to heat only a little water, and no food. Pasang Picture was doing most of the work, crouched over nursing the gas stove. His tent mates, Nima Dorje and Pinzo Norbu, wanted to stay in the warmth of their bags. Pasang carried the water over to the sahibs' tents, bent over against the wind, trying to hold his footing in the gale and not spill anything.

Hour by hour, all day, the wind increased. Pasang Picture lay in his bag as it got dark, praying to Buddha for his life, all their lives, his lips not moving, just thinking the words in his head. He hoped that in the morning the sahibs would see reason and decide to go back down. He slept, and woke breathing raggedly, and slept, and woke and slept.

Suddenly Aschenbrenner was shaking him awake, shouting. Aschenbrenner was a big man, loud, his fingers digging into Pasang's shoulder. Pasang gripped his sleeping bag with both hands, burrowing inside. Aschenbrenner leaned down into his face, shouting, 'Down. Down.'

Down, Pasang Picture thought, and struggled out of his bag. It was morning. The tent was still shaking in the wind. It was going to be terrifyingly cold out there. But if they wanted to live, they had to go down now. Pasang helped Aschenbrenner wake up Nima Dorje and Pinzo Norbu. They were hard to move, groggy, lumpy, slow. Pasang pulled Nima Dorje out of his bag, found the man's boots inside, and jammed them on. Nima Dorje thanked him.

Nima Dorje was up now, rolling up his own sleeping bag and tying it to his pack. Pasang Picture and Pinzo Norbu exchanged a look, and neither packed his sleeping bag. Pasang reckoned the less weight he carried, the more likely he would make it down in one day. And they probably had to make it down tonight, or die. The bag wasn't worth it. But he didn't tell Nima Dorje to leave his sleeping bag behind. Each man was making his own decisions. And if it had to, the bag might hold two men.

They were outside the tent now, the other Austrian, Schneider, tying them onto the rope. He was furious, shouting into the storm at them, pulling the knots tight. We're standing like three children in a row, stupid with cold, Pasang Picture thought. He was ashamed, then afraid for the other two, and for himself on a rope with them. Schneider's furious, he thought, because he isn't going to the top. His chance of glory in his own country has gone. He's angry at the mountain, the wind, us. A Nepali phrase came to Pasang Picture's mind – Fuck you. But then he thought – Maybe Schneider's rage will get us all down alive.

Aschenbrenner had been conferring with the other sahibs. Now he was back, tying on, and they were leaving. Da Thundu came over and said something quickly to his brother, Pinzo Norbu. Pinzo nodded. Pasang couldn't hear what Da Thundu said. Maybe good luck, maybe something to tell their mother. If it were me, Pasang thought, I'd want to be on the rope with my brother. But it isn't us who decides who goes where.

They were off, Schneider in the lead, then Pinzo Norbu, Pasang Picture in the middle, Nima Dorje above him, and Aschenbrenner in the rear. Pasang looked over his shoulder as they left. The others were all outside their tents, roping up, packing. They'd follow right behind.

Pasang Picture struggled up to the Silver Saddle. As they passed close to the black rocks on the left, the wind fell. Then they started down the ridge, and this first part was hideously steep. New snow lay loose on the old ice, and his boots slid as the snow slipped over the ice. In places the wind had blown the ice clear. Pinzo Norbu in front of him was staggering, losing his balance, getting up, creeping forward. Pasang didn't look back, but he could feel from the tugs on the rope that Nima Dorje was struggling, too. Both men were clearly ill, from the height or not enough liquid or the cold, it didn't matter what.

Pasang had his ax in hand, planting it for each step on ice, always tensed for the moment when the man ahead would fall and he'd have to jam the ax down, loop the rope around it, and hope he could hold.

The air was full of snow, but he could see Pinzo Norbu, ten yards ahead, and most of the time he could see Schneider in the lead. Beyond that, gray darkness. The tracks they had made on the way up had been obliterated by the wind and snow. Schneider in the lead was zigzagging back and forth, unsure of the route.

Pasang had to concentrate on every move, his tense body ready for any emergency. But his mind raced, as much as it could in the grogginess of altitude, calculating:

They were now facing the consequences of Merkl's decision to abandon the system of ferrying supplies and to push on with everybody in one group. One tent was left at Whipped Cream and one below the Moor's Head. No food or sleeping bags were in those tents. It had taken them six days to get up from Camp 4 to Camp 8. Now they had to get back down in a day. Usually it was easy coming down a mountain. People were carrying less, going downhill, racing to leave their fear behind. Ordinarily, climbers and porters could go down four or five camps in a day. But this time they were on the long ridge. They had to go down to the notch at the bottom of the ridge, then back up to the Moor's Head. Exhausted men would have to climb up before they got down. Then there would be the traverse after the Moor's Head, below Rakhiot Peak. Much of that was nearly vertical. In good weather they had picked their way up slowly and carefully. It was hard to imagine how they could do it with Pinzo Norbu and Nima Dorje staggering, and no visibility. But if they made it, then they reached the fixed ropes.

Pasang Picture was an experienced climber. He knew Merkl's mistake would probably kill them.

Pasang saw Schneider, in the lead, start moving confidently, straight, and they found themselves at the edge of the Rupal Face, looking over into the murk and the long fall down to the valley. Schneider turned to lead them away from the face. Pasang knew the man was guessing.

The wind was howling now. They were on the top of the open ridge, with nothing to block it. The goggles protected Pasang's eyes, but the wind drove shards of snow like needles into the rest of his face. There was a sudden tug at his waist, and a scream in the wind behind. Pasang planted his feet and turned his upper body back to look.

The wind had picked Nima Dorje up and blown him off his feet. Pasang and Aschenbrenner, the two nearest men, struggled to hold Nima Dorje down. But the wind took his rucksack and blew it away over the Rupal face. Now the Sherpas had no sleeping bag. If they didn't get down tonight, they'd die. Pasang pulled harder, the air screaming in and out of his lungs, and they were able to wrestle Nima Dorje down.

They lay over his body, holding him down, Pasang and Aschenbrenner both winded, rasping for breath from the exertion and the fear. After a few minutes all three men were able to sit up, though they were still breathing hard. They looked down. Below them on the rope Schneider and Pinzo Norbu sat by their axes in the snow, the rope looped round each ax head. They must have hoped their weight could hold the others if they blew away.

Pasang Picture looked at Nima Dorje carefully. 'Well?'

Nima Dorje nodded, said, 'Well.'

They stood up and went on. Nobody said anything about the sleeping bag, but they knew what it meant. They went very slowly now, afraid, each step careful, using up precious time.

They were down the steepest bit, somewhere near the Whipped Cream. But Pasang couldn't see the tent. Schneider in front was still leading first one way, then another. Now that it was flatter, the snow was deeper. Schneider sank up to his knees. Pasang mechanically put his feet in the holes made by the two men in front.

Schneider stopped on a flatter place and waited for the others to catch up. When they did, he spoke to Aschenbrenner in German.

'Well?' Pinzo Norbu asked Nima Dorje.

'Well,' Nima Dorje said.

Pasang looked at Nima Dorje carefully. It was hard to tell with the goggles on, and the hood of his coat pulled tight round his face, but the man still looked terrified. Maybe I'm just imagining it, Pasang thought. Maybe it's my fear.

The two Germans were untying themselves from the rope. Pasang thought – They're insane. The five of us can't go on unroped, in this. But maybe they think if one falls, we just let him go, the rest are all right. It's immoral. But maybe they're right.

Schneider took his pack off. He untied his skis from the pack. Pasang Picture understood. The two Austrians were going to ski away and leave the Sherpas to die.

Schneider and Aschenbrenner were big men, more than a head taller than each of the three Sherpas. The Austrians were also the best climbers on the expedition. Pasang had watched them bounding up to the Silver Saddle two days before. He had felt, secretly, safer to be with them, on the first rope down.

Schneider put on his skis.[3]

Pasang knew those skis. One rest day, Schneider had tried to teach the Sherpas to ski on the ice just above Camp 1. The Sherpas had fallen over, their legs crisscross in the air, laughing at each other, Schneider laughing at all of them.[4] Schneider and Aschenbrenner, the doctor and Drexel, who had died, were all beautiful on their skis, making long loops from side to side, leaning into the mountain, their backs straight.

Aschenbrenner put his skis on, too. Schneider was talking to Pasang now. Pasang refused to look at him or reply. His body was full of rage. He didn't know what he'd do if he looked at the man.

Aschenbrenner clumped over on his skis. He used hand signals. He pointed to his chest, then down the mountain, then to Pasang, and said, 'Come after.'

They are treating me like a child, Pasang thought. And they're making me as helpless as a child.

The two big men turned on their skis. Schneider dug his poles into the snow and glided off slowly, then gathering speed, silent in the roar of the wind, unbearably graceful. He disappeared into the murk of the driving snow. Then Aschenbrenner followed, not looking back. One moment he was there, then he was a blur in the gray, and then he was gone.

Pasang thought – that would have made a good picture.

He looked at Pinzo Norbu on one side of him, then at Nima Dorje on the other. They were just standing there, looking at where the sahibs had disappeared. No way could either of them lead. They had all been sinking up to their knees in snow. Below it would be deeper. Someone would have to break trail, all the way.

I'm the leader now, Pasang thought, the burra sahib. There was no satisfaction in the thought, only anger and fear. (This was the moment in history when a Sherpa took charge on a mountain, when the 'coolies' became Sherpas.)

Pasang was roped in the middle between the two men. To lead, he would have to untie and retie himself in front. He tugged at the knot round his waist. It was frozen, wouldn't come open. He took off his mitten, telling himself to remember to put it back on, it's an easy thing to forget when you're tired stupid on a mountain.

His bare fingers undid the knot. Nima Dorje made a sound. Pasang looked up from the knot. He saw Nima Dorje thought he was untying and leaving them.

'No,' Pasang shouted. 'I'm leading. I'm tying myself in front. I'll be leader.'

Nima Dorje nodded and looked down at the snow.

Pasang tied himself on at the front, in Schneider's place. Nobody knew what to say.

I have to do something, he thought. 'Tse tso,' Pasang shouted, 'Long life,' as people shouted when they reached the top of a pass.

'Long life,' the other two shouted back, ragged in the wind.

Pasang remembered to put his mitten back on. They moved off. For a time Pasang followed the ski tracks, but they wandered from side to side. His brain moved slowly. Of course, that's how they ski, first to one side, then leaning into the other. He was losing too much time following the skis. So he chose a route he hoped was between the ski tracks. Soon he had lost them altogether.

It was very slow. They were somewhere on the ridge. If he continued, he might lead them over the edge or down and along a slope from which they could not return. They could see nothing of the route in the blinding snow. Their only hope was that tomorrow the weather would be better. They stopped and dug a little furrow in the snow, pushing at it with their mittens and boots. The furrow was just deep enough so the worst of the wind passed over them. They lay together, not talking, holding each other, waiting for darkness.

Up ahead of the three Sherpas, Schneider and Aschenbrenner moved quickly on their own. Before noon they were at the Moor's Head. Visibility was so bad they knew they wouldn't be able to find the route for the traverse below the Rakhiot Peak. So they climbed directly over the top of the Peak, something the porters behind them would be unable to do. It meant an extra five hundred feet up, and serious rock climbing, but it seemed safer.

At Camp 5 Schneider and Aschenbrenner found food and sleeping bags. By late afternoon they were down to Camp 4, friends, and safety.

Ever since the accident that had killed seven porters on Everest in 1922, British climbers had tried to make sure a sahib was always on the rope with the porters in a difficult situation. This was because the sahibs were more skilled climbers, but also so no porter would die without a European dying, too. The British had passed this established practice on to the other European climbers in the Himalayas. Schneider and Aschenbrenner had broken this rule. So after the expedition finished, German climbers were embarrassed by what Schneider and Aschenbrenner had done. But they hadn't only left the porters behind. They had also left the weaker German climbers high on the mountain. And they were the two strongest men on Nanga Parbat.

Aschenbrenner's explanation, afterward, was that Pinzo Norbu and Nima Dorje were ill and could not keep up. Moreover, once Nima Dorje lost his sleeping bag in the wind, they had only one bag, Aschenbrenner's, between five men. If Schneider and Aschenbrenner had not gone on alone, they would not have got down that night, and then they would have died. So they went.[5]

The most shameful detail was skiing away from the porters. Neither Aschenbrenner nor Bechtold mentions this in their published accounts, nor does any other German source. I have it from Ang Tsering, but it is widely known among older Sherpas in Darjeeling. Schneider and Aschenbrenner certainly had skis, and it would make sense to use them on the deep, new snow. Without skis, they would struggle, fall, and have to fight their way through. On skis they could sail over the surface. That's what skis are for. It's also difficult to see how they got from Camp 8 to Camp 4 by late afternoon without skis.

Earlier that day Pasang Picture, Aschenbrenner, Schneider, Nima Dorje, and Pinzo Norbu had set off on the first rope. The others – Merkl, Wieland, Welzenbach, Ang Tsering, Dakshi, Gaylay, Kitar, Da Thundu, Nima Tashi, Pasang Kikuli, and Nima Norbu – followed behind in a body. They were carrying a few sleeping bags, no food, and no tents. The sahibs expected to get down to help within a day, or two days at the most. The less they carried, the more quickly they could move, and the more likely they were to get down alive. They had now been at twenty-two thousand feet or above for six nights. These men were exhausted, some of them were sick, and all of them must have been afraid. Cold and fear make men groggy, and prolonged altitude makes it difficult to think straight. Packing would take energy, and they must have wanted to flee for their lives.

Soon they had to struggle against the wind with each step. The driving snow reduced visibility to a few yards, so they had trouble picking their route. The snow had covered the tracks they had made on the way up, so there was no path. When they'd set out, they had been fed and rested. Now they were exhausted. They had eaten only a little soup two nights ago.

They made it to the Silver Saddle and part of the way down. Somewhere above Camp 7 and the Whipped Cream, the sahibs said they couldn't go any farther, so everybody would have to stop. They would bivouac – sleep out in the snow.

The eleven men had three sleeping bags between them. Two men could share one bag – it was cramped but warmer. One sleeping bag belonged to the sahibs. Welzenbach left it to Wieland and Merkl and slept on the snow in his clothes that night.

At this point Welzenbach was clearly stronger than Merkl and

Wieland. He probably said to himself that the other two men were weaker and needed the warmth more. Three years before, he and Merkl together had survived an open bivouac for sixty hours on a face in the Alps. Perhaps Welzenbach was overconfident, but it seems more likely he was simply being decent.

The eight porters had two sleeping bags. Four men must have used them, and four slept on the snow in their clothes. They had sweaters and coats, but no down jackets.

Nima Norbu from Thame died on the snow that night.

In the morning Merkl had frostbite in his right hand and Wieland in both hands. They seem to have gotten frostbitten while inside the sleeping bag, though it may have been coming on the day before. These were experienced climbers. They would have seen a lot of frostbite in the Alps. They knew it was a sign their bodies were beginning to die. That Wieland had it in both hands was a sign that he was weaker than Merkl.

The porters and climbers prepared to leave the night bivouac. Dakshi, Gaylay, and Ang Tsering said they were too sick to go on. They would spend another day and a night in the bivouac, then follow if they could. The others left the three sick men in the bivouac and went down. They must have assumed they were leaving all three men to die. Nobody in his right mind would stop at this height, in this weather, unless he absolutely could not go on. And if he could not move now, he was unlikely to be stronger after a day without food and water and another night in the snow.

But they left. What else could they do?

At almost exactly the same time, down in Camp 4 Bechtold and the other sahibs were calling Lewa, the sardar, to their tent. As he came in, the wind blew snow into the tent after him. The sahibs wanted Lewa to find porters for a rescue party. Lewa calmly told them what they already knew: all the porters were now too sick to go up.

Eventually they managed to muster a small party. It's unclear if this was made up entirely of sahibs or included Lewa and a porter or two. They struggled up toward Camp 5 in 'bottomless powder snow,'[6] the residue of what was now seven straight days of snow at Camp 4. And it was still snowing. As they broke trail going up, the new snow obliterated it behind them.

At about eleven the clouds parted for a few minutes. On the ridge high above they saw a large number of men coming down from the Silver Saddle. They were stunned and confused. Merkl and the others ought to have been well below the Silver Saddle by now.

Above the main party they saw a lone figure 'wandering down.' Then the man sat down on the snow. Why, Bechtold asked himself as he watched, why? The clouds came down again, and they saw nothing more.

It continued to snow, and eventually the rescue party gave up and went back to Camp 4. 'What was unspoken between us was now dreadfully clear,' Bechtold said. 'Up there our companions and the Darjeeling porters were fighting for their lives.'

The men at Camp 4 had seen Da Thundu, Pasang Kikuli (pronounced *Pasang Kukoolee*), Nima Tashi, Kitar, Welzenbach, Wieland, and Merkl coming down from the Silver Saddle. These were the seven men who had left Ang Tsering, Dakshi, and Gaylay sick in the high bivouac that morning.

The man the watchers saw struggling alone behind the rest was Wieland, now clearly the weakest of sahibs. Welzenbach was still the strongest of the sahibs, even after his night on the snow. He drove his ice ax into the snow and fixed a rope to it for the last steep descent to Camp 7. Then he and Merkl waited for Wieland.

Kitar, Da Thundu, Nima Tashi, and Pasang Kikuli hurried on ahead of the sahibs to reach Camp 7, the Whipped Cream. In the whirling snow the snow dunes must have loomed like specters, rolling, rippled, with strange clean curves along the sides. There they found one tent still standing but full of snow. The four porters waited over an hour for the sahibs. Finally Merkl and Welzenbach appeared without Wieland. Kitar thought maybe Wieland was coming behind. None of them knew it, but Wieland was stumbling lost among the dunes of the Whipped Cream.

Six men were now at Camp 7. There was only one tent, capable of holding two men, perhaps three. Merkl told the four porters that the sahibs needed the tent. The porters should go on to Camp 6. So they went.

Going down the ridge, Kitar, Da Thundu, Nima Tashi, and Pasang Kikuli often crashed through the thin crust of new snow and sometimes got stuck up to their necks. The others would have to stop and help them claw their way out. They made it to the low point on the ridge and started up toward the Moor's Head and the Rakhiot Peak. They didn't make it up to Camp 6 that night. So they slept in the snow.[7] This was their eighth night above twenty-two thousand feet, and the fourth night of the storm. They had been without food for three days and without water for two.

In the morning it was still snowing. Again, we cannot know in detail how it was for the Sherpas. But from the bare written record, we can imagine what Da Thundu might have done and felt that day.

Everybody says Da Thundu was a good man. In any crowd of people, at a party or at work, he was the man on the edge of the group, quiet, nodding, saying little. He didn't push himself forward, but he was there if you needed him. And he looked after his family, always.

He had two relatives on Nanga Parbat that day. The day before, his younger brother Pinzo Norbu had started down on the first rope with the Austrians. Da Thundu was on the second rope with Kitar, his wife's father. Kitar was the most experienced of all of them – he had been on Everest in 1921, 1922, 1924, and 1933, and on Kangchenjunga in 1929, 1930, and 1931. Now the older man was the weakest person on Da Thundu's rope.

In the first light Da Thundu looked around the mounds of snow where they lay. Pasang Kikuli, Nima Tashi, and Kitar were all still alive. They gathered themselves together. Then they set out up toward the Moor's Head, Da Thundu breaking trail. He knew he was very much the strongest of the four men now. There had been eighteen inches of new snow that night.

They reached the Moor's Head and climbed the gentle rise toward the steep traverse below the Rakhiot Peak. Da Thundu was dreading the traverse, with three very sick men, stumbling and slipping. They didn't talk. He thought that maybe they would get down that morning, but he couldn't tell if the others would live that long.

Suddenly he saw a track ahead of them in the snow. He thought – I don't have to break trail.

Relieved, he walked on, stopping time after time as the rope came tight behind him. Then he thought – There's almost no snow in these tracks. Someone made them this morning. Who? – and he prayed it wasn't Pinzo Norbu, prayed that his brother had got off the mountain already.

Just ahead he saw a gray figure in the drifting snow. A Sherpa, by the coat. Da Thundu knew it was his brother, told himself it wasn't, but couldn't stop from shouting, 'Pinzo.'

The man stopped. Da Thundu moved as fast as he could, yanking on the rope, pulling the man behind him, not running, not even walking really, but faster than he'd been for two days. It was Pinzo. The brothers hugged. Pinzo was shaking in his arms. Da Thundu was suddenly furious that his brother was here, anger boiling out of him. He said nothing. It was clear Pinzo was glad to see him.

The others were around them now. Two men were on the rope with Pinzo – Pasang Picture and Nima Doye. 'Where are your sahibs?' Da Thundu asked.

Pinzo said nothing.

'They skied down the mountain. They unroped and left us two days ago,' Pasang Picture said. He spoke in short words, saving his breath. 'The night after they left we got lost and slept in the snow. I was afraid of falling if we went on. Yesterday we could see the way all right. But it was really slow. Last night we slept on the ice again.'

Da Thundu, in that moment, hated the two sahibs who had left his brother. He would hate them for the rest of his life. He made himself say, 'It's all right. We're all still alive.'

'Up there?' Pasang Picture asked.

'I don't know,' Da Thundu said, though in his mind he saw Nima Norbu's body in the snow in the previous morning. He was pretty sure Dakshi, Ang Tsering, and Gaylay were dead, too. But why say all that?

Then Da Thundu realized that Pasang Picture was doing all the talking because the other two on his rope were too tired to speak. Pasang could have got down, but he had stayed with the other two men on his rope. He stayed with my brother, Da Thundu thought.

The wind cleared the whirling snow, and Da Thundu saw that they were standing right at the beginning of the steep traverse. They had found the route. They would have to struggle across the traverse. If it had been terrifying coming up, it would be harder going down in the state they were in. Beyond that would be the fixed ropes, almost straight down. But there were only three fixed ropes, six hundred feet, and at the bottom of them was Camp 5. Food, maybe drink and blankets. They could make it. All of them. Please God.

He looked at the six men around him. The three men on his rope could hardly walk. He wanted to help his brother down, but thought – If we fall together, mother will have no sons.

He looked at old Kitar, his father-in-law, and said, 'How do we do this?'

Kitar understood the problem. 'I leave you and tie on with the other rope,' Kitar said, 'and Nima Dorje goes with you.' Kitar began undoing the knot around his waist. Da Thundu knew that would leave himself on a rope with the two weakest men, Nima Tashi and Nima Dorje. But not three. He thought – I'm the strongest. I have to do it.

Kitar couldn't seem to make his hands work. Nothing was happening to the knots. Da Thundu crossed the few yards of deep snow and pulled the rope free. Kitar lurched toward the other rope and stumbled to one knee. Da Thundu thought – His feet are gone, too. Frostbite.

Da Thundu didn't know it, but every man there except him had badly frostbitten hands and feet. He helped Kitar up and tied him to the other rope. Nobody said anything. The first rope – Pasang Picture, Kitar, Pinzo Norbu, and Pasang Kikuli – started along the steep traverse. The second rope followed – Da Thundu, Nima Tashi, and Nima Dorje. Da Thundu led this rope. He was afraid all the way. One slip behind him and he wouldn't have the strength to hold them.

They made the traverse.

They came to the fixed ropes. Pasang Picture and the three other men on his rope started down. Da Thundu waited until they were fifty feet ahead. Then he said to the two men with him, 'You go first. I'll come last. I'll hold you if you fall.'

They were terribly slow. The fixed ropes were almost vertical. They had no metal carabiners to clip onto the rope, and no crampons on their boots to grip the ice. They had to hold on, with all their strength, trying to grip the rope with dead hands, kicking numb feet into the ice for steps. It took both hands to hold the rope, but you had to loosen one to move down. If they lost the hold, it was five hundred feet straight down. All this took far more strength than anything they had done before, and the sickest among them had no strength left.

In front of Da Thundu, Nima Dorje kept twisting his arm into the fixed rope to hold on. He was stopping all the time now to rest, great breaths dragging out of him. Da Thundu was just behind him, saying, Put your feet here, here, there, we can make it, the tent is so close now. Food. You can do it.

They were down one fixed rope and onto the second. It had taken half an hour. The air cleared and now Da Thundu could see the four men on the first rope at the bottom of the fixed ropes, staggering toward the tent. He could see the poles of the tent, just sticking out of the snow. Pinzo was down, Kitar was down. They were going to live.

Nima Dorje had stopped, twisted into the rope to rest. 'Come on,' Da Thundu said. 'Come on. We're safe.'

Nima Dorje said nothing. Da Thundu shook him, gently so as not to pull him down. No response. Da Thundu looked at Nima Dorje's face. He took off his glove and put his hand to Nima

Dorje's mouth, felt nothing. He put his fingers inside the lips. Nima Dorje's jaw was shut rigid. He wasn't breathing. Da Thundu grabbed, burrowed inside Nima Dorje's coat, feeling for the vein in the neck. Nima Dorje, who had climbed higher than the summit of Nanga Parbat on Everest the year before, was dead. Nima Dorje, who was always laughing.

Da Thundu didn't put his glove back on because now he had to untie himself from the dead man. His fingers scrabbled at the knot on his waist. They couldn't seem to work. Da Thundu stopped. He felt stupid, knew he was crying, couldn't look at the dead man. He made himself rest there, his shoulder against the body, breathing slowly, trying to calm down. And then he undid the knot.

He clambered over Nima Dorje, reckless now, wanting only to get down. Just below was Nima Tashi, and Da Thundu knew even before he got down to him that the man was dead, too. 'Nima,' he screamed. 'Nima.' No reply. He felt the man's cold face. Then, by God's grace, he remembered to put his glove back on.

Now he was past Nima Tashi, thinking – I got them both down. So close. Both. Almost there.

And then he looked down at the tent again, and a man was lying in the snow just by it, and three men standing next to him. Da Thundu told himself he didn't know who the man in the snow was. He went down the rope frantically now, fast, lungs screaming. He was down, scrabbling through the tracks of the others to the tent.

The man in the snow was his brother. Da Thundu fell by him, reached for his face.

'He's dead,' Kitar said above him.

Da Thundu put his arms around his brother. Kitar had a hand on his shoulder, patting, and then shaking him. 'He's dead,' Kitar said. 'We have to go on.'

Da Thundu looked up at the old man. He looked strange, the hood pulled around his head, the eyes covered with black goggles. Da Thundu wanted to ask for some kind of help.

'You're still alive,' Kitar said. 'You have a wife. Children.' Kitar said their names. 'You must live.'

Da Thundu just shook. 'We need you, son,' Kitar said. 'We can't do it alone. I'm old.'

And then Da Thundu stood up. He looked around. Pinzo Norbu had died six feet short of the tent. The other men were all unroped now. Da Thundu began to lead them down toward Camp 4 and safety.

In Camp 4 they had seen the men coming down the fixed ropes. A rescue party went up.

The four survivors continued straight down, unroped. Pasang Kikuli fell off a serac and badly injured his back. He picked himself up and kept on going.

Somewhere above Camp 4 the rescue party met the four men coming down. They were making a trench as high as a man down through the deep, new snow. The man in front was hacking away at the head of the trench, the others waiting behind. Bechtold said:

The wretched men were absolutely played out, at their last gasp. All had their hands and feet more or less severely frost-bitten; Pasang had lost his snow-glasses and was snow-blind. Bernard cautiously gave them some soup, and then each of us took a porter by the arm and led him carefully down to the camp. In the big porters' tent all sahibs and porters set to work massaging the frostbitten men. Bernard distributed his orders. One man sat at each hand and foot, and rubbed incessantly with snow. When one's own hands grew moist, a relief was exchanged. There was a battle over each single toe, over each finger. One man shoveled snow constantly into the tent.[8]

They worked on the sick men from midday through the night until dawn. Aschenbrenner and Schneider were there, helping with the rest. So was Pasang Picture, the only survivor of the three men on the rope Aschenbrenner and Schneider had left behind. Da Thundu was there, too, angry for his brother.

In that tent at Camp 4 there was pain, grief, rage, and guilt, and a sort of relief that people were finally helping each other as they should. Sahibs and porters worked together, with no distinctions of color or money, skin against skin, just men all trying to be kind and do what they could. The porters, too, were thinking of friends, and sometimes kin, on the mountain. For many hours the four men were too far gone to talk. In the middle of the night, almost twelve hours after they had begun, Kitar was finally well enough to speak. He probably possessed the best English, but even his grasp of the language was not that good, and talking was still an effort. 'We had to press each word out of him,' Bechtold said.[9] From what he told them, the sahibs thought it was 'more than improbable' that any men were left alive on the mountain.[10]

They were wrong. Five men were still alive, two at Camp 7 and three bivouacked out on the snow above Camp 7.

Chapter Seven

GAYLAY

Two days before, the main party had left Ang Tsering, Dakshi, and Gaylay ill in the high bivouac just below the Silver Saddle. Ang Tsering was blind from the sun on the snow the day before – he must have lost his goggles. He knew what had happened to him. It was a common affliction in the mountains. It happened to climbers, and to Sherpas crossing passes with their yaks. On the 1934 expedition, many of the local porters had already gone blind on the passes during the march to Base Camp. The pain of snow blindness is terrible, but Ang Tsering knew it was temporary. For the moment he could see nothing and would not be able to get down safely. But if he waited, perhaps a day, perhaps two or three, it would get better.

Dakshi came from Thame, the same village as Ang Tsering. He was simply too weak to go on. The third man with them was Gaylay, from a village near Paphlu in Solu. Sherpa society is divided into clans, and like many people near Paphlu, Gaylay belonged to the highest-ranking clan, the Lamas. But he was still just a Sherpa, a workingman about forty-five years old. He was a close friend of Lewa's, which is probably how he came by this job. They lived together outside Darjeeling, near the army cantonment, and like Lewa, Gaylay worked there as a cleaner and waiter.

172

This was his first Himalayan expedition.

I asked Ang Tsering if Gaylay was a handsome man, or ugly. Neither, Ang Tsering said, somewhere in between. He was an ordinary man and seemed of ordinary character. He was thin, though. His face always looked so thin it made you think he was weak.

At this point Gaylay was weak, but not very sick. He stayed with Ang Tsering and Dakshi because they were in trouble and needed help.

The three men lay on the snow all day and slept out for a second night. In the morning Ang Tsering was still blind and Dakshi ill. They stayed another day, their second. Ang Tsering believed that if his sight came back, he was strong enough to get down. Dakshi must have known he was dying. Gaylay stayed with both of them. They spent their third night on the open snow.

When he woke up in the morning, Ang Tsering could see. The world was blurry, but he knew he could find his way down. Dakshi, though, was too weak to walk. Clearly, he would die in the bivouac. If Gaylay and Ang Tsering stayed, they would, too. So they left him there.[1] Ang Tsering didn't admit to himself what he was doing. For days afterward, he told himself he was going for help, and Dakshi might still be alive up there.

Before they started down, Ang Tsering turned to the peak and defied the god of Nanga Parbat. 'You think you can kill me,' he shouted at the god. 'But you're wrong. My god is stronger than you, and he will save my life.'

Ang Tsering's god was Khumbi La, the holiest mountain in Khumbu.

Gods live on four mountains in Khumbu – Chomolungma (Everest), Cho Oyu, Khumbi La, and Tseringma (Gaurishankar, near Thame).

Sherpas revere Buddha as the highest god. After that come many others, Buddhist teachers, ancient Sanskrit gods, and local Tibetan ones. Some are male and some female, but there is no separate word for goddess. Gender is not the most important thing about a god. Some of these gods can be found in heaven, or everywhere. Some, like mountain gods, live in one place.

Kailas, in the far west, is the holiest mountain in Tibet. It's a high peak, standing alone above a great blue lake, a white pyramid of ice on a black cube of rock. Many pilgrims go for the sacred, and difficult, three days' walk round Kailas. Those I have talked with say beauty and sanctity are everywhere around you.

Khumbi La, the mountain Ang Tsering called upon to fight Nanga Parbat for him, isn't like Kailas. You have to live in Khumbu for a while to understand why Khumbi La is the home of a god. At first, to my foreign eyes, it seemed a modest mountain. I looked in wonder at Tamserku, its fluted glaciers soaring into the air; at Kwangde, with its three-mile-long ridge of black rock and white ice; and at Ama Dablam, 'the mother's jewel box,' every trekker's favorite mountain. Khumbi La is not a white peak, not a real Himalaya. There's a bit of snow right on the top, and sometimes more on the sides in winter, but no great hanging glaciers. The rock is brown, or dark red, not particularly beautiful, and I never found a place where you could see the full sweep of the mountain.

Yet, as the months passed, I realized that Khumbi La is a mountain for which you feel, not awe, but affection. It rises behind the twin villages of Kunde and Khumjung, an hour's walk above Namche. Unlike the other mountains, it does not tower away from people, but seems to watch over them. And it is at the center of Khumbu. Thame is to the west, Phortse and Pangboche to the east, Khumjung, Kunde, and Namche just to the south. It's the right place for Khumbu's mountain.

The name Khumbi La means the 'god of Khumbu.' When monks come to a family's house to pray and read from the holy books, all the books are in Tibetan and so are almost all the prayers. The only exception is the prayer to Khumbi La.

Sherpa songs are also old Tibetan ones borrowed from across the Nangpa La. The only exception is a song to Khumbi La. Sherpas sing all these songs at parties, drunk, happy, the men dancing in one line with their arms round each other, the women in another line. For the song of Khumbi La, the singers imagine they are villagers coming from all over Khumbu to honor the God. They sing:

> *Khumbu is*
> *A beautiful frontier*
> *Like a beaten ornamental golden border*
> *On a great brass water bowl.*

> *Our God*
> *Lives on Khumbu.*

> *We come together*
> *To see our God*
> *Bringing silk scarves*
> *To honor God*
> *God sees us coming*
> *And rejoices.*

> *We gather together*
> *Bringing our lives*
> *All the lives we have lived*
> *Into this moment*
> *When we come together*
> *For a moment's joy*
> *Between the griefs of life.*

> *Please*
> *Do nothing*
> *To shatter this moment.*[2]

The sahibs and the porters brought different attitudes to the mountains. On one side there is struggle and triumph, on the other love. But something of the spirit of the German mountaineers was in Ang Tsering's words hurled at Nanga Parbat. And he chose to see his fate in a contest between mountains.

All the other Tibetan and Sherpa climbers I've talked to prayed hard in the mountains. But they did it silently, quickly, directly to Buddha, not to the mountain or another god: 'Buddha, save me. Buddha, help me.'

In Darjeeling I talked with Gonden, a Tibetan climber from the fifties and sixties, and Dawa Thempa, Ang Tsering's son. They both said that high on a mountain your lips were so cold and stiff you couldn't pray out loud. Gonden also said that usually you'd count your prayers with rosary beads, but up high you couldn't take your mittens off. Dawa Thempa, who spent almost thirty years in the army, said it was a lot like war. On the mountain, in times of sudden danger, everyone began praying like crazy, begging, promising this to God and that to God, if only they got out alive. It was the same in battle. When the firing began, soldiers crouched over their guns – Dawa Thempa stretched himself out and jerked his body like a man on top of a jumping gun – and as they fired, they, too, begged God frantically, promising anything, everything.

Ang Tsering, by contrast, did not beg Buddha. He defied Nanga Parbat.[3]

Gaylay and Ang Tsering left Dakshi to die at the high bivouac and started down. They were unroped. With his sight back, defiant, Ang Tsering was stronger than Gaylay. He went on ahead, and soon Gaylay was well out of sight behind him.

Ang Tsering never told me why he went on alone. My guess is that he thought Gaylay would not make it and was trying to save himself. But perhaps, as with Dakshi, Ang Tsering did not allow himself to think too clearly about what he was doing.

Just before Camp 7, in the Whipped Cream dunes, Ang Tsering came upon Uli Wieland's body. Two days before, Wieland had been coming down to Camp 7 after Merkl and Welzenbach, but never caught up with them. He had died thirty yards from the two men in the tent, on the other side of a small hill of snow. Perhaps he was lost in the whiteout, or maybe he just collapsed.

Minutes later Ang Tsering found both Merkl and Welzenbach

alive in the tent. They had now been there two nights. This was their third day. The tent had been full of snow when Kitar and the other three porters had left Merkl two days before. Since then neither Welzenbach nor Merkl had been strong enough to shovel it out.

Willo Welzenbach had written a note the day before, hoping some porter would come by to take it down:

> Camp VII, July 10
>
> To the Sahibs between Camps VI and VII, in particular the Doctor Sahib.
>
> We have lain here since yesterday, when Uli [Wieland] got lost on the way. We are both ill. An attempt to make VI failed due to general exhaustion. I, Willo, have probably got bronchitis, angina and influenza. Bara Sahib has a feeling of general exhaustion, and frost-bitten feet and hands. We have neither of us eaten a hot meal for six days, and have drunk almost nothing. Please help *us soon here* in Camp VII.
>
> Willo and Willy[4]

Of course there were no sahibs between Camps VI and VII. Welzenbach apparently didn't know Wieland was lying dead thirty yards away.

Ang Tsering could see Welzenbach's feet were shaking uncontrollably. From that he knew the man was close to death.

Ang Tsering said to Merkl, 'We go down now. They will close Camp 4. We get no food.'

Merkl and Ang Tsering both had limited English. Ang Tsering was suggesting they leave both Welzenbach and Gaylay behind and go down alone.

Merkl said, 'No.'

Ang Tsering looked back up the mountain and saw Gaylay, far away, coming down alive.

When he explains it all now, Ang Tsering says nothing about why he went on ahead of Gaylay to the Whipped Cream. But he does say that once he saw Gaylay in the distance, coming down alive, he knew he had to stay at Camp 7.

I think that up until that moment, he had been determined to live and was sure the only way he could was to go down alone, immediately, with or without Merkl. Now, as he saw Gaylay still alive, still moving, he was recalled to humanity. He couldn't leave Gaylay, who had stayed with him.

The Germans and the porters always had trouble communicating. Most of the porters spoke little English. One reason the sardar was so important was that he could talk to the sahibs. The German climbers, Ang Tsering says, spoke no Nepali or Hindi at all. Their English, too, was basic. Merkl probably had very little – two years before he had been the only German climber with none at all.

Ang Tsering says this made complex orders difficult to understand. Some things could be said simply. If he needed food, for instance, he opened his mouth as wide as possible, tipped his head back, and pointed down at the gaping hole with his finger, repeating, 'Food, food,' loudly in English. They soon understood.

At the Whipped Cream, Ang Tsering and Merkl spoke simply, but each understood what the other was trying to say. Ang Tsering meant that they should go down immediately and leave Welzenbach to die. Ang Tsering was worried that the sahibs down below would soon give them all up for dead. They would close Camp 4, stripping everything. Then even if he and Merkl reached Camp 4, there would be no food and no one to help. Moreover, it was still morning. They might reach the camp if they started now.

Ang Tsering also understood that Merkl was saying somebody ought to stay with Welzenbach till he died.

Ang Tsering's fear that they would soon close Camp 4 was reasonable. In other such tragedies, the people in the camps below usually wait a day, perhaps two or three, before they give up hope for survivors. When they do, they strip the camps. This is an understandable action. To leave a camp fully stocked is to admit to yourself that somebody may still be alive up above you. In which case, it's difficult to justify going down yourself. But in the aftermath of tragedy, the people in any support camp know they, too, are in danger. If they stay longer, what has just happened above may happen to them.

Merkl didn't allow himself to think they would shut down Camp 4. Even now, he was still hoping the men below would come up to rescue them. He was weak and most likely couldn't descend on his own. And Merkl was the leader. He had made the decision to push up in one group. He probably couldn't admit to himself how that choice had now left them all beyond rescue. Merkl must have known Welzenbach was dying, but as the expedition leader couldn't abandon his comrade.

Merkl was thinking like a leader of the climbers, not the porters. The first day of the retreat, when the sahibs had been too ill to go on, Merkl had insisted they stop and bivouac in the open. If he had been thinking of the porters, he would have sent most or all of them on. Now, again, he could have gone with Ang Tsering and left Welzenbach. Or he could have sent Ang Tsering on alone, to save at least one porter's life.

He didn't, presumably because once Welzenbach died, he would still need Ang Tsering. Merkl was, however, still trying to be decent and take care of somebody else, not himself.

When Merkl said, 'No,' Ang Tsering looked back up the mountain and saw Gaylay, far away, coming down alive. Ang Tsering stayed.

Gaylay joined them. He spoke better English than the other Sherpas, having learned it when working in the British army cantonment. Merkl now said to both Sherpas: We should not go now. We will stay. When Welzenbach sahib dies, then we'll go.

Merkl next told Ang Tsering to clear out the deep snow inside the tent. One was still the master, the other still the employee. But Ang Tsering was also the strongest man at Camp 7. He did as he was asked, or told.

They stayed at Camp 7 all that day and that night. Merkl and

Welzenbach were in the tent. Ang Tsering and Gaylay slept outside on the snow, with no sleeping bag or groundsheet.[5]

The next day Ang Tsering still wanted to go down. The weather was better and the wind had lessened a bit. Now that it was clearer, the three men up at the Whipped Cream could see down to Camp 4 far below. Suddenly they saw men climbing up from Camp 4.

Lobsang, Ang Tenjing, Nurbu, Müllritter, Schneider, and Aschenbrenner were trying to get to Camp 5. After six hours of hard climbing, without loads, taking turns at breaking trail, they reached Camp 5. Müllritter said they found Pinzo Norbu's body 'lying head downward in the snow, still roped, just as he had fallen' three yards from the tent, food, and sleeping bags. He tried to bury Pinzo Norbu. Lobsang, Ang Tenjing, and Nurbu stood and watched. They didn't see the point.

The bodies of Nima Dorje and Nima Tashi were still hanging in the fixed ropes just above Camp 5. Schneider and Aschenbrenner tried to reach the ropes to bring the bodies down. The wind and the snow were too strong. All six men turned round and went back down, reaching Camp 4 late that evening.

Up at the Whipped Cream, Merkl, hoping help was on its way, told Ang Tsering they would stay another day.

The next morning Müllritter and several porters took the four frostbitten men who had survived the fixed ropes – Da Thundu, Pasang Picture, Pasang Kikuli, and Kitar – gently down to Base Camp. Dr. Bernard decided not to go with them. He would stay at Camp 4 in case anyone else made it down alive. At Base Camp, Müllritter told Bechtold, 'Nobody believes that anybody can still be living [up] there, it is absolutely impossible! Camp IV will be closed tomorrow or the day following.'[6]

Ang Tsering's worries were proving right. The people below were discussing closing Camp 4. But Merkl's hopes, understandably, had been revived.

At about five o'clock that afternoon Merkl came out and said, 'Sorry, Ang Tsering. Sahib is died.'

That 'sorry' could have meant many things. It could have meant: I regret to tell you. Or: I am full of grief. Or: I apologize to you for not leaving earlier. Merkl was probably feeling all those things.

It was now too late to go down that day. That night Merkl slept in the tent with Welzenbach's body. Ang Tsering and Gaylay lay down on the snow in their sweaters and coats, without blanket or groundsheet.

Merkl didn't invite the two Sherpas into the tent. Sahibs and porters did not share tents. Even at this extremity, the rules of caste and class were still accepted on both sides. They would also have had to haul Welzenbach's body out and leave it in the snow. Perhaps Merkl could not bring himself to do that.

The next morning Ang Tsering, Gaylay, and Merkl went on together. This was their sixth day without water, the eighth day without food, and the thirteenth day at twenty-two thousand feet or more. Ang Tsering was still eating ice. He and Gaylay had slept out on the snow for five nights running.

Merkl was going very slowly, needing help from the other two. Both his hands and feet were frostbitten. He could only walk by leaning on two ice axes.

The clouds were lifting now. The men way down in Camp 4 could see much of the ridge between the Silver Saddle and the low point on the ridge. They saw three figures coming slowly down from Camp 7. They couldn't tell who the climbers were, but they knew Merkl and Welzenbach were the last people seen alive there. When the three figures reached the low point on the ridge, according to Bechtold, 'a man stepped forward and signaled. Now and then the gale brought down a distant cry for help.' That man was probably Ang Tsering. The men in Camp 4 were staggered. They had been pretty sure everyone had died up there.

Ang Tsering didn't know he'd been seen and heard. He went on.

Schneider and Aschenbrenner were the only climbers still at Camp 4. They were exhausted – they'd survived the retreat and had already been back up to Camp 5 the day before. They didn't try to rescue the figures they saw or even go to Camp 5. Nor did Bernard or the porters. Nobody went up the next day either.

Ang Tsering and his two companions climbed from the low point in the ridge, up toward the Moor's Head, Camp 6, and the Rakhiot Peak. The two Sherpas were moving very slowly, matching their pace to Merkl's. The retreat was hard now. They were going up again, after so long at altitude, in constant cold, without food or water. Merkl had severe frostbite in his hands and feet. Ang Tsering had bad frostbite – he would eventually lose all ten toes. It's very likely Gaylay did, too.

Frostbite makes it hard to walk. Numb limbs cause a climber to stumble and stagger. Ang Tsering says they almost made it to Camp 6 before dark. But not quite all the way. This time all three men lay down to sleep in the snow together.[7]

It was the sixth night of their retreat, Gaylay and Ang Tsering's sixth night in the open. Merkl, too, had been without water for six days and food for seven. Ang Tsering says they had been eating ice for days. Most climbers believed that ice or snow would make you ill, and it certainly does use up calories to melt it, but it was keeping them alive. For all three men, it was already an extraordinary feat of endurance and courage. Nobody had ever survived so long in such circumstances in the Himalayas before. And nobody has done it since.

Ang Tsering lay awake on the snow that night, thinking:

If all three of us try to go down together tomorrow with the leader in the state he's in, we won't reach Camp 4. If we don't reach it tomorrow, they're likely to close the camp. And then all three of us will die. The only thing we can do is send Gaylay ahead to get help. I'll follow slowly with the leader.

I asked Ang Tsering if he was afraid that night. He said no. He had shouted' at the god three days before. After that, he knew Nanga Parbat and Khumbi La were fighting over his life, far above his head. Whether he lived or died would depend on which god turned out to be stronger. He could do nothing about that, and so being afraid was pointless.

His son Dawa Thempa showed me a painting of Khumbi La he owns. It was done by the Kappa of Khumjung, a famous Sherpa painter, in the early 1950s. Khumbi La looks like a rich man in fine Chinese robes riding a horse. His face is long and beautiful, his smile gentle. He holds a staff aloft as a warrior holds a spear, but there are prayer flags in place of a point. In front of him are the animals associated with the god – a yak, a wild mountain sheep, and a mouse deer.

These are the animals you see around Khumbi La today. Yaks are everywhere. They're large and can be dangerous. Every few years somebody in Khumbu is gored to death. But there is also something calm and kind in their broad faces and big cow eyes. The yak in the picture is like that, and smaller than the god and the horse.

The wild mountain sheep (tahr) have big horns, and their long, thick coats of wool sweep the ground, looking blue in some lights, black in others. You see herds grazing a hillside, or one against the skyline, standing on a rock looking down.

Walk down by Khumbi La from Khumjung in the early morning, on the path toward Tengboche, and if you're quiet, you'll see the little mouse deer. It's usually alone, about the size of a Labrador dog. When it notices you, the deer stops, alert, frozen but trembling slightly, careful but not really afraid, the two horns sticking straight up. The mouse deer in the Kappa's picture has its head raised that way.

Behind the god, to one side, is a yeti, 'the abominable snowman' of Western myth. This one looks something like a man and something like a monkey. They, too, can be dangerous, but the Kappa's yeti seems naughty and happy and devoted to the god.

In the morning Merkl, Gaylay, and Ang Tsering were all still alive. Ang Tsering told Gaylay he should go down and bring back help:

Gaylay said no. He would stay with Merkl.

Gaylay and Merkl talked in English.

Then Merkl said to Ang Tsering: Gaylay stays. Can you make it, Ang Tsering?

Ang Tsering said, 'Yes.'

He went down alone.

Ang Tsering says that Gaylay could have gone down with him and left Merkl. This is also what Ang Tsering told Da Thundu and Tenzing Norgay in 1934.[8] Twice, I asked Ang Tsering why Gaylay stayed with Merkl. Both times he repeated that he had told Gaylay to go down, Gaylay had said no and talked to Merkl, and then Merkl had told Ang Tsering to go down. For Ang Tsering, the key thing was that it was Gaylay's decision, not his.

I have asked many older Sherpas why they think Gaylay stayed behind. Putting together what they said, and considering everything else, this is my best guess as to why Gaylay remained with Merkl.

Ang Tsering was clearly stronger than Gaylay. If one man had to go down, Ang Tsering had the best chance. If he made it, then the people down in Camp 4 might come up and rescue Gaylay and Merkl. If that happened, and they all lived, Gaylay could expect a substantial tip, more than his wages and the value of his gear put together. And he would have a patron, and probably a pension, for life.

Afterward, the Germans said Gaylay did what he did because he was faithful and loyal. This explanation fits the European paternalist view of Sherpas as good sons to good fathers. The flaw in it is that I have never heard a Sherpa speak of loyalty. They speak of honesty, a virtue among equals. Loyalty and faithfulness are found in unequal relationships. Perhaps, however, it's possible to see loyalty as an acceptance of inequality. Gaylay had worked as a servant for the army. In the last few days, he had stopped when the sahibs had said to stop and slept on the snow while they slept in the tent. He had followed orders for many years, and now he was staying with the burra sahib – the big boss.

Maybe, however, he was just being decent. The Buddhism that Sherpas follow enjoins love for all living things. The phrase is usually translated into English as 'compassion for all living things.' But the word the Sherpas use is *nyingje*. It means 'heartlike' and is used for the love of a mother for her child, or a man for his wife of forty years. Their Buddhism says that as you feel for those people, so you should feel for every yak and dog. Their idea of love has, perhaps, more compassion and less possession in it than the English word *love*, but it's basically the same feeling.

Of course, not all Sherpas behave with love all the time. They can be sneaky, hostile, angry, jealous, and cruel, just like anyone else. But love is there, as a value. It's a way you ought to behave.

There's one large piece of evidence that Gaylay acted out of love. Five mornings before he decided to remain with Merkl, he had faced the same choice at the high bivouac. Ang Tsering and Dakshi had been too sick to go on. Gaylay had stayed with them. It's possible he did it because he, too, was sick, but it's unlikely. I can't think of any illness besides snow blindness from which people get better with rest at that altitude. He survived five days for certain after that, and probably six, sleeping on the snow. And after all that, he was still strong enough to go on.

I think Gaylay stayed with Dakshi and Ang Tsering in the high bivouac out of kindness. No tips were to be expected there, no faithfulness to a burra sahib.

Gaylay was not the only Buddhist on the expedition, or the only moral man. But he was the only one who twice stopped to help the sick and dying. He was forty-five years old, an ordinary-looking man on his first job in the mountains. Gaylay did what he did not because he was a Sherpa, but because of the individual he was, a good man.

After he left Gaylay and Merkl, Ang Tsering walked along the ridge, past the Moor's Head and across the icy traverse below the Rakhiot Peak. He followed small footprints he found in the snow. They were mostly filled and no use as a broken trail, but they showed him the way. He went very slowly and often shouted for help. Nobody heard him.

Both his feet were badly frostbitten, and he was to spend almost a year of agony in hospital. He does not say so, but he was lucky not to slip on the icy traverse.

Ang Tsering reached the top of the fixed ropes. Now he thought he could hear somebody replying to his shouts. He was wrong.

He started down the six hundred feet of fixed ropes. His feet were in trouble, but his hands were all right. It was still difficult. He could see one dead man held in the ropes. Another had fallen from the ropes and was lying directly below. He reached the first body and couldn't get by. The man had frozen rigid, tangled in the ropes. His head was thrown back at an unnatural angle, and his right leg stuck out straight, making the body long, so that it blocked Ang Tsering's way.

He looked at the dead man's face. It was hard to tell whom he was seeing. A Sherpa, certainly, but goggles hid his eyes. A sheen of green ice lay over the face. Moisture under the skin had frozen and distorted the features. Only later did Ang Tsering work out that it was Nima Dorje, who had climbed higher than the summit of Nanga Parbat on Everest.

Ang Tsering spent a long time trying to figure out a way down, around, or over Nima Dorje. I think he shrank from embracing the corpse. He was exhausted and his feet were frostbitten. Since he wasn't thinking clearly, even simple maneuvers would have been clumsy and difficult. He was hanging on, without a rope of his own or anything to tie on with, above a fatal drop. If he slipped, he was gone.

Finally Ang Tsering found the solution. He saw that there were two fixed ropes, hanging in parallel. He lowered himself on the one the corpse was not tangled in and got round the body. Perhaps that solution had been obvious all along, and dread or a slow-moving mind had concealed it for a time.

Now he was down to Camp 5. He found Pinzo Norbu's body still lying by the tent – Müllritter must not have been able to bury it well on his own. Ang Tsering looked in the tent, but found no food. Maybe the others had taken it, or maybe his mind was confused. He did find a camera. He remembers saying to himself, I should take this down with me. There may be pictures in the camera. The sahibs will want them.

Ang Tsering started the seventeen hundred feet down from Camp 5. He had been descending since early morning, very slowly. It was dark now, and he kept losing the trail. The large camera in his hand made it difficult to balance properly. Suddenly he fell and slid helplessly down the snow. He stopped at the edge of a crevasse. Ang Tsering lay there on the snow and thought: What am I doing, dying for a camera? He threw it away.

As he went, he shouted from time to time, and now the men in Camp 4 heard him and came up to help. They were there, with him, the doctor and some porters. They had tea.

His most vivid memory of that day is that he wanted to drink all that tea, immediately, but the doctor only allowed him one teaspoonful.

Dr. Bernard made him wait a little, perhaps a minute. Then Bernard gave him two spoonfuls and made him wait. Then three spoonfuls. They all stood there, and he had four spoonfuls and waited. Then five, then six, seven, eight, nine, ten. And then they took him down to the tents.

Bernard was worried that if Ang Tsering drank any faster, he might vomit everything up.

In camp Ang Tsering was well enough to give a coherent account of what had happened on the mountain. He was tired, and his English was not perfect, but he made sense. Ang Tsering told them Merkl and Gaylay were still alive on the long ridge, and they must be rescued. He also told them Dakshi might still be alive. That could not be. I suspect Ang Tsering felt guilty for leaving Dakshi and could not accept his death.

Behind him, Merkl and Gaylay had walked from their bivouac in the open snow the rest of the way up to the Moor's Head. There they lay in the snow that night.

In the morning the men at Camp 4 heard human cries in the wind blowing down from the ridge. They looked up and couldn't see anybody. But they knew one man, at least, was still alive. Bechtold says, 'Against all reasonable calculation Schneider and Aschenbrenner made a dash for Camp V on the 15th [that day] and 16th of July, with their last remaining strength, but without prospect of success. It was all to no purpose, for in the unfathomed snowdrifts they were repulsed again and again.'[9]

Ang Tsering says one sahib and two porters left camp to rescue Merkl and Gaylay. They were back two hours later. He thought they didn't really try. He can't know for sure, he says, because he was sick inside the tent and couldn't see what was going on. But they didn't even get to Camp 5. For him, that says it all.

Let's imagine those two men, high on the ridge, crying out for help from the tents below.

Probably it was Merkl who cried. He stood, leaning on an ice ax and shouted for all he was worth. He thought Ang Tsering might have got down and explained that they were still alive when Ang Tsering had left them. If so, he had to scream now so his comrades would know he had survived the night. Then they would come back up for him and Gaylay.

Gaylay sat on the snow next to Merkl, in the bivouac where they had spent the night wrapped in each other's arms. It was a clear day now, the sky blue, light dancing on the snow.

'So they know we are alive,' Merkl explained to Gaylay after he shouted.

They waited for answering replies.

Nothing came.

Merkl shouted again, almost a scream.

They weren't far from help, if they'd been birds. The ice and snow fell steeply down in a curve toward Camp 4. They could almost see it through the drifting clouds. Both Merkl and Gaylay were pretty sure his voice could carry. But they couldn't go down the direct route. They would have to walk along up to the Moor's Head, along the traverse, down the fixed ropes, then double back.

'They will come,' Merkl said.

Gaylay's guess was that Merkl didn't believe what he was saying.

If help was coming, it would have come by now. Gaylay stood up and handed Merkl a second ice ax. Merkl would need both axes to walk.

Merkl looked at him, unsure, weak. 'We wait,' Merkl said. His English was not as good as Gaylay's.

'We will go down, burra sahib,' Gaylay said. 'They come up. We go down. We will meet them.'

Gaylay watched Merkl's face, Merkl's calculations. If they went farther, then when Merkl died, Gaylay would be closer to help and might make it. Merkl nodded. Maybe he understood. Maybe he thought he was going to live.

The two men started up. The Moor's Head looked so close now, the thin ice patches on the black rock flashing back the sun. Gaylay knew how easy it was to be deceived by distances in the mountains. But it is close, he thought. It's just that we're so slow.

Merkl hobbled, bent over on both ice axes. Gaylay went first, breaking trail. Then he would stop, wait, and let Merkl take his arm. Merkl would pull himself up, grim, breathing, not speaking.

So it went, hour after hour, unbearably slow. They stopped just short of the Moor's Head and sat in the sunlight. For a time they breathed, sitting next to each other.

Gaylay closed his eyes and thought of the laughter of a girl, in Chauri Kharka, twenty years before. Then he thought: If I die here, there will be no funeral. Nobody will guide me through the darkness to another life. I should have lived better.

He remembered the temple at the top of the Darjeeling ridge, with a Buddhist monk and a Hindu pandit facing each other, both reading from the holy books, their voices cutting across each other. A bowl of coins was next to each man. Gaylay always gave a bit to both, to be safe. He remembered the long line of beggars on the steep steps up to the temple. One on each step, old, thin, eyes milky, faces twisted, their bodies mangled, limbs missing and stumps. Each time he passed them, he knew one day he might find himself in that line. But he never gave to them, saved all his money for the god. Now he thought: Probably that was wrong. Probably I will pay for it when I'm dead. But I had so little money.

A few minutes later Merkl died, sitting up. Gaylay heard the noises and understood them. I can go on now, he thought. I can get down on my own. I'm glad he's dead. That's wrong. I shouldn't feel that.

I'll just sleep for a bit, then go on.

Four years later, in 1938, Fritz Bechtold came back to Nanga Parbat and found Merkl and Gaylay frozen on the snow, side by side, just short of the Moor's Head.

Chapter Eight

DARJEELING

The next day Schneider and Aschenbrenner wanted to try another rescue attempt. All the porters refused to go with them. They said they didn't want to walk past the body of Pinzo Norbu again.

Lewa and the porters helped Ang Tsering down to Base Camp. Lewa was Gaylay's friend, but he now thought any rescue was impossible. Only Nurbu Sonam and Ramona, the cook, stayed with Schneider, Aschenbrenner, and Dr. Bernard at Camp 4. The two climbers made another attempt to reach Camp 5, and failed.

In Bechtold's book there is a photograph of Ang Tsering arriving in Base Camp. It was probably posed, but the emotions are real enough. Ang Tsering is utterly exhausted, almost staggering. His face seems full of pain and haunted. Peter Müllritter gazes across at him, a much bigger man, with a blond beard. There is horror on Müllritter's face, and many questions. Between and behind the two men stands a porter, Aiwaa from Thame, looking at Ang Tsering with shocked compassion.[1]

Lewa told the sahibs at Base Camp that Merkl and Gaylay had still been alive the day before. They immediately started packing for a rescue and set off that night with 'eleven more or less sick porters.' Lewa told them it was useless. Bechtold says, 'We brushed such thoughts aside.'[2]

Two of the three scientists attached to the expedition had already gone up. Walter Raechl was a geographer, and Peter Misch a geologist. They were not climbers, but they were rested. They reached Camp 4 the night of the same day that Ang Tsering and Lewa got down to Base Camp. Hearing the news, the scientists decided to try for Camp 5 the next day. Aschenbrenner and Schneider told them it was hopeless. The two scientists tried anyway, but the snow was more than three feet deep and they had to turn back.

In the morning the two climbers, the two scientists, the doctor, the cook, and Nurbu Sonam, the last porter, closed Camp 4 and went down. Aschenbrenner had frostbitten feet from his rescue attempts and wore special felt shoes. Bernard's hair had turned gray. Just above Camp 2 they met the sahibs and porters coming up. The sahibs sat on their rucksacks, talked, and agreed there was no hope. They all went down to Base Camp.

The lower camps still had to be cleared. All the Darjeeling men refused to go anywhere on the mountain now. The sahibs understood. The Balti porters went up to strip the lower camps. Bechtold wrote:

Flowers are in bloom before our tents, and one can reach out a hand from the sleeping-sack to pick them. . . . As evening falls, we gather round the glimmer of the blazing camp-fire. Conversation flickers up . . . and now they are again with us: Willy, Uli, Willo, Alfred, in their gentleness and purity of heart, stern of will, rejoicing in battle, pressing toward the mark. . . . In the midst of our talk comes the groping, ever-recurrent question: wherefore then these things?

Over there, beside the camp-fire of our Darjeeling porters, we might learn the answer. Deep-rooted in their primitive Asiatic souls rests the idea of destiny, the desire for light and consummation, a firm belief in the immutability of Kismet, untroubled by harassing questions of the causality of events. We town-bred Europeans, with our practical minds, our gift for mechanising thought, are strangers to their outlook upon the world.[3]

Kismet is a concept in the Arabic language meaning fate, what is written, and more generally the will of God. Muslims and Christians use this idea sometimes, although of course they also have natural explanations for most events. Hindus and Buddhists do not use the concept. Ang Tsering's understanding of causality was that all those people died because Merkl had abandoned the system of ferrying loads and went for the top in one last push. Ang Tsering's understanding of why he had survived was that Khumbi La had saved him. But this was not fate – it only happened because Ang Tsering defied the god of Nanga Parbat and called up Khumbi La.

There is a photograph of Schneider, Aschenbrenner, Bechtold, and Müllritter at Base Camp after the tragedy. They sit on the ground, arms around each other. Aschenbrenner and Schneider, thin, almost wasted, look straight at the camera. Schneider seems suddenly old and sad. Aschenbrenner's face under his pith helmet is stunned, and full of questions. Bechtold looks down at the ground. Müllritter alone appears rested, his big, blond beard carefully trimmed.

Three of these men would return to Nanga Parbat, and one of them would die there.

There is another photo of the four Sherpas who survived the fixed ropes. They sit in front of a tent, in long woolen underwear, not touching or looking at each other. Da Thundu has bandages wrapped around his left hand. Pasang Kikuli, Kitar, and Pasang Picture wear bandages around both hands and both feet. None of them look at the camera. Perhaps they are ashamed of their ragged clothing or their suffering. Maybe they resent Müllritter's camera. All four are clearly in pain. Da Thundu's head is cast down, his eyes almost closed. Pasang Kikuli looks to one side. He seems lost. Kitar is hunched forward with pain. He seems to see nothing – he may still have suffered from snow blindness. Pasang Picture looks away, into the distance.

Within five years three of these four men would die in the mountains.

Back in Darjeeling the women waited.

Tenzing Norgay was in Darjeeling when the news came from Nanga Parbat. He wrote later: 'There was mourning and grief in many homes in Toong Soong Busti, but there was also a certain deep pride in what our men had borne and accomplished.'4

In Darjeeling in 2000 I wanted to know what those grieving women had felt. I couldn't find any of the widows of 1934. But two other women told me what it was like to lose your husband. One was Lhakpa Diki, whose husband, Lobsang, died in the mountains in 1947. She was born in Pare, across the river from Thame, in 1912. It was a hard life in Khumbu then. Lhakpa Diki was twenty-four when she and three friends ran away to Darjeeling without telling her parents. Life was good in Darjeeling. Nobody starved. She could get by as a trekking porter working only in season, carrying sixty-pound loads. In Khumbu she had to work year-round.

She fell in love with Lobsang, who was also working the treks. (This was not the Lobsang who was on Everest in 1924 and Nanga Parbat in 1934, but another Lobsang, called Lobsang II by the Himalayan Club.) When he couldn't get portering, Lobsang worked on the rickshaws. He got work in the mountains, too. I asked Lhakpa Diki if they fought about that. No, she said. In those days both of you just wanted the money. Then she laughed, and so did her son Ang Purba, who was translating.

Lobsang did well on Everest and by 1940 was awarded the eleventh Tiger Medal. The two years from 1945 to 1947 were the couple's best time. They had finally saved enough money to buy two horses. Lhakpa Diki and Lobsang worked together, taking sahibs on trips round Darjeeling. It was easy, and companionable.

In 1947, Lobsang got work on an expedition going to Green

16 Nanga Parbat, 1934: Climbers crossing a crevasse in the ice field.

Rakhia Peak (23,195 ft)

Fixed ropes

Camp 6 (22,618 ft)

Moor's Head

Camp

Camp 5
(21,950 ft)

Route to
Camp 4

Nanga Parbat Group from the Southern Chongra Peak

17 Nanga Parbat: the route of the 1934 expedition.

Summit (26,642 ft)   Southeast peak (24,705 ft)   Silver Saddle (24,446 ft)   Northeast peak (24,925 ft)   North peak (25,541 ft)

18 Nanga Parbat, 1934: Alfred Drexel's comrades carry his body to the funeral. Note the swastika on the flag.

19 Aschenbrenner and Schneider making the route up to Camp 2. Note the skis.

20 Nanga Parbat, 1934: Looking from Camp 6 down towards the Moors Head, then along the ridge and up to the Silver Saddle between the two dark peaks. Wieland is breaking trail down to the Moors Head.

21 Nanga Parbat,
1934: Ang Tsering, on
the left, arrives at Base
Camp after the retreat.

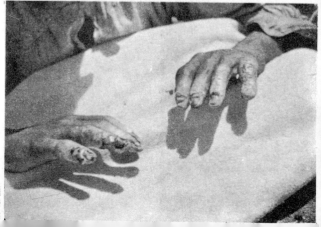

22 Pasang's frostbitten
hands.

23 Nanga Parbat, 1934: Pasang Kikuli being helped into Camp 4 on the retreat.

24 and 25 Nanga Parbat, 1934: At Base Camp after it was all over.
Top: Schneider, Aschenbrenner, Bechtold, Mülritter.
Bottom: DaThundu, Pasang Kikuli, Kitar, Pasang.

Lake, on the north side of Kangchenjunga. It was partly a pleasure trip, but partly a reconnaissance for a planned expedition to
the mountain. There were two sahibs, Lobsang, and another
porter. The other porter became ill, and they left him in a cave
with some food and went on. Lobsang and the two sahibs never
came back. The sick porter recovered and returned.

Lhakpa Diki waited. For a long time there was no definitive
word. Then she was told there would be an air search, but nobody
was found. She had to accept it.

She had two small children. Ang Purba was three, and his
brother was about nine months old. Lhakpa Diki was forced to
put the head strap back on. As Lhakpa Diki told me this, she
began to cry. I had never seen a Sherpa man or woman cry, and
I was ashamed at my questions.

She continued crying silent tears as she told how she would
go to Chowrashtra each day, leaving the baby in a basket round
the corner by the stable where the ponies were kept. She told the
three-year-old Ang Purba to play, but not to go too far from the
baby. Then she worked all day, carrying loads and fetching shopping for the planters who came into town.

The Tibetan agent who had arranged the expedition to Green
Lake came to her house and told her there was no insurance for
her husband because the two sahibs had also died on the expedition. The agent gave her three thousand rupees, from his hand
to her hand, without paperwork. She did not know if this was
compensation or insurance or just the money her husband had
made on the expedition. But she took it. She didn't see what else
she could do.

Lhakpa Diki didn't cry when she told me of her happy memories or of Lobsang's death. She cried when she began to talk about
working afterward, and her loneliness.

She worked eleven more years with the head strap. Ang Purba
has always been grateful to her because she made sure he went
to school. He never had to work himself as a child. He watched
his cousin, another boy who'd lost his father, picking through
rubbish for things to resell, and working on the roads carrying

and breaking rocks. Lhakpa Diki was able to make sure that didn't happen to her son. When Ang Purba was fourteen, he went on a training course at the Himalayan Mountaineering Institute in Darjeeling. When he finished it, he told his mother to stop work, it was his turn now. He did a bit of climbing and trekking work, then became a soldier. Ang Purba retired as a major in a British regiment of Gurkhas.

The other widow I talked to was Lhamoo Iti. She married Da Thundu, one of the survivors of Nanga Parbat, in 1952. Lhamoo Iti was his second wife, as Kitar's daughter had died several years before they married. Lhamoo Iti's parents arranged it. This wasn't usual then. Most women married for love. But when Da Thundu came back to Khumbu in 1952, as a porter on the Swiss expedition to Everest, he was obviously a successful man. Her parents thought he looked to be a good catch. She'd never seen him before. Lhamoo Iti came from Khumjung, Da Thundu and Pinzo Norbu's home village. But they had left for Darjeeling before she was born.

As soon as the Swiss expedition was over, Da Thundu took her straight to Darjeeling. At first she missed her family terribly and dreamed of them every night. Now she's been in Darjeeling forty-eight years and speaks mostly Nepali, but her dreams are still in Sherpa. More and more the friends of her childhood come to play in her dreams.

Darjeeling had electric lights, rice was cheap, and living was easy. Her childhood in Khumjung had been work, work, work – carrying wood for fuel and grass for the animals, digging potatoes, taking the family sheep and goats to pasture. What we did in Khumjung, she said, was we ate potatoes. Period.

In time she came to love and respect Da Thundu. His spirit was good, and he took care of his family. He took work on expeditions when he could. Between times he worked as a laborer on construction sites in Darjeeling. And he was a quiet man, not pushy. That, too, made him a good man.

She showed me his Tiger Medal, and his Himalayan Club book.

Beginning in 1938 the club gave each porter a book in a thick leather pouch. On each expedition the leader wrote a chit in the book. Da Thundu had climbed on Everest in 1933 and was twenty-eight years old on Nanga Parbat in 1934. After that, among other expeditions, he was on Peak K36 in 1935, Everest in 1936, Kangchenjunga with Bauer in 1937, and Annapurna with Herzog in 1950. On his chit for the Swiss Everest expedition in 1952, when he was forty-six, Dumont wrote: 'No challenge was too great for his courage and there was a time, namely in the assault on Camp VI (25,850 feet) when he pushed himself forward to the utmost of human endurance.'

Da Thundu was on Everest with Tenzing and Hillary in 1953, and back to Everest and Lhotse with the International expedition in 1955. After that Gunther Dyhrenfurth wrote in his book: 'He appears to be ageless, since he can still keep up with the fastest and strongest of the younger Sherpas.' His last expedition was in 1966. I couldn't read the name of the peak in the leader's hand-writing in the book, but it was 20,680 feet. Da Thundu made the summit. He was sixty.

After that he fell ill and did not climb again. He died at sixty-six. It was a hard death, eighteen months of pain. A stomach ulcer killed him, caused by his drinking too much, as did so many other climbers of his generation. Lhamoo Iti was left with three daughters. The last twenty-eight years have been difficult, and lonely.

I ask if she was afraid when he went on expeditions. Of course, she said. But if he didn't go, there was no money for the family. So they both accepted the necessary risks. When he was away, she prayed every day, morning and evening, asking: Please, God, let my husband come home alive. She knew he was praying on the mountains, too.

She says the main fear men had in the mountains was what would happen to their family if they died.

Expeditions in both India and Nepal are now legally obliged to take out insurance on their high-altitude porters, and the compensation is generous if a man dies. But until the 1960s, payouts were small. Before 1939 there was no insurance. The sahibs were supposed to pay two thousand rupees for a married man, and one thousand for a bachelor. Even that was not binding.

The porters on Nanga Parbat had to fear their own death and worry for their family's welfare.

They had to carry Ang Tsering from Nanga Parbat Base Camp to the hospital in Srinagar where all his toes were amputated. A few weeks later the local secretary of the Himalayan Club gave him enough money for the train home to Darjeeling. There he went straight into the Victoria Hospital, where the staff found twenty-four large, white maggots in the holes left by his amputations. He says the flies in Kashmir must have been different from the flies in Darjeeling. The maggots didn't hurt, but they unnerved him.

He spent about six months in hospital in Darjeeling. The pain was constant and severe. The treatment was free, and the Germans paid him a pension of sixteen rupees a month, about what he would have earned working on the rickshaws. Mrs Henderson, a tea planter and secretary of the local Himalayan Club, visited Ang Tsering often. She explained to him that if he went back to work after he left the hospital, the Germans would no longer pay the pension.

The Germans did pay compensation to the families of those who died on Nanga Parbat. In 1934 the standard rate was as above. There was no standard compensation for injury – many expeditions paid nothing for anything less than death.

Money for frostbite was always a problem. Pasang Phutar, for instance, got frostbite on a British expedition to Masherbrum in the Karakoram in 1938. He, too, went to the hospital in Srinagar, where they amputated five fingers on his left hand and parts of two fingers on his right hand. They did it, as so often, knuckle by knuckle, trying to save as much of each finger as they could. But the mosquitoes in the hospital were bad, and Pasang Phutar made a formal complaint about them. In retaliation, the doctor removed another knuckle on one finger. Pasang Phutar was unaware that this was a punishment until the doctor was replaced and the new one informed him.

After a few weeks Pasang Phutar was homesick for Darjeeling. He went to see the local secretary of the Himalayan Club, to ask for money for the train home. The secretary said Pasang Phutar would have to get a letter from the hospital saying he was sick. As the secretary knew who he was, and he had very obviously just lost seven fingers, Pasang Phutar was annoyed by this, but he did it.

The train trip home involved several changes and took eight days. When he got to the Victoria Hospital, Pasang Phutar had maggots, too. He ascribed this to being unable to change the bandages on the train. He stayed in the hospital for several months, almost a year in total in Srinagar and Darjeeling.

Did it hurt? I asked Pasang Phutar.

'AAIIEEEEE,' he said, waving his hands in the air and smiling broadly. It hurt the whole time. The British expedition was unwilling to pay him any compensation. He was unmarried then, and his relatives in Darjeeling advised him to move back to Khumbu. Without his fingers he wouldn't get work in Darjeeling. But he wanted very much to stay. Finally the family found a lawyer who took the British climbers to court. In the end the judge said Pasang Phutar should be paid compensation of seventy rupees. 'Ten rupees a finger,' Pasang Phutar says, flourishing his stumps in my face, laughing as he often does when he speaks of injustice.

Pasang Phutar managed to buy a cheap horse with that money and set up as pony man in Chowrashtra, giving short rides to tourists. He slept in the stables every night, to make absolutely sure nobody stole that horse.

So Ang Tsering didn't have much chance of formal compensation when he got out of hospital in the spring of 1935. He was soon off to the north of Sikkim as a porter with a trekking group. According to the chit he received, Ang Tsering tried hard but his frostbitten feet had not recovered and he had to go back early.

Mrs Henderson stepped in. She was kind to many Sherpas. Ang

Tsering's son Dawa Thempa remembers her coming to Toong Soong Busti every Sunday. She would inquire who was ill and bring them medicines. If somebody had no money, she would make sure they got help. In September she and her husband hired Ang Tsering as a porter on a trek to Dzongri in Tibet. Afterward Mrs Henderson gave him a chit saying that his feet seemed recovered, he did heavy marches, and he kept up with the others. He did not work on snow because the trek didn't go on snow, but he did walk and work in up to twenty-four degrees of frost.[5] I think she took him just so he could get that chit.

She also bought him a horse with her own money. For the next several years he worked, liked Pasang Phutar, at Chowrashtra and the stables alongside Pasang Phutar. It was traditional work for Tibetans in Darjeeling, and a person could do it without carrying loads. Over the years Ang Tsering managed to build up a business with several horses, for pony rides and trekking groups. In season there were races at a course below Darjeeling, and two of his horses did well there.

Ang Tsering keeps a photograph of Mrs Henderson in the same pouch as his book of chits from the Himalayan Club. She eventually left Darjeeling in 1956 and opened a tea plantation in Chile.

Soon after Ang Tsering got out of hospital he married Nima Dorje's widow, Pasang Diki. She had originally been a nun near Tengboche in Khumbu, but ran away to Darjeeling to earn some money and see what other places were like. She and Ang Tsering had eight children, four boys and four girls. Like most Sherpa marriages in those days, she married for love. Now many Darjeeling Sherpas marry people chosen by their parents. I asked Ang Tsering if the old ways were better.

Yes, he said. We sat and smiled at each other for a while. There was a lot in his smile. Remembered love, and remembered pleasure in shared passion. They were married for thirty-seven years.

PART III

The Shadow of Nanga Parbat

Chapter Nine

THE GERMAN SIEGE

E rwin Schneider returned from Nanga Parbat determined to organize another expedition to the mountain. But Paul Bauer, the Munich lawyer who had led two previous expeditions to Kangchenjunga, had other plans. Bauer was worried about the effects of the Nanga Parbat tragedy on German climbing:

> In view of the heavy sacrifice incurred in this bold venture, many people felt that the risks were not commensurate with the stake, and the assault on the highest peaks on earth did not promise useful results. The Nanga Parbat disaster threatened, therefore, to sound the knell of German Himalayan expeditions, if not for ever, then at least for a very long time, in the same way that the deaths of Mallory and Irvine checked British attacks on Everest for nine years.[1]

Bauer was also worried that Erwin Schneider might become the leader of German mountaineering. He wrote to the Reich sports führer, von Tschammer und Osten, in December 1934:

> It is today incomprehensible for mountaineers who respect comradeship, how Schneider and Aschenbrenner could leave

their porters behind in a snowstorm and leave them to a certain death. The explanations I have heard are all excuses. . . . It is a hard and fast rule that in bad weather the team must stick together and those in the lead have to wait for those coming later. Anyone who runs away without consideration for stragglers, like Schneider and Aschenbrenner, cannot be seen as a good comrade in the mountains. It is very dangerous when people of such doubtful behavior behave as heroes. . . . The bad example they provided on Nanga Parbat could spoil a generation of new mountaineers.[2]

Bauer also diminished the dead to von Tschammer:

Welzenbach was a man who strived for records. He felt himself to be, and continuously strived to be, a mountaineering wizard. In contrast, I represented a totally different perspective. My perspective was victorious over Welzenbach's in the AAUM [the Munich University Alpine Club] of which we were both members. I always felt like an old soldier, and in the AAUM consistently pursued a national and socialist direction. In 1923 Adolf Hitler was already, for us, the man we would not see touched. In contrast Welzenbach belonged to the Bavarian People's Party and stood with a few of his kind in opposition, which for their characteristic reasons they never made public, as they found no support in the AAUM. For the club was sure of its goals and we were dogged in our attitude.

Bauer trashed Merkl, too:

Welzenbach and Merkl gathered round them mainly people with money. I constructed a united team, each of whom I had known for years. Welzenbach and Merkl, and . . . Schneider, who [was] close to them, also failed to understand that it was a national affair. They based their plans of

1930, '31, and '32 on the participation of wealthy foreign·
mountaineers. Schneider ... went in 1930 with Dyhrenfurth,
a man of Jewish background, to the Himalayas, and they
didn't even have the courage to hoist the German flag, but
instead hoisted the 'Swabian' and 'Tyrolean' flags.[3]

These arguments worked. The sports führer put Bauer in charge
of the national foundation for Himalayan climbing, and
Schneider was unable to secure government funding to lead a
return to Nanga Parbat. Bauer led another expedition to
Kangchenjunga in 1936. He then sent one under Karl Wien back
to Nanga Parbat in 1937. Bauer also managed to turn the tragedy
of 1934 into a crusade. He argued that 'the object of the next
German expedition to the Himalayas had once more to be Nanga
Parbat if the efforts and last sacrifice of so many of our dead
comrades were not to be in vain.'[4] He later said that for Wien 'it
would have been intolerable to attack another Himalayan mountain as long as Nanga Parbat held his comrades unavenged.'[5]

Sacrifice, attack, vengeance – this is the language of war, or even
of a personal and murderous feud. There are conscious echoes
here of Germany's defeat in World War One and the cry to avenge
it.

While Bauer was raising the money, Pasang Picture was trying to
get work on the 1936 British expedition to Everest. With his
younger brother Mingma, Pasang Picture approached John
Morris, one of the British liaison officers in charge of hiring
porters. Morris felt torn:

There was at first considerable doubt whether Pasang would
be selected. .... His hands had been terribly frost-bitten on
Nanga Parbat in 1934, and it was only too apparent that it
would be unfair to let him go high again. If he himself realized that to be again frost-bitten would probably mean
losing the use of his hands, he showed not the slightest sign
of it, and came almost daily to plead with me to include

him in the party. Eventually I left it to Humphreys and Warren to decide. They both agreed with me that from a medical point of view his inclusion in the party was not warranted. But who could resist Pasang's astonishing persistence and ever-smiling face? We just had to take him, and a satisfactory compromise was effected by making him Smijth-Windham's personal servant. By giving him this particular duty he would not be required to go beyond Camp 1, where there was no danger of further damage to his hands. Nevertheless, in spite of all our precautions for his safety, Pasang one day escaped from the boredom of the Base. He was always a front-line solider, and before any of us knew what was happening, he had carried a load up to the North Col. The next day he was back again with his master, smiling and happy once more. He had proved to his own satisfaction that he could still do as well as any of the others. There was just no stopping that man!

Pasang's younger brother Mingma was an altogether different type, being of a rather quiet and mild disposition. He was, if anything, rather stronger physically than Pasang, but lacked such splendid strength of will. Perhaps I can better explain the difference between the two brothers if I say that I shall always retain a picture of Pasang in my mind – nothing, I think, can efface it – whereas the picture of Mingma is already fading, and in a year's time I shall have forgotten how he looked.[6]

The next year Pasang Picture and his brother Mingma were both back on Nanga Parbat with the 1937 German expedition. So was Peter Müllritter, the photographer from 1934, and Da Thundu, whose brother Pinzo had died three paces from the tent at Camp 5. Da Thundu had not forgiven the Germans. But when work was available, he took it.

The German climber Hans Hartmann was on the expedition, too. He had been to the Himalayas before, on Kangchenjunga in 1931 with Paul Bauer. There had been some question whether he should go this time because he had lost all his toes and the front halves of his feet to frostbite in the Alps. But as they left Kashmir for the march to Base Camp, Hartmann remembered a moving speech by Nazi sports führer von Tschammer und Osten at a memorial service in 1934 for Willy Merkl and his companions. Von Tschammer had quoted some lines from the poet Flex:

> *Let cold and pain do what they will*
> *One binding oath will I fulfill*
> *Which burns like firebrands*
> *Through sword and heart and hands*
> *Whate'er Fate may decree*
> *Germany, I stand by thee!*[7]

Now Hartmann told his diary that those lines

have since remained in the forefront of my mind; they have in fact haunted me. My [earlier] decision to join the 1931 Kangchenjunga expedition was reached with some difficulty, for I had to admit to myself that others with sound feet would probably be more useful there than I. But will and enthusiasm finally triumphed and it was with a grateful and humble heart that I claimed this great experience. Then came the 1937 Nanga Parbat project . . . and here I am once more! But there were not many who understood or approved of my joining this expedition.

'What about his wife and children? . . . His scientific work will suffer! . . . Why must he go again? . . . He only just escaped alive last time.' Criticisms of this kind were heaped upon me from every side, but I regarded the matter differently. 'Let cold and pain do what they will.' I was always browsing in Scott's diary and in the account of Alfred Wegener's last journey. 'One binding oath will I fulfill . . .' I thought of my Kangch comrades – Pircher, after Schaller had fallen, bent low over his ice ax, breathing heavily, waiting for the strength to return; Bauer, whose iron will caused his eyes to shine when, above Camp 10, his heart nearly gave out.[8]

The 1937 expedition again employed both Darjeeling men and local Balti porters. They followed the 1934 route, but more slowly, because of heavy snowfall. On June 14, by chance, most of the climbers and porters were together at Camp 4. Wien sent down a message that they would try to establish Camp 5 and push on to the summit as soon as the weather cleared. Uli Luft at Camp 2 heard nothing more for four days. On the fifth day he took a few Balti and Sherpa porters up to see what was happening:

I hurried on alone over the smooth slopes from Camp III to Camp IV, my gaze continually sweeping Rakhiot Peak in an effort to find Camp V on its flank or a trail there showing that my comrades had moved on – but in vain. By midday I reached the first site of Camp IV, which I knew had been evacuated on the 10th. . . . Breathing heavily I plodded upwards, expecting in a quarter of an hour to be able to hand my friends their eagerly awaited letters. I paused in a shallow basin from which my unobstructed gaze could sweep from Chongra Peak along the ridge to Rakhiot Peak. An oppressive silence reigned. An almost obliterated trail stretched away towards the ridge in the east as if into eternity.

With merciless force the truth dawned on me.

Where I was standing an avalanche of terrific proportions had covered a surface of nearly fifteen acres with gigantic ice-blocks. There was not a single trace of the camp. It lay buried beneath thousands of cubic feet of ice.

The porters came up and confirmed that the camp was standing here when they had descended on the 14th. Far below we discovered some tins and three empty rucksacks which had evidently been carried along on the surface of the avalanche. After three hours search it became clear that we could never hope to extricate the deeply buried camp

with our light picks, for everything had frozen together into
a rigid, immovable mass.⁹

The avalanche had covered an area five hundred by thirteen
hundred feet. Pasang Picture, his brother Mingma Tsering, and
Peter Müllritter were dead. So were Jigmey Sherpa, Gyaljen Monjo,
Chang Karma, Ang Tsering II, Nima Tsering, Kami Sherpa, Nim
Tsering, Karl Wien, Hans Hartmann, Pert Fankhauser, Gunther
Hepp, Adolf Gotner, and Martin Pfeffer, all crushed or quickly
suffocated under the weight of ice.

Müllritter and Jigmey Sherpa had both been on Nanga Parbat
in 1934, though neither had been trapped in the storm. Jigmey
had been on Kangchenjunga three times, and on Everest in 1933,
1935, 1936, and 1937. Hugh Ruttledge had called him 'everlast-
ingly willing and cheerful.' Nima Tsering, Wien had said, was
'staid and thoughtful, attacking everything with amazing calm
and assurance.' Ang Tsering II was not Ang Tsering I, the hero of
Nanga Parbat, but another man who lived in Khumbu and had
climbed on Everest three times.

There were no survivors at Camp 4. The only climbers and high-
altitude porters left alive were the men who had been at Camp
2 the night of the avalanche – Luft, the sardar Nursang, another
Darjeeling man, and Da Thundu. Now those four men stood on
the snow, the dead men below them, gradually taking in what
had happened.¹⁰

It's hard to imagine what Da Thundu felt, standing next to
Luft, looking around the silent waste. Camp 4, this very place,
had been his refuge after he had come down the fixed ropes.
Here they had massaged his frostbitten hands all night in the
porters' tents. A few hours above, at Camp 5, his brother Pinzo
had died.

Da Thundu was a quiet man, always. There is no record of him
crying or making a fuss, even here. He was probably in shock,
but he must have asked himself: Why me?

I asked his widow Lhamoo Iti what she thought was most

important to a climber's survival: strength, intelligence, or luck? I put that question to many climbers. The strong ones tended to say strength. The intelligent ones said all three. Da Thundu's widow said it was luck that saved a man.

Two days after Luft and Da Thundu discovered the avalanche, Paul Bauer got the news in Germany. He immediately organized a trip to Nanga Parbat, taking along Fritz Bechtold and a climber named Kraus. They flew to India, where a Royal Air Force plane took them to Gilgit. Twenty days after they had heard the news, Bauer and Bechtold arrived at Base Camp. There they met Nursang, the Sherpa sardar, one of the lucky survivors. Bauer and Nursang knew each other well. They had been together on Kangchenjunga in 1929, where they had discovered that they had fought from opposite trenches on the Ypres front in World War One. Nursang had been a Gurkha sergeant, and Bauer a German officer.

Bauer immediately led an attempt to retrieve the dead Germans from the snow-covered mountainside. Da Thundu went back up to help.[11] So did Bechtold, too nauseated to eat. Jussup Khan, a local porter, went up with them and saw in a vision how the fairies of Nanga Parbat had killed the climbers and porters: 'In the dusk dozens of naked women had danced on the glacier near Camp IV in front of the Sahibs, and then destroyed the entire camp when all were asleep.'[12] Later, in Gilgit, an Englishman showed Bauer a photograph he had taken on the Rakhiot glacier in 1934: 'It showed one of those fairies silhouetted against an ice-wall.'[13]

At Camp 4, Bauer, Luft, Kraus, Shukar Ali, and Satara dug down ten feet and gradually found the dead, all peaceful in their tents, with their possessions unbroken. They seemed to have died immediately. Bauer and the others managed to dig out five of the seven Germans and rebury them in a mass grave. They left the Sherpas. Bauer said this was because Nursang, the sardar, wanted to leave them where they lay. Perhaps Nursang did, perhaps he was obeying orders, and perhaps he thought the whole project strange.

In fact it was pretty mad to climb to twenty-two thousand feet and risk more lives to dig up and then rebury five bodies. Recovering diaries for families had some point. Bauer must have felt guilty, since he'd organized the expedition. He must also have been aware that this latest accident threatened German Himalayan climbing as a whole. This time there was no long retreat or heroic bivouacs. Sixteen men had died in their sleep, like sitting ducks waiting for the hunter's shot. There'd been little warning before tons of ice and snow had hit their camp.

What Bauer was doing was turning a helpless accident into another battle in a long war. And it worked. The German government gave him more funding to return to Nanga Parbat the next year, 1938, with another expedition.

That expedition wanted Darjeeling men again, and Nursang returned as sardar. H. W. Tilman, the British climber, was in Darjeeling hiring for the British 1938 expedition to Everest.

> Besides picking twelve porters for ourselves we had to choose twenty for three other parties coming to the Himalaya later. After this was done there seemed to be no good experienced men left. One, Nursang . . . was collecting porters for Nanga Parbat, and was having some difficulty in persuading men with the memory of so many dead comrades fresh in their minds, to go again to that unlucky mountain. Nursang's forcible appeals reminded me of the exhortation of Frederick the Great to his wavering troops. 'Come on you unmentionable offsprings of scoundrels. Do you want to live forever?'[14]

Nursang eventually found ten porters, 'all of them young men without much experience'[15] – Gyaljen, Nima Sherpa, Pasang, Pasang Chikadi, Pemba Bhutia, Pemba Sherpa, Pintso, Phuttar, Thuthin Bhutia, and Sonam. These were new men, even if many of them have the same names as people we now know well. Da Thundu refused to go. But Uli Luft, the sole German survivor of 1937, was back. And so was Fritz Bechtold, Willy Merkl's best friend, now on his fourth trip to Nanga Parbat in six years. There is madness at work here, and a survivor's guilt, and perhaps grief and heroism as well.

Heavy snow made climbing difficult. For the fourth expedition in a row, the German climbers found the weather against them. Perhaps they were simply not prepared for the weather on Nanga Parbat. To make up for the small number of porters, they had arranged for a Junker plane to drop supplies to them on the mountain. This didn't work out – parachutes failed to open, and boxes rolled down the mountain into crevasses.

On July 19 the German climber Ruths found the body of a dead Sherpa frozen in the fixed ropes below the Rakhiot Peak. The sardar, Nursang, identified the body as Nima Dorje, who had climbed higher on Everest than the summit of Nanga Parbat and had died on the ropes just before Camp 5. Nursang and the Germans cut Nima Dorje down and buried him quickly before any of the other porters could see him. They were worried that the sight, on top of the accident the year before, would scare the porters so badly they would refuse to work.

Three days later they made it round the Rakhiot Peak and onto the North Ridge, just below the Moor's Head, where Bauer saw something. He turned around to check if the two Sherpa porters behind him had seen it as well. Luckily for Bauer the closest, Phuttar, was fifteen paces back. Bauer 'called out to Zuck to lead the two porters some distance back.' Then he asked Bechtold to come forward.

Bechtold said, yes, the man sitting frozen on the ice was his childhood friend Willy Merkl. The man lying next to him under a thin sheet of ice was Gaylay.[16] Bechtold now knew that both men must have left their last bivouac and climbed, or crawled, this far. Bauer wrote later: 'We bared our heads in the presence of the dead. Then we removed the ice. Merkl's face was perfectly intact, as if modeled in wax. In his pocket was a letter, Willo Welzenbach's last call for help. . . . We buried [Merkl and Gaylay] where we found them.'[17]

Before they buried the two men, they took a photograph of

Gaylay's mummified body, his face round, his eyes staring. (Out of respect, they did not publish the photo, and I have not either.[18]) Then Bechtold and Bauer guided the porters back down to Camp 5. But at least one of the porters, Phuttar, had seen the bodies. The next day they established Camp 6, and the day after that two German climbers got to within five hundred vertical feet of the Silver Saddle. Five days after Merkl and Gaylay were found, four German climbers and one porter, Pintso, were at Camp 7 on the ridge up to the Silver Saddle. The other porters said they were too sick to climb above Camp 5. They may have been – or may have dreaded what Phuttar had seen.

At that point Bauer, at Camp 5, just below the Rakhiot Peak, laid out a red parachute on the snow, which was the agreed signal for a general retreat. 'Naturally the eager vanguard felt unhappy over this decision,' Bauer says.[19] But he had only one working porter. Though he does not mention it, Bauer had also dug up a lot of dead people in the last twelve months. Iron-willed he might be, but another failure on Nanga Parbat was preferable to another tragedy.

Bauer led the sick porter Phuttar down from Camp 4. 'The Sherpa,' Bauer said, 'still had the same fixed stare that he had ever since we found the dead near the Moor's Head.'[20] They rested at Base Camp, then tried one more time, but got no farther than Camp 5.

Bauer wasn't giving up. The next year, 1939, he sent a small German expedition of four climbers and three Darjeeling porters to have a look at the Northwest, or Diamir, Face of Nanga Parbat.[21] Bauer was worried about the constant avalanches on the route of earlier expeditions. He knew the Northwest Face was much steeper, almost vertical. Also, perhaps the more direct Northwest Face would enable climbers to avoid the long traverse across the North Ridge and up to the Silver Saddle. This 1939 expedition would have a look, then another expedition in 1940 would have a real try.

The 1939 expedition included Heinrich Harrer, one of the four men to make the first ascent of the North Wall of the Eiger in the Alps. While tourists in the village below watched through telescopes, Harrar and the others had inched their way up the wall that had killed so many before them. In Berlin, Adolf Hitler had listened to the live reports of the climb on the radio. After their success, Hitler met and honored the four men as exemplary new German heroes. Andre Heckmair, a guide and one of the four men on the Eiger, said years later he was not impressed: 'It could have happened to a dancing bear.'[22] Harrar, already a lieutenant in the Nazi SS, certainly was impressed.

Now Harrar was on Nanga Parbat. The four German climbers found the Northwest Face narrow, austere, and intimidating. In June there were constant avalanches, and in July rockfalls. Much of the climbing was technical, and clearly too difficult for most Darjeeling porters. The Germans did manage to climb to a point just above twenty-two thousand feet and thought they could see a reasonably safe way higher up.

When they came down from the mountain, war between Germany and Britain seemed imminent. The Germans headed for Karachi and their ship home, but it failed to arrive. Harrar left town fast, heading west across the Baluchistan desert toward Iran, but was caught in Las Bela. All four German climbers were interned as enemy aliens.

Their prison camp was in the foothills of the Himalayas. In 1944 two of them, Harrar and Aufschnaiter, escaped along with three other German prisoners. They walked across the foothills into the mountains. Sometimes they hid by day, and sometimes they trusted local villagers to feed them and see them on their way. Finally both climbers made it to Tibet, where the Dalai Lama's government, neutral in the war, gave them asylum. The war ended the next year, but both men stayed on in Tibet. Harrar became a trader, and a friend and tutor to the young Dalai Lama. He stayed until the Chinese army invaded, and finally left after seven years in Tibet.[23]

But the German siege of Nanga Parbat wasn't over yet.

Chapter Ten

THE SHERPA SURVIVORS

In the spring of 1936, General Bruce came out to Darjeeling. The five Sherpa survivors of the summit attempt on Nanga Parbat – Ang Tsering, Kitar, Pasang Kikuli, Pasang Picture, and Da Thundu – were called to a ceremony on Observatory Hill. Bruce presented each of them with a certificate from the German Red Cross, honoring them for their courage.

Kitar and Ang Tsering were living together, with Ang Tsering's new wife and Kitar's son. Later that spring Kitar and Pasang Kikuli found work on a British expedition to Nanda Devi in the Indian Garwhal Himalaya.

Pasang Phutar, who was on the Nanda Devi expedition, says the difficult part was the walk in, along narrow paths above high gorges. There was also something wrong with the food on the approach march. Several of the porters got dysentery, Kitar very badly. The other porters wanted to carry Kitar in or take him back to the road. Tilman, the leader, refused to allow this, saying it would only slow them down.

Pasang Phutar says Tilman was a difficult man to work for. Tilman would plunge across a fast mountain stream, confident because he could swim. On the other side he would stride off, not looking back. The porters, who couldn't swim, would stand at the edge, hoping Tilman would return to help them across. He never did, and they crossed the stream as best they could.

Tilman was the same on rock, Pasang Phutar says. He mimes a man scrabbling wildly up an overhang, hands enthusiastically grabbing air. Then he says, in English, 'Very danger man.' Pasang Phutar means Tilman was both a man who loved danger and a dangerous man to work for.

By the time they reached the Nanda Devi Base Camp, Kitar was quite sick, with blood in his stool. He lay there for the rest of the expedition. Tilman, Shipton, and Odell made it to the summit, which in 1936 was the highest mountain ever climbed. Kitar died at Base Camp. Tilman later wrote that Kitar 'did not seem to us a very likable type of Sherpa.'[1]

Pasang Phutar held Tilman responsible for Kitar's death. Ang Tsering went further. He felt Tilman was a murderer and never forgave him.

Kitar left one son, a disabled boy with a hunched back, living in Ang Tsering's house. The boy was smart, and Ang Tsering looked after him and paid his way through school.

Pasang Kikuli had a luckier time on the Nanda Devi expedition. Tilman said that of the four Sherpas, Kikuli was the 'only one worth a place on a serious show.'[2] He carried high and became friends with the only American climber on the expedition, Charles Houston. In 1938 Houston returned to India as the leader of an American expedition to K2 and hired Pasang Kikuli as his sardar. The small expedition did a reasonable job, although getting nowhere near the top. Pasang Kikuli was the only Sherpa allowed to climb to the higher camps with the Americans. The next year a second American expedition returned, and Pasang Kikuli was the sardar again.

The 1939 K2 expedition marked two turning points in Sherpa history. It was the first time a Sherpa was a member of the summit party for a great Himalayan peak. And Pasang Kikuli, haunted by the memory of Nanga Parbat, changed everyone's idea of what a Sherpa should do.

A photograph of the high-altitude porters was taken in a garden in Srinagar just before the expedition set out to walk from Kashmir to K2.[3] The nine men wear European wool jackets, white shirts, and sweaters, although three of them have baggy Indian pants. Their hair is cut short and carefully combed. They are proud. These men have come a long way since they first walked from their homes to Darjeeling with long hair tied up in braids and decorated with semiprecious stones.

Seven of the nine men look directly at the camera with the stern expressions people put on for pictures in those days. Pasang Kikuli's brother Sonam, on one end of the row, is the only one smiling. At the other end is Da Thundu, who had survived Nanga Parbat in both 1934 and 1937. (His name was now spelled Da Thundup, Dawa Thundu, and Dawa Thundoop, his own preference. It was usually pronounced Da Thundu.)

Pasang Kikuli is in the center, the most expensively and carefully dressed – a wool suit with matching knee-length shorts and waistcoat. Though one of the smallest men in the row, his well-cut waistcoat shows off the size and musculature of his chest. He is twenty-eight years old and has been climbing professionally for the last ten years.

Pasang Dawa Lama stands next to him and is the only man with a part in his hair. With his coat unbuttoned to show off his white shirt, he looks raffish and stylish. He is already twenty-eight, one of the least experienced porters, but known for his strength, and already deputy sardar. Five of the other porters on the expedition – Kikuli, his brother Sonam, Phinsoo, Pemba Kitar, and Tsering Norbu – had been on K2 with Houston and Petzoldt the year before. Da Thundu had Nanga Parbat behind him. Pasang Kitar and Tse Tendrup made it nine. Nine men weren't really enough high-altitude porters for K2, but this team was strong and experienced.

The American climbers were something else altogether. The only strong or experienced climber was the leader, Fritz Wiessner, who'd been on the first German expedition to Nanga Parbat in 1932. At that time he'd been a German citizen, but in 1933 he'd settled in the United States and taken American citizenship. In part he was following his business interests, but it seems likely that he was also deciding to disassociate himself from the new Nazi government. He was, however, a social conservative. Andrew Kaufman and William Putnam were American climbers who knew him well in later life. In their excellent 1992 book, *K2: The 1939 Tragedy*, they describe Wiessner thus:

> Fritz was no humanist. Rather he preached Darwinian naturalism with its emphasis on the survival of the fittest. The weak must perish so that the strong may live – such was his philosophy. . . . He could be good company, especially for the people he liked, which in the 1930s meant the rich and the influential – 'the good people' he called them. He could ooze with central European charm and knew precisely how to do 'the proper things in the proper situation' with grace and courtesy, but he could be brutally curt with those he disliked or who meant little to him.[4]

Five foot six inches, bald, broad-shouldered, muscular, and strong, Wiessner belonged on K2. He put together a team that included both experienced climbers and rich men willing to shoulder the costs of the expedition. But before the expedition left New York, all the experienced climbers pulled out. Now none of Wiessner's four fellow Americans was capable of leading climbs and finding routes on K2. This was crucial, for it was complex rock and ice all the way up. The Abruzzi Ridge was the easiest way up to the slopes below the summit, but even on the Abruzzi there was a continuous steep stretch of six thousand feet where a moment's loss of concentration would mean a fatal fall. Wiessner solved this problem by leading all the way himself, from Base Camp almost to the summit. Since that time people have climbed the great peaks solo, quickly, without fixing ropes and without looking after other climbers. Nobody, before or since, has led as Wiessner did on K2.

The question was: Who could stay with him? The most difficult

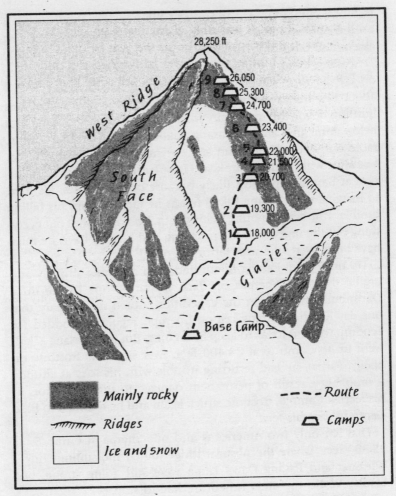

28,250 ft

9 26,050
8 25,300
7 24,700
6 23,400
5 22,000
4 21,500
3 20,700
2 19,300
1 18,000

West Ridge

South Face

Glacier

Base Camp

Mainly rocky

Ridges

Ice and snow

Route

Camps

K2 in 1939

technical climbing was the House Chimney, just above Camp 4 on the Abruzzi Ridge. It was only eighty feet high, but the first ascent had taken Bill House four hours the year before. On July 11, Pasang Kikuli's brother Sonam was halfway up the chimney on a fixed rope when he slipped. Sonam fell forty feet, rolled about two hundred feet down the snow slope below, and was hurtling down the mountain with a fall of three thousand feet below him. In Camp 4 Pasang Kikuli saw his brother falling, raced out, and grabbed him as he went by. Sonam was bruised, but alive with nothing broken. He spent the rest of the expedition at Base Camp, most likely because of his injuries. It's hard to imagine what Pasang Kikuli felt as he raced toward his falling brother, who was tumbling to his death. Even if he shut out everything but the urgency of the moment, and he may have, he must have been overcome with terror afterward.

Up until then, Pasang Kikuli had been climbing strongly and urging the other Sherpas on. Jack Durrance, one of the three Dartmouth students on the expedition, noted in his diary that one day Kikuli, climbing last on his rope, regularly prodded Tse Tendrup with his ice ax to keep him going. But then Pasang Kikuli went up to Camp 6, at 23,400 feet. Ever since his frostbite on Nanga Parbat, he had recurring trouble with his toes at altitude – probably a result of permanent damage to the circulation in his feet. At Camp 6, frostbite struck again and he returned to Base Camp to save his feet.

That left only two Americans and one Sherpa at Camp 8, at 25,300 feet, where the Abruzzi Ridge joined the summit ridge. Wiessner and Pasang Dawa Lama were still going strong, but Dudley Wolfe, the other American, had to stop.

Wolfe had no business being at Camp 8. He was forty-three years old, heavily overweight, a clumsy and awkward man. He had done all his previous climbing with guides. In the Alps and the Rockies, it often took two guides to get him up the difficult pitches, one pushing his bottom from below and one hauling on his arms from above. He was now on the most difficult mountain on earth, within three thousand feet of the summit.

Complicating matters even more, he led a rather pampered existence, with a great mansion in New York where servants had looked after him all his life. Now he was unable to cook his own food – he didn't know how – and even had great difficulty lighting a pressure stove at altitude to boil water.

At least two of the other climbers believed that in return for Wolfe's financing the expedition, Wiessner had agreed to guide him as high as he wanted. But Wiessner also had to have a companion for the summit, and in 1939 it was assumed that companion would be another white man. Despite being fat and clumsy, Wolfe was strong, the only American other than Wiessner capable of reaching Camp 8.

From there, Wolfe, Wiessner, and Pasang Dawa Lama set off for Camp 9, the last camp before the summit attempt. Almost immediately, Wolfe discovered that he could go no farther. Wiessner then asked Pasang Dawa Lama to accompany him to the summit.

This was something entirely new. A few men, such as Alexander Kellas and Charlie Bruce, climbing without other sahibs, had gone to minor summits with porters. Sometimes two or three sahibs had taken a porter to the summit with them to carry their spare gear. But no sahib on a big expedition had asked a porter to share the glory.

In one way, Wiessner had no choice. Pasang Dawa Lama was there, he was strong, and he was Wiessner's only chance of success. But Wiessner was also unusual in the way that he treated Sherpas. On the lower slopes of K2, he had the porters carrying fifty-pound packs while the sahibs (except Wolfe) carried thirty-five. On the higher slopes the sahibs *and* the porters all carried forty pounds – and Wiessner carried this weight himself, with the added burden of leading the climbing. This fairness and equality was new.

At one camp there were only two tents, one for Durrance, Wolfe, and Wiessner, and one for several Sherpas. With Wolfe's bulk, the sahibs were too crowded in their tent, so Wiessner took himself off to share the Sherpas' tent. This may seem a small point, but as late as 1955 the distinguished Swiss mountaineer Gunther

Dyhrenfurth still assumed that Sherpas and sahibs could not share a tent. Writing of the 1938 K2 expedition, he said that at first only four sahibs and three Sherpas stayed at Camp 3 – 'It was the only feasible arrangement, for one more Sahib and one more Sherpa would have meant two more tents, with all the necessary gear.'[5]

Sherpas had been climbing for eighteen years now. Year by year, mountain by mountain, they had been changing the sahibs' idea of them and what they could accomplish. Pasang Dawa Lama was an exceptionally strong climber. So in that moment just above Camp 8 the relations between sahibs and Sherpas changed because of the necessities of the moment, because of the personal characters of Wiessner and Lama, and because of all that a generation of Sherpas had demonstrated they could do.

Wiessner and Pasang Dawa Lama pitched their tent at Camp 9 that night, only 750 feet above Camp 8, and 2,200 feet short of the summit. The next morning they set out at 9 A.M. The late hour was unusual. Nowadays summit parties leave at three or four in the morning. In those days most left at six or seven. The timing may mean that Wiessner and Pasang Dawa Lama were already exhausted, but on the 1939 expedition they tended to make a late start every day.

Wiessner came to a point where he had to choose between two routes. One followed the difficult, steep, and jagged ridge. The alternative route was to branch sideways across the snowfields on the face. That looked easier, less steep, but also slower. Wiessner took the rock ridge, a reasonable guess, but a mistake. Every successful attempt since has taken the route across the snowfield.

Nine hours after they started, at six in the evening, Wiessner had surmounted all the difficult pitches but one. Only a twenty-five-foot traverse sideways stood before him, and that didn't look impossible. Above that it was a snow walk. He estimated they could do it in three or four hours, climbing in the dark, and come down in the light the next morning.

Pasang Dawa Lama said no. There is little doubt that they could have made the summit. But Pasang Dawa Lama felt that they wouldn't survive the night, and he was probably right.

They stood together and argued. Wiessner held firm to his desire and turned to climb. Pasang Dawa Lama, who was belaying him, refused to pay out the rope. That left Wiessner no alternative. They went down to Camp 9. Pasang Dawa Lama's good sense and insistence had saved their lives.

It is worth pausing a moment to underline what they had achieved. They were climbing without oxygen. Wiessner had been above Base Camp for thirty-six straight days and above Camp 6 for six days. He had led all the way up the mountain, except for a few hundred feet. That much time at altitude destroys the body. These days no one, ever, stays that high for that long. K2 is the hardest mountain on earth to climb, much harder than Everest. It was not until 1978, forty years later, that the first two people climbed Everest without oxygen. It was the 1980s before anybody climbed K2 without oxygen. Those climbers on Everest and K2 also had the benefit of much better gear and were far more rested. Nobody has ever climbed K2 on the route Wiessner and Pasang Dawa Lama tried on summit day. Yet they got to within eight hundred feet of the top. It was certainly the most impressive single climb before 1978. Since they didn't make the summit, however, it was forgotten.

They turned round sometime after six. Abseiling down in the dark, Pasang Dawa Lama got tangled in the rope and lost their crampons. They reached their tent at Camp 9 at two-thirty in the morning. The next morning was sunny and warm, the wind still. Wiessner lay naked on his sleeping bag, the tent flaps open, gradually recovering. Pasang Dawa Lama lay next to him. That afternoon Pasang Dawa Lama told Wiessner he was ready for another try. They were two very tough individuals.

But without those crampons they had to cut steps in the ice, and it was hopeless. That night they rested in Camp 9 again –

climbers still didn't understand altitude. In the morning they packed to go down. They left the tent and Wiessner's sleeping bag. Pasang Dawa Lama carefully put his own small sleeping bag and mattress in his pack. They were still an important part of his pay for the expedition. His sleeping bag was smaller than the ones the sahibs had, in part because the climbers reckoned the Sherpas were small men. The expedition may also have been saving money.

On the way down to Camp 8, Pasang Dawa Lama fell again, but Wiessner belayed with his ax and held him. At Camp 8, Wiessner expected to find more supplies and more porters. They saw nobody, and only one tent stood. For a moment they thought that anybody inside must be dead. Then Dudley Wolfe crawled out of the tent on his hands and knees. Because Wolfe was such an awkward climber and needed help to get up each stage, he had spent the last forty-three days above Base Camp. He couldn't really navigate the mountain, so he had climbed up one camp, rested about a week, and then climbed to the next. He'd now been at Camp 8 for seven days. After Wiessner and Pasang Dawa Lama had left him there four days before, he'd almost immediately used up all his matches. Without servants, exhausted and groggy, he must have lit one match after another as he tried to work the stove. Then, without matches, he'd no way to cook food. More important of course was melting water. Luckily, it was sunny. Wolfe had put snow on a tarpaulin outside the tent to melt in the sun. That was how he had survived.

The three men set out down to Camp 7 immediately. On the way Wolfe fell and pulled Pasang Dawa Lama behind him. Wiessner only just managed to belay them. Pasang Dawa Lama's chest was badly bruised, and by that evening his kidneys were painful. Wolfe had lost his sleeping bag in the fall.

They slept at Camp 7 that night, fitfully, all three men trying to fit into Pasang Dawa Lama's one small-size sleeping bag. The next morning Wiessner and Pasang Dawa Lama faced a decision. Below Camp 7 was the hardest ice pitch on the whole mountain. The fall the day before, on a relatively easy stretch, was evidence enough that Wolfe would likely pull all three men to their death on the ice pitch.

Wiessner believed that in the next camp down, Camp 6, he would find willing hands to rescue Wolfe. He didn't know that the Sherpas and Americans below had waited a week for the summit team to return, then concluded that they were probably dead. Tony Cromwell, the deputy leader, had given orders to clear the mountain, leaving the tents standing, but carrying down the sleeping bags and food. There was shelter below Wiessner, Pasang Dawa Lama, and Wolfe, but no help.

Wiessner and Pasang Dawa Lama decided to leave Wolfe at Camp 7. Wiessner did not admit to himself what he was doing. Dudley Wolfe, like Pasang Dawa Lama, probably understood that he could accidentally kill the other men. Wolfe had always been a decent, uncomplaining man. He did not complain now.

Wiessner and Pasang Dawa Lama got down the mountain in two days. As they passed each camp, finding no one, Wiessner began to understand what had happened. They reached Base Camp. Tony Cromwell and the others came out to meet them. Wiessner was barely able to talk. In a low, rasping voice, he called Cromwell a murderer. Wiessner must have felt, somewhere inside, never publicly acknowledged, and probably never even admitted to himself, that he himself had murdered Wolfe.

The next morning Jack Durrance, Pasang Kitar, and Phinsoo went up to try to rescue Wolfe. Pasang Kikuli, the sardar, did not go with them. The frostbite still affected his toes.

The three rescuers made it to Camp 2, three thousand feet above, in one day, and to Camp 4, another twenty-two hundred feet, the next day. There Durrance realized he could go no farther. The next day he went down, and Pasang Kitar and Phinsoo, to their undying credit, continued on alone to Camp 6. There they stopped, thirteen hundred feet below Wolfe and Camp 7. They may have been reluctant to climb the steep ice pitch between 6 and 7, and may have felt Wolfe was probably beyond help. But they did not come down.

Durrance reached Base Camp the same day. Now, finally,

Pasang Kikuli, the sardar, said he would go up to rescue Wolfe. He must have known that even if he survived, he would lose his toes, and perhaps his feet. Later Wiessner's enemies, who included most of the other Americans on the expedition, accused Wiessner of ordering Pasang Kikuli to his death. Actually, though, Kikuli's later actions leave little doubt that he volunteered.

We cannot know why he did so, but we can make reasonable assumptions. From his point of view, now not only one man was in danger on the mountain, but three – Wolfe, Pasang Kitar, and Phinsoo. Kikuli had been on Nanga Parbat. He must have been able, all too easily, to imagine what all three men were feeling up there. His lesson learned on Nanga Parbat was that in extremity only the Sherpas could be counted on to behave decently and look after each other and the other climbers. And it probably followed that if he was the only person who could lead a rescue, it was his duty to do so. Again, we can only guess, but I don't think his decision arose out of loyalty to sahibs. It was a matter of *nyingje* – love.

Whatever his reasons, Pasang Kikuli went up. In that moment he redefined what it was to be a Sherpa sardar. In 2000, listening to me tell the story of Nanga Parbat, the experienced Namche climber Anu Sherpa suddenly asked me where the sardar had been in all that tragedy. He assumed that it was the sardar's job to take charge in such an emergency. The answer was that the sardar, Lewa, was in Camp 4, with all his toes amputated years before, trying as hard as he could to ascend. But nobody in 1934 commented on the role of the sardar, because nobody assumed he had the main responsibility. A rescue, or a retreat, was to be led by the sahibs. What Pasang Kikuli did in the next four days changed that, for all Sherpa porters.

Pasang Kikuli took Tsering with him. They climbed from Base Camp to Camp 6, seven thousand vertical feet, in one day. This was climbing of an extraordinary order. There they found Pasang Kitar and Phinsoo, safe. The next morning Kikuli led Pasang Kitar and Phinsoo over the ice pitch to Camp 7. Tsering, unwilling to risk the ice pitch and probably exhausted from the previous day's effort, stayed behind.

Pasang Kikuli and the others found Wolfe still alive, but in desperate shape. He had been above twenty-two thousand feet for thirty-eight days. For the last sixteen days he had been at an average height of twenty-five thousand feet. He had no matches again. He'd been unable to eat hot food, and more seriously, unable to melt water. For the last five days he appeared to have drunk nothing. It was a wonder, and a sign of his physical toughness, that he was still alive. But he lay on his sleeping bag, too depressed to read his mail or the note from Wiessner that the Sherpas had brought him. He had not been out of the tent for days. What distressed Pasang Kikuli and the others most was that Wolfe had defecated all over his sleeping bag, and all over his food. They made him some tea and told him they would take him down. Wolfe told the Sherpas to come back the next day, when he would be strong enough to go with them.

By this point Wolfe probably understood that he wouldn't make it down the next pitches without falling, and he didn't intend to take three men with him. Pasang Kikuli, Pasang Kitar, and Phinsoo still persevered. They got Wolfe outside the tent and stood him up. He staggered around, and the Sherpas soon saw what Wolfe was trying to tell them. So they left him there, saying they would come back the next day. They meant it.

They made it back down to Camp 6 and Tsering. That night it snowed, and all the next day a storm trapped the four Sherpas inside their tent, where they talked about what to do. In the end, they decided to try one more time. They would attempt to get Wolfe on his feet, then lead and lower him down. If they could not get him started, or he refused again, they would ask Wolfe for a written chit saying that they had tried and it was his decision to stay.

They wanted a chit because their future work, and particularly Kikuli's, might well depend on it. Since 1937 there had been an important change in the chits that porters got from climbers. That year the British-run Himalayan Club in India drew up a register of high-altitude porters and issued each man an official notebook. That notebook came with a thick, waterproof, brown leather case, and another black leather case to put that into. The casing would help the notebook withstand the rigors of expeditions for years. In each book, Mrs Henderson, the secretary of the Himalayan Club entered a short record of the man's service before 1937. After 1937, the leader of each expedition would write an evaluation of the man's service. The point was that a Sherpa porter couldn't now simply lose a bad reference. All his references would be in one book, and a dissatisfied or vindictive employer could wreck a man's livelihood.[6]

Pasang Kikuli must have known that, even without a bad entry in his book, what was happening on K2 was of such importance in the climbing world that good and bad versions of his conduct on the mountain would soon spread. That he felt the need of a chit also means that he was pretty sure many sahibs wouldn't believe his word about what had happened.

The next morning the weather was better. Tsering, still leery of the ice pitch, stayed in Camp 6. The other three men went up to help Wolfe down or to get a chit. Tsering waited forty-eight hours for their return, then made his own way down to Base Camp. Pasang Kikuli, Pasang Kitar, Phinsoo, and Wolfe were never seen again.

Wolfe and Phinsoo had no children. Pasang Kitar left a widow and two children. It detracts nothing from Kikuli's generosity, and his heroism, to say that he also died because he was a workingman with a wife and two children and he needed a good reference.[7]

During World War Two there were no expeditions; Darjeeling climbers found other jobs. Ang Tsering found work with a British officer who took him to the Naga tribal areas of Assam, in eastern India along the border with Burma. Ang Tsering's officer's job was to try to persuade the Nagas not to side with the advancing Japanese army. He promised them more schools, free schools, and more services. One day, while at a British army camp, Ang Tsering heard gunfire. When all the soldiers jumped into the trenches, Ang Tsering did, too. Japanese planes flew over, diving low and firing. The eerie thing about them was that they were silent – the British planes were noisy. The soldiers returned fire.

After that Ang Tsering wrote a letter to himself in Nepali. The letter stated that his father was sick and near to death, and Ang Tsering had to come home. He took the letter to his British officer.

The British officer said: You can't go. But I'll write a letter to the authorities in Darjeeling and get them to make sure that a really good doctor visits your father.

That won't work, Ang Tsering said. My father isn't in Darjeeling. He's in Solu Khumbu in Nepal, many days walk from the road.

The British officer said: You're lying. (As he told me this, Ang Tsering drew his finger across his throat, meaning – now I knew I was dead.)

What I will do, the British officer said, is give you just fifteen days' leave. But I won't give you any money, none of the wages due to you. So you'll have to come back. (As he tells me this, Ang Tsering draws his finger across his throat again.)

He took the fifteen days' leave. When he got to Darjeeling, he was so happy to be with his children – he's laughing as he talks, ninety-five years old, his whole body bobbing up and down in the stuffed armchair, his big shoulders straightening, the exuberance of life exploding up through him, eyes shining with mischief, inviting me to share the joke – 'so happy I never went back. Forget the money.'

After the war, work on the mountains picked up again. Then, on Kedarnath in 1947, the memory of Nanga Parbat drove Wangdi Norbu to a desperate act.

Wangdi Norbu was Tibetan. He almost died of altitude sickness at Everest Base Camp in 1932 and was with Drexel when he died at Camp 2 on Nanga Parbat in 1934. After that Wangdi Norbu didn't climb beyond Camp 4. As you'll recall, Merkl chose only Sherpas for the final push. Wangdi Norbu talked to the survivors, though, and what he heard and saw scarred him for life.

He was by nature a confident and swaggering man. Frank

Smythe describes below Wangdi Norbu on the expedition to Kamet in 1932, two years before Nanga Parbat. On the march in, several of the Darjeeling porters hired local people to carry their packs:

> Strolling along like Sahibs, able to pay for substitutes to carry their loads, their prestige in the valley around would be enormously enhanced; not only would the villagers offer them liquid refreshment, but they would find favour in the eyes of the village belles. I noticed that, among the Darjeeling men, Ongdi [Wangdi Norbu], who was the first to find a substitute, invariably found favour with the feminine element of the villages through which we passed, although when we looked at him we used to wonder why, for he is by no means prepossessing in appearance.[8]

But he did have charm and style. Smythe, writing five years later, said:

> He is a little fellow, all bone and wiriness, who does not carry an ounce of superfluous flesh and has one of the hardest countenances I have seen; he looks a 'tough,' but in point of fact he is sober and law abiding. He has less pronounced cheek bones than many Tibetans and his lips are thinner and firmer. His eyes are usually slightly blood-shot in the whites, which give them a ferocious, almost cruel look, but Wangdi is not cruel; he is merely hard, one of the hardest men I know. . . .
>
> Wangdi is illiterate, but in addition to his native language he can speak fluent Urdu and Nepali. He is quick and jerky in action and speech; it is as though some fire burns within him which can never properly find a vent. Like many of his race he is an excellent handy-man, but failing his kukri [carved Gurkha knife] prefers to use his teeth, and I have seen him place the recalcitrant screw of a camera tripod between [his teeth] with the screw as an axis until the latter

was loosened, then calmly spit out such pieces of his teeth as had been ground off in the process. Last, but by no means least, he is a fine climber . . . [and] never so happy as when exercising his magnificent strength and undoubted skill.[9]

On Everest in 1936, he got altitude sickness a second time and again recovered completely once he went downhill. In 1937, Wangdi Norbu was on a small expedition with Frank Smythe when news came that an avalanche had killed sixteen people on Nanga Parbat. Wangdi Norbu was upset – many of them were his friends. That night he told Smythe about Nanga Parbat. Smythe wrote:

> There is nothing that promotes an intimacy of spirit better than a campfire. He is dull and unimaginative who cannot sense the spirit of comradeship that persists within this warm circle of dancing light . . . I can see him now, cross-legged on the ground, the red firelight in his face, his lips clenching the inevitable cigarette-holder [and saying] . . . 'I have always felt that Nanga Parbat is different from other mountains. There is something in it that will kill you if it can. It is a cursed mountain. I was asked to go again this year, but I said no, I would rather come with you, because I am quite sure there will be another accident and then many lives will be lost.'[10]

In 1938 the Himalayan Club selected ten particularly distinguished Darjeeling porters, five Tibetans and five Sherpas, to honor with a special award as 'tigers.' Wangdi Norbu was one of them.

Nine years later, in 1947, he was the sardar on a small Swiss expedition to the Garwhal Himalaya. The first peak they attempted was Kedarnath, 22,770 feet.[11]

Five men formed the summit party. Andre Roch and Rene Dittert, two experienced climbers, were on one rope with the Alpine guide Alex Graven. On the other rope were Wangdi Norbu and Albert Sutter. Sutter had less experience than the others and, as so often in these situations, seems to have been the richest member of the party. Wangdi Norbu, with his immense experience, was the natural partner for Sutter.

On the final ridge leading to the summit, either Sutter or Wangdi Norbu slipped. Whichever one, and it was probably Sutter, he dragged the other off the ridge. They fell a thousand feet, tangled together. When they came to a stop, the other climbers couldn't see if they were alive or dead. Nor could they climb down directly to the two men – they had to go back down the ridge and then traverse across the face. This took some time. They finally found Sutter alive and shaken, but not badly hurt. Wangdi Norbu couldn't stand or walk. One leg was broken, and the other had been badly sliced by Sutter's crampons as the two men fell together.

The only way down for Wangdi Norbu was if the Swiss carried him. They felt too exhausted. So they made him comfortable on a ledge inside a crevasse, sheltered from the wind, and said they'd be back the next day. There is little doubt that had a Swiss been injured, Wangdi Norbu or one of the other climbers would have stayed with him in the crevasse.

The next morning Roch sent a party of Sherpas back up the mountain to rescue Wangdi Norbu. The Swiss didn't go – they slept all morning. The Sherpas found the approximate area, but were unable to locate the crevasse. Wangdi Norbu could hear them calling to him and moving around. In his weakened condition he shouted as loud as he could. But the walls of a crevasse often trap sound, and so it proved in this case. The Sherpas went back down and at one in the afternoon told the sahibs they'd been unable to find Wangdi Norbu. None of the Swiss went back up.

Wangdi Norbu was a hard man. Seventeen years before he'd been climbing alone on Kangchenjunga and fallen into a crevasse. He had spent three hours wedged helpless in that crevasse, not knowing if he would ever be found. He'd also been close to death on Everest twice. Now he had one leg broken and the other lacerated and wounded. He must have been weak, cold, and in pain. As dark came on he gave up hope. Since the Sherpas had not found him, and the sahibs had not come back for him, he thought the sahibs had left him to die. The reason for this assumption, I think, was his memory of what the sahibs had done on Nanga Parbat in 1934.

Wangdi Norbu took out his knife – the Sherpas seem to have stopped searching each other for knives after the war. Lying between the crevasse walls, he began to cut his throat. Weak as he was, it was difficult work. With his throat cut partway across, Wangdi Norbu suddenly remembered his wife and children. He decided to try to stay alive one more night for their sake and drove the knife into the wall of the crevasse.

It was a long night. He lay absolutely still, bleeding from the open wound in his neck. He hoped that if he didn't move, the blood would clot. The pain must have been excruciating.

Tenzing Norgay was a porter on that expedition. He had been down at Base Camp with another climber, but at seven that evening he reached the high camp. He was an old friend of Wangdi Norbu's. Tenzing does not say so directly in his autobiography, but reading between the lines, he was furious. He organized the Sherpas to go back up at first light. This time Tenzing took Andre Roch with him, and they found the crevasse.

The ice inside was covered in blood. Wangdi Norbu lay there, his neck red, but alive. After lifting him out of the crevasse carefully, Tenzing and the other porters carried him down the mountain, on their backs and sometimes on a stretcher. At first they moved slowly and with great care, but as they descended, they realized his neck wasn't going to open again.

They got him down to the hospital in Mussoorie. Tenzing later wrote: 'And after some time there in the hospital his injuries had healed and he was able to go home. He was never the same again, though. When I saw him later in Darjeeling it was obvious that what he had suffered had had a lasting effect, not only on his body, but on his mind. Old Tiger Wangdi never climbed again, and died in his home a few years later.'[12]

Dorjee Lhatoo went to school with Wangdi Norbu's son in Darjeeling. Dorjee says that when Wangdi Norbu came back from Kedarnath, he swore he'd never climb again, even if he had nothing to eat but water and had to beg in the streets. And none of his children, he said, would ever go work in the mountains. None of them ever did.

With Wangdi Norbu incapacitated, the Swiss had to find a new sardar. They offered the job to Tenzing. A new era in climbing had begun.

Chapter Eleven

TENZING MEETS THE GUIDES

Tenzing Norgay was different from other Sherpa climbers. Tenzing himself said the difference was that where other men had two lungs, it seemed as if he had three. The higher the altitude, the stronger he became. But people who knew him emphasize two other things – willpower and intelligence.

If Da Thundu was a quiet man, never pushing himself forward, Tenzing was the opposite. As a boy he always dreamed of greatness. In 1933 he joined the lineup of men looking for work on that year's British expedition to Everest. He was devastated when he was not chosen. The other Sherpas told him to relax, he was only eighteen, too young for the mountains. But he was burning for the experience. Two years later he tried to get on the next Everest expedition. He had no experience, and no chits, and was not taken. But this time Eric Shipton needed two last-minute replacements. All the hopefuls lined up. Without speaking to them, just by eye, Shipton picked out Tenzing and one other man. On that expedition, and every one that followed, Tenzing went as high as any other porter.

Willpower and strength, though, would not have mattered without intelligence. It wasn't just that Tenzing had fire inside. He knew how to make his dreams reality. Every sahib who worked with Tenzing commented on his brains. The Sherpas who knew him best say he was the smartest man they had ever met.

Nawang Gombu was seventeen when he first climbed with his uncle Tenzing on Everest in 1953. He later became the first person to climb Everest twice and worked under Tenzing at the Himalayan Mountaineering Institute in Darjeeling for twenty years. Gombu says he would be working along with Tenzing and something unexpected would come up. Tenzing would do something about it, and then a bit later that would turn out to be a brilliant thing to have done. Gombu would realize that Tenzing had figured out months before what was likely to happen, had worked out a plan, and knew what the results of his plan would be. 'Like this,' Gombu says. He holds his right arm out as far as he can, raises one finger, and squints to stare at the finger. 'Tenzing was always thinking ahead.'

Tenzing first became a sardar just as the Alpine guides came to the Himalayas. They changed climbing, Sherpas, and Tenzing.

When the first British climbers came to the Alps in the nineteenth century, they employed local farmers to guide them up the mountains.[1] Like the Sherpas, these villagers feared the mountains and had never climbed them. But, again like the Sherpas, some of them saw a good living and taught themselves, and their sons and grandsons, the necessary skills. Being a mountain guide became a trade, usually confined to a local guild. From 1950 on, the best of these Alpine guides came to the Himalayas. The Sherpas had never seen anyone like them. They made it possible for Tenzing to imagine his own greatness.

The impact of the guides on the Sherpas was immense for two reasons. First, the guides were working men themselves and treated the Sherpas like equals. Second, until then Himalayan climbing had been dominated by gentlemen. Two examples, one British and one American, will illustrate this.

In 1921, George Finch was probably the most accomplished Alpinist in Britain, an obvious choice for the Everest expedition that year. However, there was a nervous feeling in the Alpine Club that he was not quite a gentleman. For one thing, he had been born in Australia. He had not attended a British public school, Oxford, or Cambridge. Instead, he had been raised on the continent of Europe by a rich but bohemian mother. Finch did have a Ph.D. from a Swiss university and a lectureship in chemistry at Imperial College, London. It was not enough. He was thrown off the 1921 expedition team after failing a medical checkup that many thought was fixed.

This created a small scandal, and there was considerable pressure to include Finch on the 1922 expedition. One of the people selecting the team approached George Mallory privately. He asked how Mallory would feel sharing a tent with a man like Finch. Mallory replied that he would sleep with anybody if it increased the chances of climbing Everest. Finch was accepted.

Because he had a job, Finch was late joining the expedition in Tibet. Before he arrived, the deputy leader, Lieutenant Colonel E. L. Strutt, saw a photograph of George Finch in a magazine. The photo showed Finch apparently repairing his own climbing boots – performing manual labor *in public*. 'I always knew the fellow was a shit,' Strutt said.[2]

Similar, although more polite, class distinctions existed in American climbing. We will take the example of Paul Petzoldt on K2 in 1938.[3]

Petzoldt started climbing alone at the age of nine, on the walls of the Snake River Canyon near the family ranch in Idaho. When he was fourteen, his widowed mother lost the ranch, and Petzoldt left school and began seven years of hitching and bumming – riding the railway freight cars without paying. His proud wife, Patricia, later boasted that 'one time he even caught the Twentieth Century Limited out of Chicago. This is recognized among bums as an almost impossible feat.'[4]

By the time Petzoldt was twenty-two he had summer work out of Jackson Hole as a mountain guide in the Wyoming Tetons. He put himself through two years of college with money from guiding, washing dishes, playing poker, and golf hustling.

The dean of Windsor Castle came climbing in the Tetons and invited Petzoldt to visit. Petzoldt saved, hitched, rode the rails to New York, and begged passage on an ocean liner. He enjoyed Windsor Castle, played golf, and read a lot. Petzoldt loved books. He'd started going into libraries to get out of the cold when he was bumming, found they didn't throw you out if you pretended you were reading, and soon got hooked.

From Windsor Castle he rode his bicycle to the Alps. Petzoldt couldn't afford lodgings, so he camped out in the mountains. The Swiss climbers in the nearby hut sent two young men to find out what was wrong with him. Patricia wrote that 'when the two young men discovered they were speaking with an American they were really alarmed. For most rich Americans – and they all appeared to be rich – had one guide ahead to pull, another to push, and one to carry the lunch.

'They assured Paul that mountain climbing was a very dangerous sport and that he must not attempt it without a guide.'[5]

That week Petzoldt climbed the Matterhorn twice in one day, up one side, down the other, back up and back down.

He wrote to Patricia, a college girl he'd met in Wyoming, and asked her to marry him. She thought it over for a few seconds and wrote back to say yes. He replied, 'Darling, you may have a hard time with me. I haven't much to offer you in the way of material things. I'm not even sure that you will always have enough to eat. But I know we'll have a wonderful life. There are so many interesting things for us to do together.'[6]

They skied, worked on dude ranches, and climbed and guided in the Grand Tetons. One winter she got cabin fever in Jackson Hole and went home. Her mother saw Patricia coming up the path and got worried. Patricia reassured her that 'as a married woman I considered myself a howling success.'[7]

The couple were in Mexico in 1938 when Paul got a telegram asking him to join the American expedition to K2. William Loomis had dropped out of the expedition and recommended Petzoldt as his replacement. Loomis also offered to pay Petzoldt's share of the expenses. He could never have gone otherwise. The other four climbers were all rich men with Ivy League educations.

It was Paul's dream – the Himalayas. Patricia, like any climbing wife, was afraid.

Paul spent some money on film for his movie camera and left the rest for Patricia. In New York he discovered that Loomis's money had gone into the expedition kitty, which paid for Paul's fare and meals and nothing else. For the voyage out on ocean liners, and the whole time in India, Petzoldt refused invitations to bridge or drinks because he could not buy his own. He worried that he seemed curt and unsociable. But he couldn't bring himself to tell these rich men about his situation.

The gulf between Paul Petzoldt and the other four climbers was enormous. Patricia explains:

> Remember this was 1938, and mountain climbing was still not widely popular in the United States. The American Alpine Club, composed of a relatively small group of people, most of whom lived in the eastern part of the United States, dominated the climbing scene. It was a rather exclusive club. . . . By far the greater majority of them agreed implicitly with the British tradition. . . . The early literature of British mountain climbing assumed that only those of a certain class were privileged to establish a climbing reputation. The early literature never compared the ability of the 'gentleman' and the 'guide.' Regardless of how much more skilled the guide might be, or even if the gentleman had to be pulled or pushed most of the way, it was always the gentleman who climbed the mountain. If he had a famous and skilled guide, that fact was mentioned only as another valuable piece of judgment in choosing him, as one would applaud the climber's judgment in picking a strong rope or the right pair of shoes.
>
> A good many Americans, who fostered these preposterous ideas, would have been highly embarrassed had they been reminded that they themselves were not 'gentlemen' by British standards.

Later Paul discovered that there had been some doubt expressed in the club as to whether he would be able to adjust himself socially to the rest of the party. The fact that he was a professional, a guide, had been questioned; and then of course he was a Westerner and, although he was known to have had some education, he had not attended an Ivy League college. But finally practical considerations won out. The group realized perfectly the advantages they were getting in a climber whose great skill and tremendous endurance had won him, among the elite of mountain climbers, a very fine reputation. Not to mention the fact that his years of continuous climbing as a guide would certainly be of value.[8]

Once they began the march to K2, Petzoldt did something no other climber had ever done. There were five Sherpa porters from Darjeeling on the expedition, including Pasang Kikuli. Because Paul was a working guide, he could see what they needed. So he 'started a climbing school for the Sherpa porters. Although all of them had mountaineering experience, they had not acquired the necessary skills that go with acrobatic climbing. Paul showed them how to drive pitons, how to use carabiners, and how to rappel. He made a game of the climbing school, using the canyon walls for practice, and the Sherpas took to it eagerly.'[9]

And once they got to the mountain, of course, Petzoldt climbed higher than anybody else.

The British climber Tom Longstaff and the Italian Duke of Abruzzi had both brought Alpine guides to work for them in the Himalayas before World War One. Between the wars, guides like Paul Petzoldt on K2 and Peter Aschenbrenner on Nanga Parbat were isolated exceptions. But in 1950 the French came to Annapurna. The leader, Maurice Herzog, was from Chamonix, at the foot of Mont Blanc. Three of the climbers – Louis Lachenal, Gaston Rebuffat, and Lionel Terray – were professional guides from Chamonix. They set the tone for the whole expedition and taught the Sherpas how to climb ice and rock.

On the march up to Annapurna Base Camp, they had to cross the Mristi Khola River. A slip might send a man tumbling downstream to his death. Herzog 'spotted some tree-trunks which the others had placed the day before, but our coolies refused to venture on them with their loads. Rebuffat and I did not hesitate: we would take the stuff over ourselves. Now Rebuffat was transformed into a porter; he had the straps supporting the containers placed round his forehead, and his head, his neck and his long body swayed dangerously.'[10]

But he made it across.

I asked Khansa of Namche who was the best foreigner he ever climbed with. Lionel Terray, he said. They worked together on Makalu in 1956, and what Khansa liked about Terray was that he taught the Sherpas all the way up the mountain. I said that Terray was a guide, and that the grandfathers of the guides had been farmers like the Sherpas when the climbers first came. Khansa said all the Sherpas knew that, and they loved that the French had learned from their ancestors how to carry weight on the head strap.

Higher up on Annapurna the sahibs carried loads of forty-five pounds each. Herzog wrote later:

Our breathing was short and uneven as we approached the 20,000 feet level.

'We're not Sherpas,' said Lachenal bitterly.

'We didn't come to the Himalaya to be beasts of burden,' growled Rebuffat.

Terray was stung to answer:

'A climber ought to be able to carry his gear,' he said, 'we're as good as the Sherpas, aren't we?'

Lachenal was bent over his ice-axe, Rebuffat had flopped down on his rucksack. Their faces were scarlet and running with sweat; they didn't usually show their feelings, but they looked really angry.

'If we wear ourselves out now with this ridiculous porterage, how on earth shall we manage in a few days' time.

It isn't the Sherpas who'll be making a safe route through the seracs.'

At this, Terray saw red:

'And you call yourselves Chamonix guides! Just bad amateurs, that's what you are.'[11]

Ang Tharkay was the sardar on Annapurna. Ajiba, Ang Tsering's younger brother, was one of the Sherpas. And so, of course, was Da Thundu, now forty-three years old. He made it to 23,500 feet.

As the pitches on Annapurna got steeper, Herzog and Terray kept pushing the Sherpas into the lead. Da Thundu and the rest, at the edge of their competence, kept trying to give the lead back. This was, on both sides, the exact opposite of what normally happened. On one steep pitch Herzog led Da Thundu and Angdawa, knowing that if any of them slipped all three were gone. A British, German, or American climber would have fixed ropes. Herzog treated the Sherpas like the guides they were, both honoring and terrifying them.

Ang Tharkay and Sarki were the strongest Sherpas, carrying to Camp 5. There Herzog

had a brief conversation with Angtharkay in our pidgin-English.

'Tomorrow morning Lachenal Sahib and Bara Sahib go to the summit of Annapurna.'

'Yes, sir.'

'You are the Sirdar and the most experienced of all the Sherpas. I should be very glad if you will come with us?'

'Thank you, sir.'

'We must share the victory! Will you come?'

At that moment I felt it my duty to take into consideration the Sherpas' very understandable feelings. After a pause Angtharkay replied. He was grateful for the choice of action I had given him, but he held back:

'Thank you very much, Bara Sahib, but my feet are beginning to freeze. . . .'

'I see.'

'And I prefer to go down to Camp IV.'

'Of course, Angtharkay, it's as you like. In that case go down at once because it is too late.'

'Thank you, sir.'

In a second their sacks were packed and, just as they were setting off, they turned round and I could guess their anxiety at leaving us alone.

'Salaam, sir. Good luck!'

'Salaam – and be careful.'

A few minutes later two black dots were on their way down the slope we had just come up. How oddly their minds worked. Here were these two men, proverbial for their trustworthiness and devotion, who quite certainly enjoyed going high on the mountains, and yet, when on the point of reaping the fruits of their labors, they prudently held back. But I don't doubt that our mentality struck them as even odder.[12]

Ang Tharkay thought that Herzog and Lachenal were quite likely to die and didn't want to perish with them. Also, frostbite was beginning in his feet. In the event, both men got to the summit, but were badly frostbitten on the way down and almost died. Ang Tharkay felt guilty then and wished he had gone with them. But his judgment had also been confirmed.

Tenzing Norgay, on the other hand, would have gone with them.

Two years later Tenzing got his chance on Everest.

In 1950 the Chinese army invaded Tibet. After that, only Russian or Chinese expeditions could get permission for the old route up Everest. But in 1950 a revolution in Nepal threw out the Ranas, the old feudal rulers and Britain's allies. There was now in place a very limited democracy under a king. The old government had closed off Nepal from the world to keep out democratic ideas. The new government opened the borders. Everest could now be climbed from the south.

The British assumed it was still their mountain. From aerial

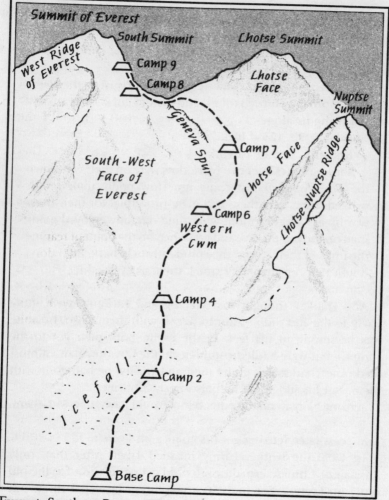

Everest, Southern Route, 1952–3

photographs, one route looked possible. They saw a four-mile-long, relatively flat glacier they called the Western Cwm. (*Cwm*, pronounced *koom*, is the Welsh word for 'valley'.) On one side of the Cwm was Everest, and on the other side was a long ridge between the great peaks of Lhotse and Nuptse. A steep wall of ice and snow was at the head of the Cwm, but it looked possible to climb. At the top of that wall was a plateau they called the South Col. The Col was the low point in a ridge that ran down from the summit of Everest and then back up to Lhotse. That ridge too seemed climbable.

The difficulty was getting into the Cwm. At the lower end a massive, tangled icefall blocked the entrance. It looked dangerous indeed. In 1951 the Himalayan Committee in London, the successor to the old Mount Everest Committee, sent an expedition led by Shipton to see if the Icefall was possible.

They didn't make it through the Icefall. Ang Tharkay, who was the sardar, thought nobody ever would. Shipton reported back to London that it could probably be crossed, but to supply a large expedition teams of Sherpa porters would have to ferry loads across it again and again. As the Icefall moved, it would sooner or later lead to deaths. Shipton had his doubts that any mountain was worth those lives.

But the Himalayan Committee in London wanted Everest and decided on a full-scale assault the next year. Then they discovered, to their shock, that the Nepali government was rationing permits for Everest to one expedition a year, and the 1952 permit had gone to the Swiss.

The British decided to send Shipton back in 1952 to climb Cho Oyu, the world's ninth-highest mountain and Everest's neighbor in Khumbu. That would give them practice. In the meantime, in the nicest possible way, they hoped that the Swiss would fail.

It was a stroke of luck for Tenzing that the Swiss had the permit. Two of the Swiss climbers chosen for Everest, Roche and Dittert, had been in the Garwhal Himalaya with Tenzing when he first became sardar after Wangdi Norbu's accident. Now they wanted him as sardar on Everest. He jumped at the chance.[13]

Ang Tharkay refused to go and bet Tenzing twenty rupees they wouldn't even get through the icefall.

Tenzing had difficulty recruiting all the porters he wanted because the men who had come back the year before had spoken bitterly about Shipton's expedition. Many of the Nepali low-altitude porters had not been paid their full wages. There was an argument over a camera the sahibs claimed had been stolen. And the Sherpa high-altitude porters had received no tips at the end of the expedition. Tips were customary, even on treks, and an experienced mountaineer like Shipton knew it.

But Tenzing finally found 'thirteen good men.'[14] One was his old friend Da Thundu, now forty-six, a veteran of Nanga Parbat, K2, and Annapurna. Another was Ajiba, Ang Tsering's younger brother, not the smartest of the family, but a big man and tough.

It took the expedition sixteen days to walk from Kathmandu to Namche, across the lay of the land, up hill and down all the way – there was no road in 1952. The Swiss were a wonderful surprise to the Darjeeling porters. Four years later Tenzing explained why he preferred them to the British. He did not dislike the British, he said:

I have climbed more with the British than with any other people, and been happy with them; and some . . . I have counted among my close and dear friends. But . . . the British in general are more reserved and formal than the men of most other countries whom I have known; and especially this is so because they have so long been rulers in the East, or perhaps it is only something in their own nature. But it is a thing which we Sherpas have had much chance to observe, since we have climbed, in recent years, with men of so many nations. With the Swiss and the French I had been treated as a comrade, an equal, in a way that was not possible for the British. They are kind men; they are brave; they are fair and just, always. But always, too, there is a line between them and the outsiders, between sahibs and employee, and to such Easterners as we Sherpas, who have experienced the world of 'no line' [with the Swiss], this can be a difficulty and a problem.[15]

It should be said that the formality and reserve Tenzing mentions were characteristic only of that small minority of British people who belong to the upper class. The rest of the British people have always resembled Ringo Starr and John Lennon more than Bertie Wooster and Hugh Grant. By 1951 a new generation of working- and middle-class British climbers were driving fresh routes up the rocks of Wales and Scotland. It would be a few years before the first of them arrived in the Himalayas. But there were individual exceptions to the stiff-upper-lip stereotype even then – Ang Tsering says that what he liked about George Mallory was that the man was so friendly.

However, in general the difference was striking to the Sherpas. The Swiss climber Tenzing was most drawn to was Raymond Lambert. Lambert, like the French climbers on Annapurna, was an Alpine guide. When the Swiss climbers reached Tengboche monastery in Khumbu, the abbot and monks held a formal reception for them, serving Tibetan tea with melted butter.

Butter tea is more than just a delicacy in Sherpa country. It's the paradigmatic food of hospitality. When guests come, you say in special formal language, 'Sit, sit,' and then, 'Butter tea?' In the ordinary run of things, most Sherpas used to drink tea with salt, and no milk or butter. For poor people everywhere in the world, fat is a luxury food, and especially welcome in very cold places. Tea with salt and butter was a treat.

No travel book on Tibet or Nepal is complete without the ritual sneer at what is always called tea with rancid yak butter. In fact, butter does not go off in Tibet – the country is a natural refrigerator. But I have heard many tourists in Khumbu say they have tried that tea with rancid butter, when I knew the butter wasn't off.

Sherpa hosts always offered me butter tea. In polite formal Sherpa, it isn't possible to use any other word for tea, even when all you have is Indian tea with milk. Then my hosts would check, carefully, that I really meant I wanted Tibetan butter tea. When I said yes and drank it, they were pleased and told me they were surprised.

True to form, all but one of the Swiss climbers refused to drink the tea the monks poured for them. The exception was Raymond Lambert. He drank his, smiled politely, and then drank the cups poured for every one of his companions. He won Tenzing's heart.

This didn't necessarily mean that Lambert liked butter tea. What it meant was that he felt Sherpa hosts should be treated with the same politeness he would show to people in his own country.

Lambert spoke no Hindi or Nepali, and hardly any English. Tenzing said that therefore 'our conversations were mostly with the hands; but after a while we grew to understand each other very well.'[16]

There was another reason the Darjeeling men warmed to the Swiss. In 1952, Tenzing's nephew Nawang Gombu was sixteen and still living in his home village of Thame. He went to Everest Base Camp to visit his uncle. Gombu says what really impressed the Sherpa porters that year was the quality of the clothing and equipment the Swiss brought – much better than the British had ever used. Unlike the earlier expeditions, the Swiss provided exactly the same gear for high-altitude porters as they used themselves.

For the villagers in Khumbu, the Swiss expedition was like having the circus come to town. When the climbers arrived in Namche, people came from all over, and most had never seen white people before. Mingma Chering was a teenager in Khumjung then and remembers standing in a crowd staring silently at the sahibs in their camp. It was fascinating, he says. No one in the crowd moved or spoke. He was there for hours and got a bad cramp in his neck from staring.

It was an emotional moment for Tenzing. His father was dead, and he had not seen his mother since he'd left home. Now here she was, in front of him, holding one of her grandchildren in her arms. 'After eighteen years, we held each other.'[17]

For all the Darjeeling Sherpas, it was the best way to go home.

Most of them had been poor boys when they'd left, of little account. Now they had money, jobs, and glamor. Older men in Khumbu remember how sophisticated the Darjeeling men looked, how sharp their clothes were, and how they swaggered through the villages. There was endless home-brewed *chang* with relatives and friends. They were a young woman's dream, and they knew what to do about that.

The expedition made Base Camp and went into the icefall. 'It was like finding your way through a white jungle,' Tenzing said, but they did it. 'Aha, Angtharkay,' he thought, 'that's twenty rupees you owe me.'

They put Camp 3 at the top of the Icefall. Tenzing supervised the ferrying of the loads through the Icefall, with help from Sarki, Ajiba, and Da Thundu. For three weeks, they worked their way up the Western Cwm, which the Swiss called the Valley of Silence. Tenzing grew closer to Lambert. They shared a tent often, as sahibs had not done with him before. Whatever happened, good or bad, Lambert would say, 'Ça va bien,' the French for 'It's going well.' Tenzing began to say it back to him.

Camp 5 was set up at the head of the Western Cwm. The shortest route to the South Col was straight up a four-thousand-foot rib of rock that they called the Geneva Spur. Confident Alpinists, up the Swiss went. All along, they had let the more skilled among the Sherpas take turns in the lead, finding and making the route. 'I was working mainly with Lambert,' Tenzing said. 'No one had ordered it that way. It had just seemed to happen. And I was happy about it, for we got along fine and made a strong team.'[18]

It hadn't just happened. Tenzing was thinking ahead again, making himself the climbing partner of the man most likely to be chosen for a summit attempt. This time, finally, Tenzing knew he had a chance at the summit. The Swiss had made him a climbing 'member' of the expedition, just like the sahibs, as well as sardar. He felt it was the greatest honor he'd ever received, and 'in my heart I swore I would prove myself worthy.'

By late May they had pushed the route almost all the way up

the Geneva Spur to the South Col. The summit team was chosen: Aubert, Flory, Lambert, and Tenzing.

Those four men set off with six porters from the Western Cwm up the Geneva Spur to the South Col. An hour into the climb, Ang Tsering's brother Ajiba said he had a fever and had to go down. The others shared out his load.

After eight hours Ang Norbu and Mingma Dorje dropped their loads and said they were finished and afraid of frostbite. Tenzing tried to argue with them, but the sahibs said the porters had done as much as they could. Tenzing knew they were right. That high, in that situation, you had to let people make their own decisions. If you don't, they may die.

Ang Norbu and Mingma Dorje descended. The remaining seven men divided up what they could of the two loads, leaving a lot of supplies behind in the snow. They climbed for ten hours, into the dark. At 7 P.M. they realized they wouldn't reach the Col that night and dug out a flat, temporary bivouac for two tents.

The tents were designed to hold two men each. There were three sahibs in one and four Sherpas in the other, and no space for sleeping bags. The wind threatened to blow them off. Lambert drove his ice ax into the snow and tied himself to it, just in case. In each tent they huddled together, piling on top of each other for warmth, too cold to sleep all night.

At first light the weather was good, and they could see the Col was close. The three sahibs and Tenzing started up. Phu Tharkay and Da Namgyal went down to get the loads Ang Norbu and Mingma Dorje had dumped the afternoon before. Pasang Phutar Jockey said he would wait for them. (This was a different Pasang Phutar from the man we have met before who lost seven fingers to frostbite. Pasang Phutar Jockey was a small man and rode horses in the races at Darjeeling.)

At ten in the morning the three Swiss and Tenzing reached the South Col, at 25,850 feet. Tenzing was ecstatic. They were close. He handed his rucksack to the Swiss climbers and went back down to see what had happened to the three Sherpas.

They were all down at the temporary bivouac. Phu Tharkay

and Da Namgyal had fetched the loads, but then stopped. Pasang Phutar Jockey was in his tent groaning. He told Tenzing:

'I'm ill and I'm going to die.'

'No, you're not,' I answered. 'You're going to be all right. You're going to get up and carry a load to the South Col.'

He said he couldn't. I said he must. We argued, and I swore at him, and then I began slapping and kicking him to prove to him he wasn't dead. For it was a different thing now from when the others had turned back below. If the loads did not get up to the col the three sahibs there would surely die. And if I left Pasang where he was he too would surely die – and this time not only in his imagination. He was ill, yes. . . . But he could still move, and he had to move.

Tenzing finally got Pasang Phutar Jockey on his feet, then led him, Phu Tharkay, and Da Namgyal up to the South Col. All three men were shattered when they got there. They erected a tent and crawled into it. Tenzing went back down to the temporary bivouac and brought up another load of food and gear. When he'd brought that up to the Col and was still feeling fine, he went down and got another load.

Tenzing was now functioning as a climber, a sardar, and four porters. There was a selfless part to what he did – Tenzing very much wanted the expedition to succeed. But he was also making it clear that he was the strongest man on the Col.

That night he shared a two-man tent with Lambert. In the morning they knew they still had to make one camp higher on the summit ridge, halfway to the top. But Tenzing could see that Pasang Phutar Jockey was now very sick, and Phu Tharkay and Da Namgyal were 'not much better.' The Swiss offered Da Namgyal and Phu Tharkay a money bonus if they would carry one camp higher. Both men said they couldn't and begged Tenzing to stay and help them down. He said no, he was determined. So they stood Jockey up, tied him into a rope with Phu Tharkay and Da Namgyal, and those three started down. Without their loads, it would be difficult or impossible to stock the high camp above the South Col with enough for a summit attempt. Tenzing was not confident.

The summit was just over three thousand feet above the Col. Flory, Aubert, Lambert, and Tenzing started up the summit ridge, carrying light packs. There was one two-man tent in those packs, no sleeping bags, and food for only one day. Tenzing thought the sahibs were planning to have a look at the route, leave the tent and a few supplies at a campsite, then come back down. When they had more porters, they would stock those camps properly. Tenzing had ascended the Geneva Spur with the six strongest porters he had. Now he didn't know who else he could get up, but he kept his mouth shut.

The men climbing now were the four who had been selected for the summit attempt. They were using oxygen cylinders for the first time. The closed-circuit sets only allowed them to breathe when they were standing still or sitting down. This was almost useless. On they climbed, slowly, hour after hour.

Two thousand feet above the Col, just over a thousand feet below the summit, they knew they could go no higher that day. But Tenzing could see the weather was ideal for a summit attempt, and he and Lambert were both going well. He saw a possible campsite, pointed to it, and said to Lambert, 'Sahib, we ought to stay here tonight.' Lambert smiled back at Tenzing, and both men knew what the other was thinking. The three sahibs talked. They agreed that Flory and Aubert would go down, and Tenzing and Lambert would stay in the tent and try for the summit the next morning.

Willpower, strength, intelligence, and knowing when to keep his mouth shut had brought Tenzing to this place, to his chance. But he could never have done it if the Swiss hadn't treated him as an equal, and if Lambert hadn't been his friend. The two men set up the tent. The weather was beautiful, and they sat outside together, looking at the view. They couldn't talk much because of the language problem, but Tenzing didn't mind. 'Once I pointed up, and said in English, "Tomorrow – you and I." And Lambert grinned and said, "Ça va bien!"'

That night they had no sleeping bags – the consequence of carrying such light packs. They thought that if they slept, they would die. So they stayed awake, lying 'close together, slapping and rubbing each other, to keep the circulation going.' Tenzing kept warm this way, but he worried that Lambert was 'so big and husky that I could warm only a small bit of him at a time.' Lambert was worried about Tenzing. The Swiss climber had had all his toes amputated after frostbite in the Alps. Now he said to Tenzing, 'For me it is all right. I have no toes. But you hang on to yours.' Tenzing was touched.

In the morning it was cloudy and the wind was rising. They hesitated and looked at each other, not speaking. 'Lambert jerked his thumb at the ridge with a wink, and I nodded, smiling.' They went up, very slowly.

Lambert and Tenzing had slept one of the last three nights. Their oxygen sets worked only when they rested, so they stopped often. It seemed steep, and in places both men crawled upward on their hands and knees. They took turns in the lead, so the other could rest. Lambert said something, and Tenzing couldn't hear it. Soon, he repeated it, and Tenzing saw he was smiling.

'Ça va bien,' Lambert was saying.

'Ça va bien,' Tenzing replied.

But he knew it wasn't.

Tenzing thought of home, his wife and children. He thought they would not make it, and a second team of Swiss climbers would. He thought, no, they had to do it. He stopped thinking and climbed like a machine. Just ahead of him, Lambert stopped. Tenzing could see he was thinking whether to go on. Tenzing was too tired to think. He left it up to Lambert. They had climbed six hundred and fifty feet in five hours. They were still seven hundred feet below the summit. If they went on, they might make it. But they wouldn't get back alive.

They turned round.

The Swiss didn't climb Everest that spring. They decided to send another expedition in the fall.

The British had the permit for 1953, and the Swiss thought they'd probably make it. In the nicest possible way, the Swiss wished to prevent that. Nobody had ever tried to climb Everest in the fall. Now people do it all the time, but then it was thought that winter would come too quickly. This time the Swiss felt there was no alternative. Four of the Swiss climbers were new, but Lambert was back, and so was Tenzing.

The icefall was all right again. But the Western Cwm, which the Swiss had called the Valley of Silence, was full, all the time, of the roar of the wind. They began climbing the Geneva Spur. On October 31 twelve men were climbing together when a small avalanche of ice fell on them. Eleven of them pressed themselves into the wall of the Spur. Mingma Dorje probably looked up. A dagger of ice sliced into his face, and he collapsed unconscious.

Several men began lowering him carefully down the steep ice. Aila, Norbu, and Mingma Hrita were coming down on another rope. Maybe they were unnerved by the accident. In any case, one of them slipped and all of them fell, tumbling down two hundred yards.

Finally, all four men were brought to Camp 5, at the foot of the Geneva Spur, and laid on air mattresses. Mingma Hrita had a broken collarbone. Aila and Norbu were only bruised. But Mingma Dorje, in addition to his face, had a spear of ice stuck through his chest. He was dead a few hours later.

The Sherpas, Tenzing said, were 'badly upset.' But so were the Swiss. So they did something quite new in Himalayan climbing. They asked Tenzing to question the porters if they wanted to continue the expedition. If a majority wanted to go on, the Swiss would go on. If a majority wanted to call off the expedition, the Swiss would do that.

The porters met with Tenzing and talked 'far into the night.' Tenzing said 'no one . . . was very happy. Some were very pessimistic. . . . But in the end they all agreed that they could not let their sahibs down.'[19]

The Swiss were intelligent employers. Had they ordered the porters to continue, possibly nobody would have obeyed. The tactic worked because behind it was as much decency as calculation.

Mingma Dorje was the first person to die on Everest in eighteen years. He was buried in the Valley of Silence. The Swiss and the Sherpas gave up on the Geneva Spur as too dangerous. They tried another route, up the less steep slopes on the Lhotse Face and then across to the South Col. But the weather worsened, and they had to turn back, leaving the field open for the British the next year.

I asked Nawang Gombu why his uncle Tenzing was the first Sherpa to get to the top of a great peak. Why was he driven, in a way other Sherpas of his generation were not? I said some people told me it was because Tenzing had grown up poor and didn't truly care if he lived or died. Other people said it was ambition.

No, Nawang Gombu said, it was Raymond Lambert. When you work with people of a new kind and become friends with them, it changes your idea of who you are, Gombu said. You say to yourself, I can be a person like that. That's what happened to Tenzing. Raymond Lambert treated him as a friend and an equal, and Tenzing said to himself, I can be Raymond Lambert.

This is not something that Tenzing ever said to Gombu. But all the way up Everest in 1953, Tenzing confided in Gombu, perhaps because he was kin, perhaps because he was only a boy. And later Gombu came to know Tenzing as well as anybody.

I think he's right. And there's no doubt that Tenzing Norgay loved Raymond Lambert.

Chapter Twelve

THE TRIBULATIONS OF A SARDAR

The Swiss and their porters marched out from Everest to Kathmandu in December. Galtzen of Namche was worried. In later life he became a successful trader between Nepal and Tibet, but in 1952 he had never made more than a rupee a day. Now Tenzing had given him a job as sardar in charge of the low-altitude porters.

It was a big opportunity, but also a headache. Before they set off back to Kathmandu, Tenzing had sent a Sherpa named Pemba down from Base Camp to hire porters. Pemba had drunk quite a lot on his way down the valley and rather lost track of what he was doing. So he told everybody he met to turn up at Base Camp for work. When the time came, more people were at Base Camp than the Swiss had promised to pay. Galtzen and Tenzing didn't feel they could send away people who had come so far. They went to the Swiss and sorted it out.

So far, so good. As soon as they started out, Galtzen discovered that five more young Sherpa women had been added to his payroll as porters. They were the new girlfriends of five of the Darjeeling porters (not Tenzing). They were carrying loads all right, and they needed the money, but Galtzen couldn't see how he was going to meet their wages. He couldn't see how he was going to explain it to the Swiss, either. He would have liked to fire the women politely, but their boyfriends were tough men. They all intimidated him, and one was really scary.

So he just worried. He might have to meet their wages from his own. And he could see Tenzing was at the end of his tether. In those days most sardars drank. They could afford *rakshi* liquor after a lifetime of *chang* beer. The job told on a man's nerves. But Tenzing was drinking hard indeed. He carried a flask of *rakshi* in his pocket and kept stopping for a swig. Galtzen says – You know how American trekkers are now with their water bottles on a hot day? Tenzing was drinking liquor like that.

Tenzing's view of himself, and what he could do, had changed so much. And then he couldn't do it. He had been so near, and yet so far. On two major expeditions in one year, he had been both sardar and climber. The two jobs pulled against each other, all the time. The sardar was supposed to stay back, manage, and work hard. He was the place in the structure where all the hassles met. The climber was supposed to lead, to break trail, but also to rest and conserve himself for the summit. Tenzing was exhausted.

Ang Tsering was with Galtzen and Tenzing as the expedition walked out from Base Camp to Kathmandu after the failure of the second Swiss attempt. In recent years Ang Tsering had developed a speciality as head cook on treks and expeditions. The work allowed him to travel and be part of the old life and paid reasonably. On this fall expedition he was the head cook.

About halfway to Kathmandu, they all stopped one night at a village where Tenzing had an auntie. She served *chang*, there was a party, and everybody got drunk. As often at Sherpa parties, tempers exploded. Ang Tsering's brother Ajiba attacked Tenzing with an ice ax.

Why? There was certainly a lot of tension between Tenzing and Ajiba. Dorjee Lhatoo remembers an exciting fight in Darjeeling between Tenzing and Ajiba at around the same time. Dorjee was a small boy in Darjeeling then, and the Sherpa community held a New Year picnic. They were on the ridge near Observatory Hill, where the British had made a park with a fireplace for barbecues. Dorjee and the other small boys were harassing monkeys with their slingshots. It was fun, and absorbing. Suddenly there was a great shout. Dorjee Lhatoo turned round and there was Ajiba, a big man, arms above his head like a weight lifter at full stretch, holding Tenzing suspended. Everything stopped, and Ajiba threw Tenzing down the steep hill. Tenzing crashed through the trees. There was a moment of total hush. Nobody was sure if Tenzing was alive or dead. Then many people hurtled down through the trees to find out. They brought Tenzing back, bruised but very alive.

From a small boy's point of view, it got better. The adults were all drunk, as they usually were on New Year. The men immediately began to take sides with Ajiba or Tenzing and hit each other. Even better, when one man hit another, their wives faced off. But they didn't just trade blows. They insulted each other. One would bare her breasts and private parts and flourish them in the other's face, shouting obscenities. What was wonderful, the now middle-aged Dorjee Lhatoo says, was that back then women wore no underwear.

Now a fourth set of fights started. Every time a woman flashed her privates, the other children would tease her sons, disparaging the appearance of their mother's bits. The boys, ashamed, would strike out at their tormentors. Then all the other children would have to take sides, and knots of flailing kids swirled around the pummeling men and shouting women.

That was a great party.

At Sherpa New Year parties in Namche now, drunken people still fight over land, debts, business deals, and jealousies. Sometimes this is jealousy over a current affair. More often, somebody has been festering over an affair his wife had twenty years ago when he was away working on a trek. When the drink gets to him, he starts needling his old rival.

Galtzen thought the fight between Ajiba and Tenzing in 1952 was over a woman. Perhaps it was. Today the sexual rules among Sherpas are quite similar to those in Europe and the Americas.

People ought to be faithful, but sometimes they cheat. If and when anybody finds out, everybody's hurt. When a man comes home from trekking or climbing work today, a helpful relative or neighbor may tell him that his wife has been seeing somebody while he was away, and he seethes. Wives, on the other hand, look carefully at the husband's sleeping bag when he gets home. Woe betide him if she finds the wrong sort of hair in there. This similarity between Sherpa and Western ways is one of the reasons that so many Sherpa men and women have married visiting foreigners.

But Dorjee Lhatoo points out that fifty years ago Europeans were more reserved than they are now, and Sherpas were more relaxed. He connects this to the equality that has always existed between Sherpa and Tibetan women and men.

It would be wrong to say that Sherpa women are not oppressed. But Sherpa relationships were, and are, strikingly more equal than those among Nepalis and Indians of the plains. They are also more equal than those among men and women of the professional classes in the United States. Sherpa husbands and wives are companions. In 1995 I stayed in a small Sherpa-run tourist lodge in Nepal during the summer monsoon. The husband was home from trekking work, and there were no tourists but me. The man played with his children happily, changing them, cuddling them, keeping an eye out. The wife ran the lodge. She did it year-round while he was away – it was her business. When she needed water to cook, she said to her husband, 'Get some water,' and he fetched it, without a murmur. Sherpa men can and do cook, Sherpa women can and do work as porters.

One area where men and women are unequal is in the higher reaches of religion. Monks, not nuns, come to people's houses to read from the holy books. Some learned and respected monks can aspire to a far higher status than any nun. Still, there is a friendly equality among younger monks and nuns. You see them on the path in mixed groups, off on pilgrimage or a trip to Kathmandu, laughing and teasing together.

There is also inequality in the arranged marriages that have become more common, particularly in well-to-do families. The boy has a choice, and the girl usually does not. But she can still leave the marriage after a while and go back home. When her father gets drunk, he picks on her and says, 'He was the right man, you made a big mistake.' The daughter snaps back at him, 'No, he wasn't. It was your stupid mistake. You're the jerk.'

Sherpa men certainly have ideas of masculinity. But being mean to women is not at the core of them. I once spent two days unsuccessfully trying to find a Sherpa word for 'macho.' They do have a word for pushy, competitive, argumentative people (*angchermo*), but it's used for both men and women. Nepali has a word, *bahadur*, which means brave, strong, masculine, and tough. Sherpa doesn't have one. Sherpa men and women certainly act with and respect bravery. But the word for fear is the same as the word for danger. In Nepali you can ask, 'Were you afraid on Everest?' In Sherpa you have to say, 'Was there *jiwaa?*' That means both 'Was there danger?' and 'Were you afraid?' Because, of course, if there is danger, anybody in their right mind is afraid and not ashamed of it. Sherpas think that acting bravely is not the same as not feeling fear.

One aspect of this equality between the sexes was that there was no sexual double standard. What was all right for men was all right for women. Almost no Sherpa women, or men, were virgins when they married. After all, Dorjee Lhatoo says, boys and girls went out to gather wood together all the time. Again, husbands and wives were angry about infidelity. But they usually forgave the other. Forgiveness is not forgetting, of course. Dorjee Lhatoo was trying to explain this to me. I told him that I grew up in America in the sixties. I remember clearly what it is like to believe in sexual equality, have an open relationship, and still want to kill somebody. 'Yes,' Dorjee said, 'it was like that.'

Maybe that's what was happening between Ajiba and Tenzing. If so, nobody then would have thought anybody was doing much wrong. But there is another possible explanation.

Remember that many fights at New Year are over money, in one way or another. The tension between Tenzing and Ang

Tsering's family was part of a wider competition among Sherpa sardars. Quite a lot of money was at stake.

In 1952 a small number of men could be thought of as leading climbing sardars: Tenzing, Da Namgyal, Ang Tharkay, and Pasang Dawa Lama.[1] Ang Tsering was almost one of these men and without his injured feet would certainly have been. Da Thundu was a climber on the same level, but not ambitious and so was less of a competitor as a sardar.

An expedition sardar stood to make quite a lot of money. Some skimmed the porters' wages. Some still do, and some don't. On one of the large Everest or Nanga Parbat expeditions, a percentage of the wages of six hundred local porters and thirty high-altitude men could come to quite a lot of money. Tenzing says in his autobiography that he did not do this and so had far less trouble with the porters. But he says other men did, and the porters knew and resented it.

Even without corruption, though, a sardar did well. In 1952, Dorjee Lhatoo says, young Sherpa men were always hanging around the houses of the important sardars, asking if they could please fetch wood, carry shopping, or run errands. These young men wanted work, and the sardars had it. When an expedition came, the sahibs would want some men and know the names of others. A sardar could still pick some of his own kin, protégés, and old friends. His recommendation carried weight with the climbers. Moreover, a noted climbing sardar would also get a lot of work as a sardar on treks, and there he could hire his own more easily.

I asked Lhakpa Diki if anybody paid bribes to a sardar for work in the thirties or the fifties. She said it never happened when she worked as a porter on treks, or when her husband worked on expeditions. Ang Tsering also says sardars never took bribes then. Now some do and others don't.

However, opportunities were opening for sardars to become businessmen organizing treks in their own right. Karma Paul was a Tibetan orphan, raised by evangelical Christian missionaries and educated in English. By 1920 he was a skilled car mechanic with two taxis in Darjeeling. He also worked as a translator, and sometimes as a sardar, on every British Everest expedition from 1921 to 1938. At the same time, he built up a trekking agency, hiring and training men like Tenzing and Ang Tharkay. His daughter, Colonel Paul, says that Karma Paul was a rock of integrity. That was a wonderful thing in a man, she says, and she has always tried to live that way herself, but it was not a perfect thing in a father. He would have left them far better off if he had been corrupt. But with what they learned working for him, Ang Tharkay and Tenzing and others were able, in effect, to run their own trekking agencies. That meant they could make reasonable profits without any corruption.

So perhaps the enmity between Tenzing and Ajiba was rooted in competition. All of these men – Tenzing, Da Thundu, Da Namgyal, Ang Tharkay, Ang Tsering – had been friends, often close friends, in their youth. They had climbed together on many expeditions, putting their lives in each other's hands on the rope every day. And they had found each other work. By 1952 these ties were under strain. There were only so many expeditions, and only one Everest. They were comrades on the mountain, but also businessmen in the marketplace. Ang Tharkay, for instance, found it impossible to work for Tenzing, who had once brought ritual gifts of *chang* to Ang Tharkay and asked for work. And Ang Tsering and Tenzing had been growing apart for some time.

On the surface, the split is usually ascribed to an argument over a horse. Tenzing rented one of Ang Tsering's horses to carry loads on a trek. The horse died and Ang Tsering asked for compensation. Tenzing refused, on the reasonable grounds that one of Ang Tsering's close relatives had been working on the trek looking after the horse.

People who knew both men say the horse was really only the occasion for crystallizing a rivalry that had been building a long time, between a man who had been one of the greatest climbers and a man who was becoming the greatest of all.

For whatever reason, Tenzing and Ajiba got into more than one fight. We return now to the fight on the march back from Everest to Kathmandu in 1952. Galtzen says that two men, an uncle and his nephew, attacked Tenzing with ice axes. Tenzing fought back – he was always a strong man – and the others pulled the two men off. Tenzing seemed unhurt that night.

Ang Tsering was there, too. He says it was his brother Ajiba fighting Tenzing, nobody used an ice ax, and he didn't see any second older man fighting Tenzing. Galtzen was pretty sure there were two men. He was impressed that Tenzing could fight off two men with axes and come out without a mark on him. Possibly the second man was Ang Tsering, going to his brother's aid. In any case, these things happen when people drink. Nobody was killed and nothing was broken.

Next morning, though, Tenzing was too sick to walk. They had to carry him out to Kathmandu, day after day. He became delirious, and the Swiss doctor said he thought Tenzing might die.

Tenzing doesn't mention the fight in his autobiography. He says his illness seemed like a recurrence of malaria, but he thought in fact it was the stress of two hard expeditions where he had to be both sardar and climber. Certainly the fight had not left him injured. But it may have been the last straw emotionally. Ajiba had climbed with him on the Geneva Spur, and Ang Tsering was an old friend. Tenzing was certainly finding the job of sardar lonely. Perhaps it was not his body that was hurt by the fight.

The Swiss climbers flew Tenzing from Kathmandu to a hospital in Patna, India, where he recovered. He had already been asked to be the sardar for the British expedition to Everest the next year. It was the logical choice – he was good at his job and had now been higher than any other Sherpa or British climber.

Tenzing was torn. Mrs Henderson urged him strongly to go. Her word carried weight. She was influential in giving out work, she had behaved with great kindness to many Sherpas over many years, and she had integrity. But the stress had made him so ill he had nearly died. Ang Lahmu, his wife, told him:

'You will get ill again, or you will slip on the ice and fall and kill yourself.'

'No, I will look out for myself,' I told her. 'Just like I always have.'

'You take too many risks.'

'I am paid for climbing. They don't pay me for play. I must do what I am paid for.' . . .

'You care nothing about me or the children, or what happens to us if you die.'

'Of course I care, woman. But this is my work – my life. Don't you understand that?' . . .

'You will die.'

'All right, I will die.' By this time I was getting angry. 'If so I would rather do it on Everest than in your hut!' . . .

We got angry, made up, then got angry again. But at last Ang Lahmu saw that I was determined, and said: 'All right, you win.'[2]

So he went. He took with him young Khansa from Namche, who was eighteen, his own nephew Topkay, also eighteen, and his seventeen-year-old sister's son Nawang Gombu, from Khumjung. Galtzen Sherpa from Namche had been promoted from low-altitude sardar to high-altitude porter. And Da Thundu, now forty-seven years old, came, too.

It was Tenzing's seventh expedition to Everest. He was thirty-nine years old, and it was probably his last chance.

The British were determined, too. If they did not succeed, the Swiss were coming back the next year. The Himalayan Committee in London was worried that Eric Shipton, their first choice as leader, would not push the attempt hard enough. He was known to be reluctant to risk lives in the Icefall. More important, he had led a 1952 expedition to Cho Oyu while the Swiss were climbing Everest. Little climbing was done on Cho Oyu. So the committee replaced Shipton with John Hunt.

Hunt was forty-two years old, with considerable experience in the Alps and Himalayas, a good climber but not a great one. He was a colonel in the British army, a staff officer's staff officer. Hunt ran the expedition the way a really good officer runs a campaign. He was polite, never yelled at anybody, and didn't make speeches about bravery. Instead, he concentrated on making sure that he got enough supplies to the right places at the right time, so his troops would be warm, well fed, well supplied, and healthy. There were no dashes for the summit under Hunt. On his Everest expedition, one porter got frostbite in one finger. This was partly because Hunt was lucky with the weather. But it was mainly because whenever somebody had to come down the mountain in trouble, Hunt had made sure there were people in the next camp down to look after him.

Hunt was also Indian born, in Simla, with its view of the Himalayas, and a native speaker of Hindi. His expedition had the best climbers among British gentlemen, including former presidents of both the Oxford and Cambridge mountaineering clubs. But along with them Hunt made sure he had three aces in the hole.

One was George Lowe, a primary-school teacher from New Zealand and a strong climber. The second was another New Zealander, Edmund Hillary, who had been on the 1951 Everest expedition and on Cho Oyu in 1952. A man of Hillary's class would not have been on a prewar expedition. His father had been a sergeant in World War One, and Hillary himself had been a sergeant in World War Two. He had dropped out after one year of university – it wasn't for him. Hillary worked for his father in the family beekeeping business, making a living with his muscles. He was tall, big, strong, a superb climber, deeply egalitarian, and an utterly decent man.

Hunt's third ace was Tenzing. When they met, Hunt told Tenzing that he would be both the sardar and a member of the expedition, as he had been with the Swiss. Publicly, Hunt said he did this because without Tenzing they had thirteen members, and that was an unlucky number. Privately, he promised Tenzing a chance at the summit, although not necessarily first crack. Hunt was thinking ahead.

Tenzing was thinking ahead, too. Nawang Gombu said the obvious evidence for this was that Tenzing left Darjeeling with an Indian flag in his pack. Tenzing was already thinking about his loyalties and future career after he reached the summit.

At some point on the climb Tenzing asked Hunt if he could take the Indian flag to the summit when he got the chance. Hunt, Indian born, said yes.

Tenzing also took the red scarf Raymond Lambert had given him when they'd parted. He would much rather have been going with the Swiss. But if he couldn't get to the summit with Lambert, he would wear his friend's scarf on the top.

As soon as the expedition began, Tenzing was torn between his hunger for the top and his loyalty to his fellow Sherpas. When the expedition met up in Kathmandu, the climbers were housed in the British embassy. The Sherpas were put in the garage, which had once been the stables. They complained that there were no toilets. What really galled them, of course, was that both Hunt and the ambassador assumed they were people who did not need toilets.

The symbolism, and memory, of Empire was strong on both sides. Britain had entered World War Two one of the great powers, with a greater colonial empire than any other. The 'jewel in the crown,' in Winston Churchill's phrase, was India. By 1946 the United States and Russia were the superpowers. Britain was just another country in the American alliance. What made it worse for the British establishment was that, just before the war ended, Churchill's Conservative government had lost the election to Labour. Then, in 1947, the Indian National Congress, and the Indian people, finally won independence.

For the establishment, Everest was to be a symbolic reversal of all this. It had always been Britain's mountain, part of the Empire. As British men had conquered the world, quietly, with grit and no whining, a few gentlemen all by themselves, so they had gone to Everest. The hope was that victory would coincide with the coronation of the new Queen, Elizabeth II, and a new Elizabethan age.

But if Everest was slated to be a symbolic reversal of all that had happened to the British upper classes, John Hunt's expedition benefited from those changes. After 1945, working people all over Western Europe had far more dignity and respect. Without that, Hunt would not have been able to take Hillary. Without Indian independence, and without the Swiss, he would not have been able to imagine making Tenzing a member.

But let's return to the toilets. For the Sherpas, the toilets were a symbol of all those times they had been sitting on a bench at Chowrashtra in Darjeeling, and a British climber had come along and made them get off the bench and squat at his feet. Now they didn't have to put up with that anymore. And they had seen, in the French and Swiss, alternative ways for white people to be.

All this put Tenzing in a bind. He had to keep the sahibs happy or he wouldn't be allowed to the summit. He had to keep the Sherpas happy or the loads wouldn't get to the South Col. So he spent the night in the garage, trying to calm the Sherpas. The next morning, against his advice, they publicly pissed on the embassy driveway in protest. It was going to be a long, long expedition for Tenzing. The Sherpas expected him to be their leader, by which they meant their representative. Hunt expected him to be the Sherpas' leader, by which he meant their officer.

They started the long trek from Kathmandu to Base Camp. Khansa Sherpa of Namche, only eighteen, wasn't annoyed by the British. He was just ecstatic to have the job. All the money for wages and supplies was carried in Indian rupee coins. The coins filled twelve stout wooden boxes, carried by twelve low-altitude porters. Five Gurkha soldiers accompanied those twelve porters all day to make sure nothing was stolen. At night, Khansa says, the Sherpas took turns on a rota, sitting in the tent with the Gurkhas and the money, watching the Gurkhas. It was the Sherpas' money, too.

There were complaints about supplies and gear all the way to Base Camp. Nawang Gombu, who was there, says even the unrest at the embassy wasn't really about toilets. It's true, he says, that the expedition was run along military lines. The military are the same in every country, he says, you know what I mean? I nod. But what mattered to the Sherpas, Gombu said, was gear. The Swiss had had wonderful equipment, state-of-the-art, and shared it. With the British the Sherpas were back to basics.

There were many little complaints, but the crunch came at Base Camp. The British told the Sherpa porters that there would be a bonus of three hundred rupees for every man who managed to reach the South Col. But beyond that there was no guaranteed baksheesh. More important, the high-altitude porters usually took home the boots, coats, and sleeping bags they were issued, as of right. This time, they were explicitly told, there were no promises. If a man did well, and the sahibs were happy with him, he could keep his equipment. If not, they would take it back at the end of the expedition.

This was offensive to both feelings and established rights. It also mattered financially. Khansa's father, for instance, had worked as a high-altitude porter on just one of the British Everest expeditions in the thirties. When he came home, he sold his boots, his sleeping bag, and his coat to one of the five rich men in Namche. With that money he bought the house Khansa was born in.

The Sherpas protested about the gear, argued among themselves, and threatened to strike or even go home. Tenzing wrote later: 'This was the worst time I had on the whole expedition. Along with Major Wylie, who was also trying to make peace, I felt like the middle of a sandwich pressed between two slices of bread. Each side thought I was working for the interests of the other side, and the Sherpas especially seemed to think that I was being paid big money by the British to argue against them. Half the time I wished I was just an ordinary Sherpa.'[3]

The leader of the resistance was Pasang Phutar Jockey. It was probably not a coincidence that he was the same man Tenzing had slapped and kicked to make him carry to the South Col. Tenzing says they worked out a compromise. Pasang Phutar Jockey and Ang Dawa either refused to accept it or were fired. In any case, they left and things settled down. The expedition started into the Icefall.

The only person Tenzing had to confide in was Nawang Gombu. I think he talked to Gombu because he was kin, and only a boy, so not a competitor. But Gombu is a wise and decent man now and probably was then, too.

Tenzing told Gombu that this time he would get to the summit or die trying.

Chapter Thirteen

1953

During the same spring that Tenzing returned to Everest as sardar of the 1953 British expedition, the 1953 German expedition to Nanga Parbat was having another try at their old mountain. The leader this time was Karl Herrligkoffer, who had been seventeen when his half brother Willy Merkl died on Nanga Parbat in 1934:

> I was saddened, naturally, for I had lost my big brother, my hero, but it was not until 1937 when, at one blow, seven more of my countrymen, all renowned climbers, together with their faithful Sherpas, lost their lives on Nanga Parbat, that I felt the full impact of the tragedy associated with the mountain. I determined, there and then, that come what may, I would myself organize a new German Himalayan expedition, whose task it would be to set a seal of victory upon the heroic efforts of our dead comrades, to fulfill, in fact, a sacred trust.[1]

It took Herrligkoffer twenty years. He went through the war, became a doctor, wrote a biography of his brother, walked and scrambled in the hills. In 1951, with Germany finally recovering

270

from the war, he felt the time had come to lead an expedition. However, he had almost no climbing experience and had never been to the Himalayas. Since no one in the mountaineering world had ever heard of Herrligkoffer, few climbers would go with him, especially to Nanga Parbat. The Austrian Alpine Club agreed to sponsor him, but the much larger German club refused to. Herrligkoffer was a determined man – 'I had to begin fighting for my ideas. . . . I was not disposed to be deterred.' He raised the money, but it was obvious he couldn't actually lead the climb. For that he turned to Peter Aschenbrenner.

Aschenbrenner had been on Nanga Parbat in 1932. He had gone back in 1934 and skied away from the porters just below the Silver Saddle. He was now in his fifties, working in Kufstein as the custodian of the Stripsenjoch mountain refuge. Aschenbrenner told Herrligkoffer he couldn't spare the time from work. It wasn't a convincing story, but I can imagine many reasons why Aschenbrenner might not have wanted to see that mountain again. Herrligkoffer persisted and finally Aschenbrenner agreed. Then Aschenbrenner and his wife had their only serious fight in twenty years of married life.

It was a stroke of genius on Herrligkoffer's part. Now he had an expedition led by Merkl's brother and by one of the veterans of '34. Herrligkoffer also sent word to Ang Tsering in Darjeeling, asking him to come. Ang Tsering said no, you never did anything for me. Why should I do anything for you?

Aschenbrenner was in his fifties and made it clear that he would do little actual climbing. Only four men under forty were on the expedition. Hermann Buhl, an Austrian from Innsbruck, was the strongest of these 'youngsters,' as they came to be called. He was part of a new wave of working-class climbers. When he was growing up, Buhl said, 'ours was a modest home. My father was a small craftsman in State employ, whose restricted salary was just enough to provide the bare necessities of life. We usually had dry bread for breakfast, and I had to buy my lunch out of my pocket money, which I earned as an apprentice in a forwarding agent's business.'[2]

Buhl was now twenty-nine, working in a sports store in Munich and supporting a wife and baby. His regular climbing partner, Kuno Rainer, thirty-eight, was a foreman bricklayer and guide. Hermann Kollensperger, twenty-seven, was a mechanic. The only youngster with a middle-class job was Otto Kempter, twenty-seven, a businessman.

The expedition hired five Sherpa porters, led by Pasang Dawa Lama, who had almost made the summit of K2 with Wiessner in 1939. But India and Pakistan were now separate countries. Nanga Parbat now lay in the Pakistani sector of Kashmir, and India and Pakistan had gone to war over Kashmir six years before. From the Pakistani point of view, the Darjeeling Sherpas were Indians. They were allowed into Pakistan, but denied permission for Nanga Parbat.

So Herrligkoffer and company had to rely on Balti and Hunza porters, just as Willy Merkl's first expedition had done in 1932. Their relationship with the porters was the same old same old. The low-altitude Balti porters were not volunteers, insisted on better rates of pay, and really only wanted to get back to their crops. The liaison officer in 1932 was Lieutenant Frier of the Gilgit Scouts. In 1953 it was Rhabar Hassan, an officer in the Gilgit police. The high-altitude porters were Hunzas. On the approach Herrligkoffer told the Hunzas they had to carry loads up to Base Camp twice in one day. Then, he said, 'They ostentatiously removed their pullovers, anoraks, boots and various other garments and struck. Hassan knew it was all bluff for it was quite clear the Hunzas could not simply down tools and go. . . . If any of them returned home now without apparent reason and no testimonial from me, they would be put under arrest at once and sentenced to forced labour.'[3]

Ten days later the expedition was finally ready to carry supplies to Camp 1 in the Icefall. Here the real work, and the real ~~iger~~, would begin.

~~l~~errligkoffer again:

The porters were to start off with their loads at 9 A.M. but for the second time they went on strike, demanding more clothing, still more food, more pay, the issue of spare clothing such as extra shirts, socks and underwear, as well as the reduction of their loads from 28 to 18 kilograms [62 pounds to 40 pounds]. I immediately ordered them to remove all their clothing and other equipment and pile it in a heap. I then dismissed them. Five of them took to their heels and fled barefoot over the snow back to Tato without even waiting for the pay which was due to them. They would now rank as deserters in their native villages, but obviously they had been scared of the mountain. They had enquired more than once if their families would get their clothing if they died. Hassan advised me to give the others rather more to eat – for they could put away vast quantities of food – and then everything would be in order. They were really like children and I made them apologize to me in person before I would take them back into the ranks of the high altitude porters. One of them was reduced to tears as he fought to overcome his feeling of shame.[4]

Or possibly his feeling of humiliation.

Herrligkoffer could force the porters not to desert, but he couldn't make them climb high on the mountain. Again and again, the Hunza porters claimed sickness in the higher camps, and the German climbers did not believe them. In effect, the Hunzas were refusing to risk their lives.[5]

Note, also, that they were asked to carry sixty-two pounds on the mountain. The largest standard loads I have been able to find records of on other expeditions were fifty pounds, and thirty or forty pounds was more common. Herrligkoffer probably demanded such heavy loads because he was short of men. The Sherpas could not come up, and he had only four strong German climbers.

The Germans and the Hunzas tried, slowly, to put up a series of well-stocked camps. Short of porters, they had to skip over the Camp 3 of previous expeditions. They made their new Camp 3 at the site of the old Camp 4, where sixteen men had died in

1937. By June 30, five weeks after starting, they still had not put up a camp beyond the Moor's Head. The younger Germans, and especially Hermann Buhl, had done much of the carrying. Now only three porters were willing or able to go above the Moor's Head. Only Buhl looked able to climb high, and the monsoon would soon close in. And they had no time to establish the necessary camps on the long Rakhiot ridge and the Silver Saddle.

Peter Aschenbrenner, with a lifetime as a guide and his memories of 1934, called off the expedition. From Base Camp he and Herrligkoffer radioed the news up to the four climbers still left at Camp 3: Frauenberger, Ertl, Kempter, and Buhl.

Led by Buhl, the four refused to come down. The next day they climbed up to Camp 4, just before the Rakhiot Peak, and as they climbed, Base Camp called them three times. Aschenbrenner screamed at them, cursing at them obscenely, and they hurled Bavarian filth back.

The next morning they fought on the radio again. Buhl said later that Walter Frauenberger 'argued back and forth for half an hour before finally wringing the word of absolution from them down there at the bottom. We breathed again when we heard it: "All right, then. Go, in God's name; you have our blessing."'[6] The four climbers and three porters set out past the Moor's Head, down the long ridge to its lowest point. There they pitched a tent. The porters and two of the climbers then went back to Camp 3, leaving Buhl and Otto Kempter to make a summit attempt the next day.

This was ambitious. The summit was probably more than a day away. Even the overconfident 1934 expedition had set up their last camp just over the Silver Saddle. Buhl and Kempter were planning to climb two thousand feet up to the Silver Saddle, then turn left and follow the long summit ridge as they climbed another two thousand feet. Buhl, at least partly aware of how difficult it would be, was up at 2:30 A.M. and anxious to go. Kempter wanted a little more sleep, and Buhl charged off on his own. Kempter followed, at first half an hour behind, later an hour behind. Buhl, bullheaded, didn't stop to wait for him.

Buhl reached the top of the Silver Saddle. The long, almost flat, white summit plateau was before him. The sun reflected off the endless snow, making him sweat and parching his already sore throat. There was no wind.

Now Buhl was walking through another windless morning on the Silver Saddle. He set off across the summit plateau, taking five breaths to every step.

Kempter made it to the Silver Saddle. Already exhausted, he sat in the snow to rest and decided to wait for Buhl's return. He did, most of the day. Then, in the late afternoon, Kempter went back down alone to the tent where the others were waiting in support.

Buhl was across the great summit plain by some point in the afternoon – he wasn't keeping track of the time. He stopped and left his small rucksack by the side of the path. Even those few pounds were too much to carry. He left his thick wool sweater in the rucksack, taking only a thin pullover and an anorak. It was still warm. He took only what could fit in his pockets – some coca tea, a refreshing drink from Bolivia. A few pills to give him energy. A camera, because he was alone and knew he had to take pictures from the summit or people wouldn't believe he'd reached it. A Pakistani flag, because the expedition had promised to put it on the summit. And the pennant of his climbing club in the Tyrol. An Austrian, Buhl carried neither his country's flag nor Germany's.

Now he was at the foot of the West Summit. It was too high and too rocky for him to climb and then work his way back down to the gap between the West Summit and the higher main summit. He would have to work round the West Summit, to the left or the right. He chose the left; it looked shorter. He walked up the ridge, a great cornice of snow under his feet. He hoped the snow was resting on something. If the snow cracked, he would go down the South Face, the greatest mountain face in the world, a seven-thousand-foot drop.

He came to a rock cliff that rose two hundred feet above the ridge. To climb it alone without a rope would be to die. He worked round the rock and found himself facing another cliff:

> Fifteen feet below me there was a partly snow-filled gully leading straight up to the crest of the ridge. But how was I to get into that gully. It was protected above and below by overhanging crags. I was now prepared to risk anything. With my crampons still on my boots [so they slid on the rock] I climbed the rapidly steepening face of high, friable, rusty-brown gneiss by a crack which gave me my only hope.
>
> Once again I pocketed my gloves and jammed myself in the bottom of the crack, as I had often done in my native mountains; but now speed was of the essence [because night was coming, and his strength was going]. It was only about thirty feet, but my crampons got wedged in the narrow crevice, and my fingers threatened to give up altogether. It was climbing of the severest order, comparable to the East Wall of the Watzmann. I had that horrible feeling in my fingers again [that they would stop working]; yet only a few feet above me a new way lay clear to the gully. It just had to be done and presently I was safely in the gully. They had been terrible minutes.[7]

He was round the West Summit. He knew, but didn't seem to care, that he couldn't go back down that way. He sipped the last of his coca tea. It was still warm, and the anorak was tied around his waist.

Suddenly he understood that it was six o'clock in the evening. He'd have to stay out all night. He had a raging thirst. He was down on his hands and knees now, crawling, alone.

He would never say so publicly, but this was where he always wanted to be, alone, breaking the rules. At eighteen, in 1943, he had been lucky to avoid the war by landing a posting in an army unit that did mountain rescue. One weekend he went off on a climb and overstayed his leave. He was sent to the Eastern Front as punishment and spent two years in a prisoner-of-war camp.

He had always loved climbing alone, was famous for his solo ascents. No wonder he hadn't waited for Otto Kempter to catch up. He believed every man had the right to put his own life on the line. He continued on his hands and knees.

A friend spoke to him, urging him on, telling him it would be all right, he was safe. He looked over his shoulder and couldn't see anyone. He looked forward, at the snow in front of his gloved hands, and the friend spoke again. He recognized the voice, but could not remember the name.

Hermann Buhl reached the summit of Nanga Parbat. He had been climbing for seventeen hours. Buhl took out the pennant of his climbing club, tied it to his ice ax, and planted the ax in the snow. Sitting, he took out his camera and photographed the ax, and behind it the Silver Saddle and the North Ridge. He sat there for perhaps half an hour, in wonder.

Then he started down, walking now, suddenly feeling stronger and afraid. He left his ice ax on the summit. It was too heavy, or he wasn't thinking. He had to beat the coming darkness. The route he had taken up was too dangerous. He had to find a new one, the other side of the West Summit. He wasn't thinking clearly now. His friend was still talking to him, comforting him in his fear. He was descending a rock slab, at a fifty-five-degree angle, when he suddenly realized he was in total darkness.

He had to stop and wait for dawn. He stood on a little rock ledge, too small even to sit upon. One hand gripped a hold on the rock wall behind him. The other hand held his two ski poles. He had not used them much climbing up. Without his ice ax he needed them desperately now, going down, for balance. If he lost them, sooner or later he'd slip and be gone. Or maybe just twist an ankle as he fell. That would be enough, up here. He was exhausted. If he fell asleep for even a moment, he would drop the ski poles. He did not think of tying the ski poles to his wrists. He kept shutting his eyes, nodding off, snapping awake in terror, his ski poles still in an iron grip. He had only the thin pullover, and his feet felt strange. He was bivouacking, standing up, after eighteen hours climbing, alone at twenty-six thousand feet. He had no right to live. His friend talked to him. The weather was still kind, and there was no wind.

As the sky lightened in the morning, he was still alive. He made it down, very slowly. Forty-one hours after he'd started out, he came back to Camp 5, just below the Moor's Head.

At the Moor's Head, his friends were dedicating a new memorial over the snow graves of Gaylay and Merkl when they saw him, a black dot on the Silver Saddle. Once he reached the tent, they gave him cup after cup of tea and cried to see him. Buhl couldn't talk, and they didn't ask him if he'd made the summit. More than anything else, that touched him.

This was only the third time anybody had climbed one of the fourteen peaks over eight thousand meters. It was the first solo ascent of one, and the first without oxygen.

Buhl had frostbite, and it was clear he would lose some toes. They struggled down the next day. By the time they reached Base Camp, Peter Aschenbrenner was already gone. He'd left as soon as he'd heard the news of Buhl's ascent.

Aschenbrenner had his passage home booked and a job to get back to. Still, it was strange. Perhaps he was furious at Buhl for disobeying orders. Maybe he didn't want to meet the man who had achieved what he had almost done nineteen years before. It's possible Nanga Parbat was too full of grief for Aschenbrenner, created emotions inside him that he couldn't understand or bear. Maybe he did not want anybody to succeed there.

Herrligkoffer, too, treated Buhl coldly. The Hunza porters carried Buhl out from Base Camp to the road, with respect and care, and he lost only two toes. Home in Germany, Herrligkoffer's faction and Buhl's fell out with each other, in bitter public squabbles. Buhl had the best of the controversy because, after all, he had won, he had climbed it. So most people felt Herrligkoffer and Aschenbrenner were simply old men, stuck in the mud. The two old men, however, were right. On the mountain, they didn't have two men capable of going safely to the summit together. Buhl would have died had it not been for the gentle weather, the stillness, the lack of wind – such a rarity on an eight-thousand-meter peak. If human life is worth anything, Herrligkoffer was right.

There are two possible explanations for Buhl's phantom friend on the climb. One is that he was hallucinating, as many others have at great altitude without oxygen. The other, which fits with the extraordinary weather, is that his friend was the god of Nanga Parbat.

Meanwhile, back on Everest that spring, the British expedition had got through the Icefall without mishap.[8] Young Khansa was terrified, all the time, but simultaneously happy to have the job. He was also deeply grateful to the older men from Darjeeling. They showed him how to belay, and how to walk in crampons without slicing open his legs. He would not have survived without them.

Tenzing was having an easier time as sardar. There were still arguments. The British said the porters had to carry sixty-pound loads. The Sherpas complained, and Tenzing succeeded in reducing it to fifty. He spent most of his time at Base Camp, or just at the head of the Icefall, allocating loads and keeping the supplies moving. He was essential because he was the only one on the expedition who knew everyone's name, and his English was much better than the other Sherpas'. Khansa and the other men on his rope used hand signals to communicate with the British climbers; however, because they had no agreed system of signals, Khansa was often unsure what he had been told to do.

At Base Camp, Tenzing was continuously impressed by the efficiency of the operation. 'It was run on military lines,' he said, 'and there is no doubt that most of our men would have preferred more ease and informality.'[9] But it worked.

The hard part was not getting to lead. Edmund Hillary had led much of the route through the Icefall. Forty-five years later, when he had learned much about Sherpas, Hillary wrote:

A big party arrived with the first major lift up the icefall and everything seemed to have gone well. It was Tenzing's

first trip above Base Camp for the year and I didn't think
he seemed very happy. With the Swiss he had been one of
the lead climbers but John Hunt felt that at this stage his
influence and experience would be more valuable organ-
ising the other Sherpas and their loads up the icefall. I had
considerable respect for Tenzing's reputation but it never
entered my mind that we needed his help in tackling the
difficult ice problems which I accepted we were quite
capable of dealing with ourselves. No wonder Tenzing
always had a warmer affection for the Swiss than he ever
did for us.[10]

The loads moved up the Icefall and across the Cwm, until
Camp 6 was made at the foot of the steep slopes of the Lhotse
Face, below the South Col.

Tenzing and Hillary went down to Base Camp, on a rope
together for the first time. They were racing through a part of
the Icefall they called the Atom Bomb when Hillary came to a
crevasse. 'Instead of crossing the normal bridge, I just leaped in
the air and landed on the overhanging bottom edge. It immediately broke off and plunged into the crevasse with me on top
of it.'[11] Tenzing reacted instantly, from long experience, driving
his ax into the snow and holding the much larger man. As
Hillary climbed out of the crevasse, he thought: 'I had been
impressed with Tenzing's skill and rope work and his happi-
ness to keep going hard and fast. For the first time an idea
entered my mind – it seemed very unlikely that John Hunt
would let George Lowe and me climb together – you couldn't
have two New Zealanders getting to the top – but what about
Tenzing and me? It seemed a good idea and I decided to
encourage it.'[12]

Tenzing soon made the same decision. Both men stayed at Base
Camp. Hunt was resting them, but they wanted to show what
they could do. On May 7 they raced together from Base Camp
to Camp 4 and back again in one day. The cover story for John
Hunt was that they were testing the closed-circuit oxygen sets. In

fact they were just putting down a marker to show him what they could do.

Five days later Hunt announced his projected summit plans. George Lowe would lead the route up the Lhotse Face to the South Col. Then there would be two summit teams. First Charles Evans and Tom Bourdillon would make an attempt from the South Col, using closed-circuit oxygen sets. Whether those two succeeded or failed, Hillary and Tenzing would try the day after. Using open-circuit oxygen, they would climb partway up the summit ridge and pitch a tent. Early the next morning, they would go for the top.

(With a closed-circuit oxygen set, like divers use, they breathed pure oxygen. With an open circuit, like the oxygen masks athletes use, they breathed oxygen mixed with the air around them.)

Hunt was covering all his bases. It was a British expedition and he wanted to put two Englishmen on the top first, if he possibly could. Evans (Fellow of the Royal College of Surgeons) and Bourdillon (Oxford) were strong, but they were not in the same league as Hillary and Tenzing. If the Englishmen failed, Hunt would still have his two best climbers in reserve. He was also using two different kinds of oxygen sets. And one pair would try from the South Col in one day, and the other pair in two.

Tenzing was happy, but many of the Sherpas were not. They told Tenzing he was crazy. He would die, and what would they tell his wife? How could they show their faces to his Ang Lahmu?

Tenzing said, 'Stop worrying like old women.'

Then they came out with their larger worry. With Tenzing, the British would probably make it. And if that happened, they said, '"You will be taking the livelihood away from all of us. . . . There will be no more expeditions. There will be no more jobs."

'"It is you who are mad," I said. "If Everest is climbed the Himalayas will be famous all over the world. There will be more expeditions and jobs than ever."'[13]

Things went slowly on the Lhotse Face. George Lowe and Ang Nyima led the route, day after day. On May 15, Ang Nyima returned down and Wilf Noyce went up to help Lowe. Then Noyce descended, and Mike Ward and Dawa Tenzing went up. Lowe battled on. They established Camp 7 at twenty-four thousand feet, only partway up the Lhotse Face.

Hunt, Tenzing, and Hillary were all at Camp 4, in the middle of the Western Cwm. Hillary and Tenzing wanted badly to go up and lead. It was all too slow, and the monsoon would come soon. Hunt held them back, wanting them fresh for the summit.

Hillary wrote later: 'Time was passing and the upper Lhotse Face was defeating us. Strong winds and cold temperatures made every extra hundred feet a challenge. John Hunt decided that a desperate and courageous push was needed.'[14] Hunt sent Noyce and nine Sherpas up to Camp 7 on May 20. They had instructions to push on the next day, come what may, all the way up the face and across to the South Col.

On the morning of May 21, Tenzing and Hillary watched from Camp 4, waiting to see ten men carrying loads across from Camp 7 to the Col. The crucial thing in those loads was the oxygen. The oxygen bottles weighed twenty-one pounds each.[15] They needed enough oxygen on the South Col for two summit pairs. They also needed oxygen for the men who would support them up there and help them down, and cylinders for the climbers to breathe at night.

So Tenzing and Hillary waited and watched for the all-important carry to the Col. Instead of ten men, two emerged from Camp 7 – Noyce and Annullu. They made it across to the South Col, left their loads, and went back to Camp 7. It was not enough.

That same morning Charles Wylie and five more Sherpas were carrying up to Camp 7. They were supposed to go on to the South Col the next day. But because the others had not gone on, there would be fourteen porters cramped in Camp 7 that night.

However, if eight of nine porters had not gone that morning, it was unlikely the others would tomorrow. Tenzing was frantic to get up and urge them on. Hillary went and begged Hunt to let him and Tenzing go up to Camp 7 that night. Hunt did.

They raced up. There were now three sahibs, Tenzing, and fourteen porters in Camp 7. Tenzing talked to the porters, going from tent to tent, pointing out that Annullu and Noyce had made it to the South Col and back safely. Tenzing massaged his men's tired muscles, made tea for everyone, encouraged them. After several hours of this, they all agreed to try for the Col the next morning.

Khansa was there. Years later he said, 'Tenzing was our teacher.' He smiled then, and said, 'Perhaps he was Hillary's teacher, too.'

The next morning Tenzing and Hillary led across to the South Col. Charles Wylie and fourteen porters started out behind them. Tenzing, Hillary, and Wylie were breathing oxygen. The porters were not. Thirteen of fourteen porters, Khansa and Nawang Gombu among them, made it to the Col. Climbers and porters dumped their loads and hurried down to the Western Cwm.

By May 25, Evans and Bourdillon were on the South Col, with Hunt and Da Namgyal in support. One camp behind them, Tenzing and Hillary were on the Lhotse Face. That morning Evans and Bourdillon set off, with Hunt and Da Namgyal carrying their oxygen partway up the summit ridge. Tenzing and Hillary climbed to the South Col. 'We caught glimpses of the first assault team making excellent time up the ridge,' Hillary wrote, 'until they disappeared into the cloud covering the upper part of the mountain. I noticed that Tenzing looked decidedly subdued.'[16]

Tenzing and Hillary waited. Hunt and Da Namgyal came back down. Hunt had climbed without oxygen, beyond his strength. Now they put him to bed and Tenzing made tea. From his sleeping bag Hunt said, 'Tenzing, I will never forget this.' Tenzing was deeply touched. When he checked on Hunt a bit later, the leader said, 'It would be fine if they did it for the Queen's Coronation.'[17] Elizabeth II was to be crowned seven days later. James Morris, the correspondent of *The Times*, was down at Camp 4. Hunt was hoping Evans and Bourdillon would make it in time for Morris to get the news to London for Coronation Day.

When Tenzing heard Hunt say that, he felt bitter. That's why the two Englishmen went first, he thought, instead of Hillary and me. Then he went out of the tent and tried to put the thought out of his mind. It felt unworthy.

Evans and Bourdillon returned in the late afternoon. They had reached the South Summit, but then had to turn back, too exhausted to get to the top and down safely. That night Hillary and Tenzing shared a tent, and Hillary

> learned why Tenzing had been so morose – he thought Charles and Tom were about to reach the top of Everest. He desperately wanted a Sherpa to be in the first summit team and he was always confident that he himself was the right Sherpa for this task. I, too, had a slight sense of guilt. I greatly admired what Charles and Tom had done but I had a regrettable feeling of satisfaction as well. They hadn't got to the top – there was still a job left for Tenzing and me to do. But the storm raged on and intensified, so it was already clear there was little chance of Tenzing and myself moving upwards in the morning.[18]

Hillary was right. The weather held them on the South Col the next day. Hunt, Evans, Ang Temba, and Bourdillon went down.

The following day was clear enough. Three Sherpas were supposed to carry loads for Tenzing and Hillary to make a camp halfway up the ridge. Only one was well enough – Ang Nyima, who had made the route up the Lhotse Face with Lowe.

They had to divide up the other two porters' loads. Lowe led up the ridge, carrying forty-five pounds. Ang Nyima and the British climber Alf Gregory had forty pounds each. Behind them came Tenzing and Hillary, with lighter loads, saving themselves.

They reached the remains of the tent where Tenzing and Lambert had camped the previous year. Two days before, Hunt and Da Namgyal had left a load of supplies there. Now they shared it out. Tenzing, Gregory, and Lowe were carrying fifty pounds each. Hillary was carrying sixty-three.

With that weight, at that height, they couldn't get far. Tenzing said he remembered a possible campsite from his climb the year before. He led them off the path to the left. There was no place there flat enough for a two-man tent, but then they noticed a possible site just above.

The others left their loads, and Tenzing and Hillary dug out a campsite. Since it was so steep, they had to cut two ledges, one slightly above the other, and pitch the tent over both. Hillary would sleep on the top ledge and Tenzing below him. Hillary was a big man, and his legs hung down over Tenzing.

Tenzing did the cooking. They started with chicken noodle soup and ended with canned apricots.

They were awake at four. Hillary had taken his boots off to sleep, and now they were too frozen to put on. He spent an hour trying to warm them over the small gas stove, the smell of singed leather filling the tent. Hillary told Tenzing he had to do this, he didn't want to end up with no toes like Lambert.

This was the wrong thing to say, but Hillary didn't know it. Tenzing was missing Lambert fiercely, wishing he were there for the final try. Tenzing said nothing of this and put on the red scarf Lambert had given him.

Years later Hillary and Tenzing became friends. Now, however, they were just two men with respect for each other who'd been thrown together by shared ambition.

Between 1950 and 1956 almost all the Himalayan giants were climbed. It was partly due to luck that it occurred in those years. Norton, Mallory and Irvine had been close on Everest, and Pasang Dawa Lama and Wiessner had been even closer on K2 in 1939. Gear had improved, above all oxygen sets. The main difference, however, was human.

The guides had come to the Himalayas. So had men like Hermann Buhl and Edmund Hillary, people who had to work at ordinary jobs to live. They were hungrier than the gentlemen who'd preceded them. Mallory, Irvine, Evans, and Bourdillon were among the strongest of all the men who had been to Oxford or Cambridge. Buhl, Hillary, and Tenzing were among the strongest of the workers of the world, and there were many more workers than gentlemen.

Tenzing would not have been there without Hillary. And Hillary would not have been there without Tenzing.

Tenzing was on the ridge because he was strong, utterly determined, always planning ahead. Because of Lambert. Because India was independent. And also because of what so many Sherpa and Tibetan porters had done before him. They had started on Everest, in 1921, coolies who pulled white tourists up and down the steep lanes of Darjeeling. Year after year, mountain after mountain, one man after another had carried an extra load, helped a sahib over a difficult stretch, laughed, and made the tea. They had risked their lives, lost fingers and toes, and often died. In doing that they had changed their own understanding of who they were and what they could accomplish. Then they had changed the sahibs' understanding, too. Tenzing was there because of the particular individual he was. But he was also there because he was a Sherpa.

The Sherpas on Nanga Parbat in 1934 – Nima Norbu, Dakshi, Nima Dorje, Nima Tashi, Pinzo, Da Thundu, Kitar, Pasang Kikuli, Pasang Picture, Ang Tsering, and Gaylay – were part of the history that had put Tenzing on the summit ridge.

By six-thirty Hillary had his boots on and they started up. They made the South Summit and saw the ridge that went down and then back up to the true summit. It looked possible. Just below the low point on the ridge there was a small rock cliff in the middle of the ice. They would have to climb it. Hillary led – Tenzing was an expert on ice, not rock.

And then they were walking up to the summit ridge. It was less steep now. They went up one hump of snow, down another, up another, hoping each would be the next to last, one foot in front of the other, roped together.

Tenzing and Hillary came to a place where they could see into Tibet. They climbed the last hillock, and they were there.

Hillary, still partly an Englishman, stuck out his glove for a handshake. Tenzing waved his arms in the air and threw them around Hillary. Only then did Hillary understand how desperately Tenzing had wanted this moment. They hugged and slapped each other on the back until they couldn't breathe.

Hillary took a picture of Tenzing on the summit, holding up

his ice ax with the flags of Britain, Nepal, India, and the United Nations tied to it.

When they came down, everybody asked which of the two men on the rope had got to the summit first. Tenzing and Hillary agreed between them not to answer that question. It didn't matter, they said. They had done it together.

Chapter Fourteen

HOME

Tenzing and Hillary went down and met George Lowe on the South Col. Hillary said to Lowe, 'We knocked the bastard off.' 'Would you like a cup of tea?' Lowe said.

Hunt met them on the Western Cwm and embraced Hillary. Only then did Hillary know how much success meant to Hunt. Forty years later the two men stood together at Tengboche, looking up at Everest and Lhotse. Hunt, in his eighties, apologized to Hillary for that momentary lapse of emotion on the Cwm.[1]

When Ang Tsering heard that Everest and Nanga Parbat had been climbed, he was inclined to disbelieve both pieces of news. Soon after the conquest of Everest, the respected head of the Rongbuk Monastery died. Back in 1924 he had warned Ang Tsering and his comrades to dump their loads at the high camp and get down quick. Now Ang Tsering understood that the abbot's death was the consequence of angering Everest by climbing the mountain.

On the morning of June 2 the conquest of Everest was announced to the crowds in London waiting for the queen's coronation. My mother was there and remembers the crowd cheered madly at the news.

*　　*　　*

Hillary received a knighthood from the queen. Tenzing did not. The official explanation was that Tenzing, as an Indian, was not legally allowed to receive a knighthood. The flaw in this reasoning is that they could have offered Tenzing a knighthood and let him refuse. In reality, he would probably have accepted, and it's most unlikely that the Indian government would have done anything to stop him.

This was partly simple racism, but there was also a political context. A New Zealander and a brown man from Darjeeling had climbed Everest. The Conservative Party government in London wished to present this as a British triumph. Hillary could be recast as a sort of honorary Englishman. His grandparents had emigrated from Britain, and at that time New Zealanders were both citizens of their own country and British subjects. However, if Hillary and Tenzing were treated as equals, it would be obvious that this wasn't solely a British triumph. Between them, the two men could lay claim to five nationalities – Tibetan, Nepali, Indian, British, and New Zealander. In fact it was a triumph not for any nation, but for all people.

A controversy developed over which of the two men on the rope stepped on the summit first. Most people over sixty-five I talk to still have a firm opinion on this. Indians and Nepalis believe it was Tenzing. British people who dislike colonialism also insist it was Tenzing, while those who remember it fondly are sure Hillary was first. Younger Sherpa climbers say that based on what they have seen working on the mountains, it must have been Tenzing.

Tenzing was appalled by this controversy. He felt that what he and Hillary had done together was being cheapened on all sides for political gain. I have no intention of telling you who got there first, but if you have to know the answer, it's in Tenzing's autobiography.

In a larger sense, Tenzing's achievement was greater than Hillary's. He was thirty-nine and Hillary was thirty-three. Tenzing had been both sardar and climber. Hillary was six foot three, and robust. Tenzing was five foot eight and slim. Tenzing had grown up poor, lonely, and badly fed. The barriers of race, class, and diet he had had to cross were enormous.

Pasang Dawa Lama nearly climbed K2 in 1939. In 1953 he had been appointed sardar for the Nanga Parbat expedition, but the Pakistani government never allowed him into Kashmir. The next year, 1954, he was appointed sardar on a small Austrian expedition to Cho Oyu in Khumbu.[2] It is one of the fourteen peaks over eight thousand meters, and in 1954 only Annapurna, Everest, and Nanga Parbat had been climbed.

Pasang Dawa Lama wanted to marry a young woman in Chauri Kharka, near the present-day airport of Lukla. Her parents refused permission, pointing out that Pasang Dawa Lama was twenty years older and already had one wife. So Pasang Dawa Lama made a bet with them. If he was the first man on the summit of Cho Oyu, he could marry their daughter. If he wasn't, he would leave the girl alone and give them five hundred rupees. They took the bet.

The Austrian expedition was beaten back by high winds and the severe frostbite of the leader, Herbert Tichy. They were running out of food, so Pasang Dawa Lama went back down to Namche for supplies. In Namche he learned that a Swiss expedition had set out for Cho Oyu. He was about to lose the woman he loved.

It was three and a half days' walk from Namche over the Nangpa La to Cho Oyu Base Camp. Pasang Dawa Lama did it in one day, carrying all the food for the expedition. The next day he carried a load up to the expedition's highest camp to find the Austrian climbers. The third day he gathered up the Austrian climbers and took them to the summit.

Anu Sherpa of Namche was a boy of eight that year. He remembers Pasang Dawa Lama coming back down the valley, swaggering, planting one foot heavily in front of the other, grinning, stomping down to his new in-laws' home. Anu says the people turned out all along the valley to gaze upon Pasang Dawa Lama. They held the wedding in Chauri Kharka that week, and the whole expedition, Sherpas and Austrians, got drunk out of their skulls.

*　　*　　*

All great athletes reach their peak relatively young, then face the question of what to do with their rest of their life. The results are often unfortunate. Edmund Hillary spent the balance of his life helping ordinary Sherpas. It was, of course, the correct thing to do, but few other people would have thought of it. Many Sherpas helped Hillary to find this path. At first he continued climbing. On Makalu in 1956 he had a stroke while trying to rescue two climbers trapped in a crevasse. After that, his sardar, Mingma Tsering of Kunde, suggested he build a school. My children have eyes, Mingma Tsering said to Hillary, but they are blind because they cannot read.

Other people would just have raised money to construct a school. Hillary went to Khumjung with carpentry tools and some friends and built the school with his own hands. The Sherpas' gratitude led him to build a hospital in Kunde. When the Sherpas showed him how they felt about that, he raised money for hospitals all over Khumbu and Solu. His family traveled with him back and forth to Nepal, and his wife and daughter died there in a plane crash in 1975.

One of Mingma Tsering's sons, Ang Rita Sherpa, went to Khumjung school and then to university in New Zealand on a Hillary scholarship. He has spent the last ten years as a conservation adviser in the Makalu Barun National Park in Nepal. Ang Rita could earn far more at another job. Every time we meet, he tells me at length how much he wants a park that can conserve the beauty and fragile ecology of the mountains. Yet he also wants that park to provide a decent living, not for tour agencies and trekking sardars, but for the poor people who live there. There is only one porters' union in Nepal. It's in Makalu Barun, and Ang Rita organized it. The odds against his dream succeeding are large, but he means to overcome them.

In April 2000, Hillary came to speak at the fortieth anniversary of the founding of Khumjung school. He was eighty. For many years now his body has been unable to bear altitude, even in Khumjung at just under thirteen thousand feet. This doesn't happen to most people, but it has to Hillary. He has to fly in by

helicopter and can stay less than an hour. This April morning he
flew in and walked two hundred yards to the school. It was a
long walk, as schoolchildren, teachers, and friends came up one
after another to put silk scarves of honor around his neck.

He gave a good speech, proud of his school, telling the students
to be proud, too. He started to walk back to the helicopter. After
a few steps Hillary couldn't breathe. He said, quietly, I think I'll
sit down. The doctor at the hospital he founded ran for the oxygen
cylinder. Breathing that, held up by two Sherpas, Hillary made it
to the helicopter and flew away. After he left, an enormous pile
of silk scarves remained on the chair where he had sat. I took a
picture.

I have never heard a Sherpa in Khumbu say anything bad about
Hillary. There is a joke they often tell. Perhaps, they say, Hillary
is a god who came from 'foreign' just to help Sherpa people. It's
a joke, but not one you are supposed to laugh at. You are meant
to smile and think, that's silly, and maybe it's true.

Khumbu Sherpas sometimes compare Tenzing unfavorably with
Hillary. One man helped us, they say, and the other did not. This
is unfair. The Sherpa making the comparison is seldom as decent
as Hillary. Nor am I, and nor probably are you.

Tenzing did other things.[3] First, and most important, his 1953
climb opened the door for the generations of Sherpa climbers
who followed. Khumbu has schools now because of Hillary. It is
the richest part of Nepal because of Tenzing.

Second, when he came down the mountain and went to
Kathmandu, the authorities asked, 'Who are you? What is your
name?' They meant: What is your caste? He could have said,
Tenzing Bhotia, I am a Tibetan. He said, Tenzing Sherpa.

When he got home to Darjeeling, one of his sisters was angry
with him. We're Tibetans, she said, you should have said Tibetan.
But Tenzing knew who had put him on the summit.

Before that, Galtzen of Namche says, we were Bhotias. If you
registered your land, the government clerk wrote Galtzen Bhotia.
Your identity card, too, said Bhotia. That meant you were, in their

eyes, the lowest of the low. After that, they wrote Galtzen Sherpa.

In 1953 a Nepali pop song came out of Kathmandu: 'Our Tenzing Sherpa.' 'How did you do it, our Tenzing Sherpa?' the chorus goes. 'How did you get up, and how did you get down, our Tenzing Sherpa?' Mention that song to any Sherpa man over fifty-five, and his eyes mist over. If he's a confident singer, he sings the chorus. If not, he hums quietly to himself. That song was the moment they knew they were accepted.

The third thing Tenzing did was go home to Darjeeling and found the Himalayan Mountaineering Institute. Jawaharlal Nehru, the Indian prime minister, said to Tenzing, Train Indians, and give me hundreds of Tenzings. That's what he did. The institute produced generations of climbers, including many young Sherpas from Khumbu. And they taught me, at sixteen, to love the mountains.

When Tenzing died in Darjeeling in 1986, the names of six Asian were known around the world – Confucius, Genghis Khan, the Buddha, Mahatma Gandhi, Mao Zedung, and Tenzing Sherpa. Only one of the six was a working man who'd carried a load on his back until he was thirty-nine.

At some point in the seventies Paul Bauer came to a reunion of old climbers at the Himalayan Mountaineering Institute. The one person he was hoping to meet, he said, was Ang Tsering. Tenzing told him Ang Tsering was dead. (The two men had never reconciled.) Several of the staff at the HMI were unhappy with this, and one of the kitchen staff told Bauer Ang Tsering was alive and in Darjeeling.

In a book published in 1955, Bauer had accused Ang Tsering of being faithless for not staying with Merkl as Gaylay had.[4] Ang Tsering, for his part, had long been bitter both at the way the Germans had behaved on Nanga Parbat and because they had never helped him afterward. But now they were old men. For both, the important memory was that they had been comrades on Kangchenjunga in 1929 and 1931. Ang Tsering received a message to meet Bauer the next morning. When he arrived where

Bauer was staying, it turned out the message had been incorrect. Ang Tsering had been supposed to come the night before, and now Bauer had gone.

When I was learning Sherpa in Namche in 2000, my teacher was Anu, a former climber and still a trekking sardar. As I struggled with my verbs, there was a constant shouting from another room. It was Anu's father, Palden.

In 1953, Palden had been forty. He worked as one of the mail runners for the Everest expedition. His job was to carry bags of letters from Base Camp to Kathmandu and back. He set the record, at five days, for running to Kathmandu. It now takes a fit Nepali seven days to walk half that distance, and then a ten-hour bus journey for the other half.[5]

When the expedition finished, Palden already had a house. So he used his wages to buy the twenty-one-volume edition of the Buddhist scriptures in Tibetan. These books are block-printed, on loose leaves. The set Palden bought were particularly holy because they had previously belonged to a prosperous merchant who had lived along the trade route from Khumbu to Lhasa. Whenever a learned monk came through, he would stay with that merchant and bless the books. One of Anu's earliest memories is the arrival of those books. The family still has them. Anu has had to replace the red cloth on the wooden covers. The leaves are light orange, and the prayer scarves around the covers are bright yellow.

To me, Palden's constant shouting sounded like dementia, the same words cried over and over. I used to work in geriatric hospitals, and I could not bear to meet him, so did not ask. The family told me Palden was now blind and deaf and only lay in bed.

One day we were sitting in the kitchen when a young woman came with the usual gifts of fried sweetbread, fruit, biscuits, and *rakshi*. The liquor was for Palden. She had come, as many other people did, to ask him for a blessing and long life. His blessing counted because he was the oldest man in Namche.

Anu was polite to her. After she left, he said he wished people wouldn't do that, but he couldn't stop them. His father liked to drink, always had. Now that he was old, Anu and his wife, Ang Lhamoo, looked after him. Generally youngest sons, such as Anu, are supposed to care for aged parents. As in other parts of the world, this often doesn't work out if the youngest has work elsewhere or is not as decent as he might be. But Anu was.

He felt the liquor was bad for his father. Anu couldn't forbid it, of course. He still gave his father a generous helping of liquor twice a day, morning and evening. He didn't want to. But Anu seemed to assume that even though his father was old and helpless, he was still a person with rights and a life.

Anu said that the trouble was that his father ate so little. The good side of that was that his stools only came every few days. They were small, hard, and easy to clean up. But there was an immense amount of urine from the liquor, and Anu found cleaning that a constant chore.

I thought of my father. I said to Anu, 'You're a good son. I hope I'm as good when my time comes.'

Anu said he mixed honey into the liquor every morning and evening, to get some nourishment into the old man. Anu went to the cupboard and took two jars out to show me. He bought the honey in Kathmandu, the highest quality, Anu said. Look at it, does it look pure to you? My father wants to live. He prays all day long. That's what the shouting is. He's calling 'Lama, Lama' and 'Buddha, Buddha.' He's shouting, asking for a long life. And he's also shouting over and over 'Buddha, give my son a long life.'

I listened then and could hear the words.

Palden died in the fall of 2000, while Anu was away on trekking work. Galtzen, who was a low-altitude sardar in 1952 and a high-altitude porter in 1953, is now the oldest man in Namche.

Khansa Sherpa carried twice to the South Col in 1953, three oxygen cylinders, sixty-seven pounds in all. At the end of the expedition they were all paid off in Tengboche. Khansa got the promised three-hundred-rupee bonus for reaching the South Col. When the paying was done, the strong wooden money boxes were empty. Khansa asked if he could have one. They said yes. Khansa keeps it in the small chapel in his lodge now, using it to store the small lamps that burn butter on ritual occasions.

He got his gear, too. I think everybody did. Like his father before him, Khansa sold his boots, jacket, and sleeping bag to a rich man for fifteen hundred rupees and used the money to buy a house and get married.

In the 1980s there was another conference of famous climbers at the Mountaineering Institute in Darjeeling. This time Ang Tsering went and sat in the audience with Da Namgyal, who had carried above the South Col on the first summit attempt in 1953. They listened to famous foreign and Indian climbers talking from the podium, all about themselves and what they had accomplished. The more Da Namgyal and Ang Tsering listened, the angrier they got. Finally they both started calling out to the people on the podium: What about the Sherpas? We carried the loads. What about us? Why are you only talking about yourselves?

Ang Tsering found, to his surprise, that he was shouting in Nepali, 'You would never have done it without the Sherpas.'

As he tells me this, Ang Tsering is laughing.

NOTES

NOTES

Introduction

1. I have since looked for him in Darjeeling, and nobody from the institute in those years remembers a Pemba, so maybe I have the name wrong.

2. There was Tenzing Norgay, *Man of Everest: The Autobiography of Tenzing*, told to James Ramsey Ullman (London: Harrap, 1955), and there is now the recent book by the anthropologist Sherry Ortner, *Life and Death on Mt. Everest: Sherpas and Himalayan Mountaineering* (Princeton: Princeton University Press, 1999).

3. J.) Norman Collie, *Climbing on the Himalaya and Other Mountain Ranges* (London: David Douglas, 1902), 35. For the 1895 expedition see Collie, 1–124; Major Charles G. Bruce, *Twenty Years in the Himalayas* (London: Edwin Arnold, 1910), 212–40; Brigadier General Charles G. Bruce, *Himalayan Wanderer* (London: Maclehose, 1934), 128–36.

4. Noel Odell, 'Reflections on Guideless Climbing,' *American Alpine Journal*, 1930, 123–4.

5. Bruce, *Twenty Years*, 216.

Chapter One: The Sherpas

Much of this chapter is based on my own research in Khumbu in 1995, 1998, and 2000. But for the background I have relied particularly on Stanley Stevens, *Claiming the High Ground: Sherpas, Subsistence, and Environmental Change in the Highest Himalaya* (New Delhi: Motilal Barnarsidas, 1996), and Christoph von Fürer-Haimendorf, *The Sherpas of Nepal: Buddhist Highlanders* (London: John Murray, 1964). Also very useful are Tenzing Norgay, *Autobiography*; Ortner, *Life and Death*; Sherry Ortner, *Sherpas Through Their Rituals* (Cambridge: Cambridge University Press, 1978); Sherry Ortner, *High Religion: A Cultural and Political History of Tibetan Buddhism* (New Delhi: Motilal Barnarsidas, 1989); Christoph von Fürer-Haimendorf, *Himalayan Traders: Life in Highland Nepal* (London: John Murray, 1975); Christoph von Fürer-Haimendorf, *The Sherpas Transformed; Social Change in a Buddhist Society of Nepal* (New Delhi; Motilal Barnarsidas, 1984); James Fisher, *Sherpas: Reflections on Change in Himalayan Nepal* (Berkeley: University of California Press, 1990); and Sherpa Thupten Lama, *The Sherpas and Sharkhumbu* (Kathmandu: Eco Himal, 1999).

1. The Sherpa name for the village of Namche is simply Nauje. Namche Bazaar is the Nepali and English name. Sherpa Thupten Lama, *The Sherpas*, argues passionately for using the Sherpa names, and in general I have done so, but made exceptions for Namche, Solu, and Everest, which are now the well-known English names of Nauje, Shorung, and Chomolungma.

2. Joe Simpson, *Dark Shadows Falling* (London: Vintage, 1998, first published 1997).

3. Since this was written, Appa has climbed Everest for the eleventh time.

4. Fürer-Haimendorf, *Buddhist Highlanders*, 74. Other estimates can be found in Fisher, *Sherpas*, 189; and Vincanne Adams, *Tigers of the Snow (and Other Virtual Sherpas): An Ethnography of Himalayan Encounters* (Princeton: Princeton University Press, 1996) 210.

5. This account of Tenzing's childhood is based on his autobiography and the recollections of people in Khumbu.

6. For Darjeeling in this period, see E. C. Dozey, *A Concise History of the Darjeeling District since 1835, with a Complete Itinerary of Tours in Sikkim and the District* (Calcutta: Mukherjee, 1989, first published 1922); L. S. S. O'Malley, *Darjeeling District Gazetteer*, 1907 edition (reprinted, no date); and Jahar Sen, *Darjeeling: A Favoured Retreat* (New Delhi: Indus, 1989). Tanka Bubba, *Dynamics of a Hill Society: The Nepalis in Darjeeling and Sikkim Himalayas* (Delhi: Mittal, 1989), is about modern Darjeeling, but useful for understanding the place of Sherpas in the local system of caste and class.

7. Dozey, *History*, 24–25.

Chapter Two: The First Expeditions

For the British expeditions to Everest, 1921–24, I have relied on interviews with Ang Tsering in 2000; Peter Hansen's delightful article, 'The Dancing Lamas of Everest: Cinema, Orientalism, and Anglo-Tibetan Relations in the 1920s,' *American Historical Review* 101, no. 3 (1996): 712–47; and the written accounts of the men who were there in C. K. Howard-Bury and others, *Mount Everest: The Reconnaissance, 1921* (London: Edwin Arnold, 1922); A. W. MacDonald, 'The Lama and the General,' *Kailash* 1, no. 3 (1973): 225–34; John Noel, *Through Tibet to Everest* (London: Edwin Arnold, 1927); Charles G. Bruce and others, *The Assault on Mount Everest, 1922* (New York: Longmans Green, 1923); T. Howard Somervell, *After Everest: The Experiences of a Mountaineer and Medical Missionary* (London: Hodder and Stoughton, 1936); Edward F. Norton, ed., *The Fight for Everest: 1924* (New York: Longmans Green, 1925); John Morris, *Hired to Kill* (London: Hart-Davis, 1960); and Tom Longstaff, *This My Voyage* (London: John Murray, 1950).

For the life of George Mallory, the best sources are Peter Gilman and Leni Gilman, *The Wildest Dream: Mallory, His Life and Conflicting Passions* (Seattle: Mountaineers, 2000); David Robertson, *George Mallory* (London: Faber, 1969), and Tom Holzel and Audrey Salkeld, *The Mystery of Mallory and Irvine* (London: Cape, 1986).

1. Gilman and Gilman, *Mallory*, 231.

2. Ibid., *Mallory*, 232.

3. For Tibetan politics and the British alliance, see Hansen, 'Dancing Lamas'; and Melvyn Goldstein, *A Modern History of Tibet, 1913–1951: The Demise of the Lamaist State* (Berkeley: University of California Press, 1989), 65–138.

4. For British officers looting, Clare Harris, *In the Image of Tibet: Tibetan Painting after 1959* (London: Reaktion, 1999), 28–31. For the villagers' fears in 1921, Howard-Bury, *Reconnaissance*, 89.

5. MacDonald, 'The Lama,' 229.

6. For Charlie Bruce, see Tony Gould, *Imperial Warriors: Britain and the Gurkhas* (London: Granta, 1999), 143–53; and Morris, *Hired to Kill*, 147.

7. MacDonald, 'The Lama,' 230.

8. Noel, *To Everest*, 105.

9. George Leigh-Mallory, 'Third Attempt,' in Bruce, *Assault*, 108.

10. This and the following quotes are from Noel, *To Everest*, 155–59.

11. Somervell, *After Everest*, 64.

12. Noel, *To Everest*, 158–59.

13. Robertson, *Mallory*, 199–200.

14. MacDonald, 'The Lama,' 231.

15. Ibid., 231–32.

16. C. G. Bruce, 'The Narrative of the Expedition,' in Bruce, *Assault*, 75.

17. MacDonald, 'The Lama,' 232.

18. Patrick French, *Younghusband: The Last Great Imperial Adventurer* (New York: Harper Collins, 1995), 336.

19. J. G. Bruce, 'Local Personnel,' in Norton, *Fight*, 343.

20. Noel, *To Everest*, 174.

21. Frank Smythe, *Camp Six: An Account of the 1933 Mount Everest Expedition* (London: Hodder and Stoughton, 1937), 5.

22. Noel, *To Everest*, 180–81.

23. Ibid., 186.

24. Ibid., 108.

25. Somervell, *After Everest*, 119.

26. Ibid., 120.

27. Ibid., 104. The official account of the expedition, edited by Norton and written jointly by several climbers, hardly mentions Hazard. This is probably because the other climbers were angry with him for leaving the four porters on the Col.

28. Ibid., 120.

29. E. F. Norton, 'The North Col,' in Norton, *Fight*, 87–88.

30. This is based on what Somervell told Noel surviving porters had said to him. See Noel, *To Everest*, 202.

31. Somervell, *After Everest*, 121.

32. Ibid.

33. Noel, *To Everest*, 202.

34. Hansen, 'Dancing Lamas,' 726–27. This account of the film and its consequences relies on Hansen.

35. Ibid., 729.

36. The exception to this consensus is Ang Tsering, who says that European climbers knew more about avalanches than Sherpas did.

37. H. P. S. Ahluwalia, *Faces of Everest* (New Delhi: Vikas, 1978), 92.

Chapter Three: The Germans

The main source for the 1932 expedition to Nanga Parbat is Elizabeth Knowlton, *The Naked Mountain* (New York: Putnam, 1933.) For nationalism in the North-West Frontier Province I have relied on Stephen Rittenberg, *Ethnicity, Nationalism and the Pakhtuns: The Independence Movement in India's North-West Frontier Province* (Durham, N.C.: Carolina Academic Press, 1988).

1. Peter Mierau, *Deutsche Himalaya Stiftung: Ihre Geschichte und Ihre Expeditionen* (München: Bergverlag, 1999), 170.

2. *Pathan* is the Hindi word. In their own language, they call themselves Pushtuns or Pukhtuns.

3. Sumit Sarkar, *Modern India, 1885–1947* (Basingstoke: Macmillan, 1989), 191.

4. Rittenberg, *Ethnicity*, 67.

5. Ibid., 68.

6. Strictly speaking, the deputy commissioner was in fact the leading official in the district – there was no commissioner. But Peshawar was a provincial capital, and so Metcalfe did have a superior in the city.

7. Rittenberg, *Ethnicity*, 104.

8. Knowlton, *Mountain*, 78.

9. Ibid., 86.

10. Ibid., 92.

11. Ibid., 112.

12. Ibid., 114.

13. Ibid., 118–19.

14. I do not have sources for what it felt like to be a sharecropper in Hunza in 1932. I do know, from my own field research, what it was like to be a sharecropper in eastern Afghanistan and Pakistan's NWFP in the 1970s. Nothing I have read on northern Pakistan suggests to me that it was any different in Hunza in 1932.

15. Knowlton, *Mountain*, 120.

16. Ibid., 207.

17. Ibid., 210.

18. Ibid.

19. Ibid., 272.

20. Ibid., 280–81.

21. Ibid., 280. See also Fritz Bechtold, *Nanga Parbat Adventure*, trans. H. E. G. Tyndale (London: John Murray, 1934), 6.

Chapter Four: Chits and Knives

The main sources for the 1934 German expedition to Nanga Parbat are Fritz Bechtold, *Nanga Parbat Adventure*, trans. H. E. G. Tyndale (London: John Murray, 1935), Nebuka Makoto, *Sherpa: Death and Glory in the Himalayas* (in Japanese) (Tokyo: Yama To Keikokusha 1966), 105–48; and my interviews with Ang Tsering.

1. The discussion of German politics that follows leans particularly on Chris Harman, *The Lost Revolution: Germany, 1918–1923*

(London: Bookmarks, 1982); Donny Gluckstein, *The Nazis, Capitalism and the Working Class* (London: Bookmarks, 1989); W. S. Allen, *The Nazi Seizure of Power: The Experience of a Single German Town, 1930–1935* (Chicago: University of Chicago Press, 1965); and Ian Kershaw, *Hitler, 1888–1936: Hubris* (London: Allen Lane, 1999).

2. Quoted in Mierau, *Stiftung*, 18.

3. On mountaineering and masculinity see Sherry Ortner, *Life and Death on Mount Everest: Sherpas and Himalayan Mountaineering* (Princeton: Princeton University Press, 1999), 149–85.

4. It could be argued that Merkl only included Knowlton because she was a good fund-raiser and would write newspaper articles and a book to help fund the expedition. And technically she was only the journalist. But she is there in the photographs of the expedition members, and Merkl did allow her to climb to Camp 4.

5. Karl Herrligkoffer, *Willy Merkl: Ein Weg Zum Nanga Parbat* (Munchen: Rudolf Rother, 1937), 25.

6. All Sherpas know the year of their birth in the Tibetan calendar because your personal astrology in later years depends on your annual birth sign. Ang Tsering said in December 2000 that he was ninety-seven years old. He was using the Tibetan method of counting ages: a child is one year old the moment it is born. At Tibetan New Year, at roughly the end of February, all one-year-old children become two, and all forty-year-old men become forty-one. By the European method of reckoning ages, Ang Tsering was ninety-five or ninety-six when I talked to him in May, and probably ninety-six in December.

7. Nebuka, *Sherpa*, chapter on Ang Tsering, 105–48.

8. To see what a difference this makes, take the example of Dipesh Chakrabarty's book, *Rethinking Working-Class History: Bengal, 1890–1940* (Delhi: Oxford University Press, 1996), first published 1989. Chakrabarty generalizes about the feelings, culture, and attitudes to authority of Bengali jute workers by using only documents their British bosses left behind. These documents depict the jute workers as hierarchical, traditional, and subservient, which is also how Chakrabarty sees them. When he

did his research in the 1980s, at least one hundred thousand people were still alive who had been jute workers in this period. Chakrabarty talked to none of them. By contrast, take Shahid Amin's stunning research on the Chauri Chara riot in 1922. This riot, an important turning point in Indian history, was the work of common people who were condemned at the time by both Gandhi and the British, and whose motives and feelings were therefore long hidden from history. So the only way to make sense of what the rioters did and felt was to combine the documents with oral history, which is what Amin did. See Shahid Amin, 'Gandhi as Mahatma: Gorakhpur District, Eastern UP, 1921-2,' Subaltern Studies (Delhi: Oxford University Press, 1984): 1-61; and Shahid Amin, Event, Metaphor, Memory: Chauri Chara in 1922 (Delhi: Oxford University Press, 1994).

9. Frank S. Smythe, The Kangchenjunga Adventure (London: Gollancz, 1930), 92.

10. Ang Tsering interviews.

11. Bechtold, Adventure, 98-99.

12. F. S. Smythe, Kamet Conquered (London: Gollancz, 1932), 37, 52.

13. Ibid., 90.

14. Ibid., 96.

15. Ibid., 105-6.

16. Ibid., 91.

17. Ibid., 187.

18. Ibid., 208.

19. Ibid., 212.

20. Ibid., 213-14.

21. ibid., 224 says that Lewa refused to go down any farther without the sahibs and makes his stopping at Camp 2 seem an act of loyalty. But then he immediately says that Lewa had to be carried down from Camp 2 by four men. This makes it seem likely that Lewa in fact stopped because he could go no farther and there was no one else to carry him.

22. Ibid., 225.

23. Ibid., 229.

24. Ibid., 235.

25. Maurice Herzog, *Annapurna, Conquest of the First 8,000-Metre Peak,* trans. Nea Morin and Janet Smith (London: Paladin, 1986, first published 1952), 198.

26. Bechtold, *Adventure,* 7.

27. Ibid., 15.

28. Alfred Drexel, 'Im Angesicht des Nanga Parbat,' *Reichsportsblatt,* 1934. The following quotes from Drexel's diary are taken from the same article.

29. Bechtold, *Adventure,* 16–17.

30. Ibid., 18.

31. Hermann Buhl, *Nanga Parbat Pilgrimage,* trans. Hugh Merrick (London: Penguin, 1982, first published 1956), 355.

32. Bechtold, *Adventure,* 40.

33. I would expect his name to be pronounced *Tseen Norboo,* but listening to Ang Tsering I heard *Teen.*

34. For one example, see the riveting book by Joe Simpson, *Touching the Void* (London: Vintage, 1997, first published 1988).

35. For Tsin Norbu cutting the rope, Ang Tsering and Pasang Phutar, both of whom were on the Kangchenjunga expedition. For searching each other for knives, Ang Tsering. For another account of the accident on Kangchenjunga, see Paul Bauer, *Himalayan Campaign: The German Attack on Kangchenjunga, the Second Highest Mountain in the World,* trans. Summer Austin (Oxford: Basil Blackwell, 1937), 139–47. In this published account Bauer suppressed the cutting of the rope, saying instead that it had been sawed through by a sharp rock around which it was belayed. It is possible that Tsin Norbu lied to Bauer, that Bauer believed him, and that the other porters did not disabuse him. It is more likely that Bauer did not welcome the sort of controversy that would have followed publication of the truth.

Chapter Five: Iron Determination

1. Bechtold, *Adventure,* 45, quoting Aschenbrenner's diary.

2. For altitude sickness, see Charles Houston, *Going Higher:*

Oxygen, Man and Mountains, 4th ed. (Shrewsbury: Swan Hill Press, 1999); Michael Ward, James Milledge, and John West, *High Altitude Medicine and Physiology,* 2nd ed. (London: Chapman Hall, 1995); and John West, *High Life: A History of High-Altitude Physiology and Medicine* (Oxford: Oxford University Press, 1988).

3. Bechtold, *Adventure,* 45.

4. Ibid., 46.

5. Ibid., 49.

6. Ibid., 47

7. Ibid., 47.

8. Ibid., 49.

9. Ibid., 48.

10. Mierau, *Stiftung,* 47.

11. Bechtold, *Adventure,* 51.

12. Mierau, *Stiftung,* 170.

13. Eric Roberts, *Welzenbach's Climbs: A Biographical Study and the Collected Writings of Willo Welzenbach* (Goring, UK: West Col, 1980), 247.

14. Bechtold, *Adventure,* 55.

15. Roberts, *Welzenbach's Climbs,* 250.

16. Erwin Schneider, 'Der Letzte Angriff,' *Reichsportsblatt,* 1934.

17. Bechtold, *Adventure,* 65.

18. Ibid., 64.

19. Ibid., 69.

20. Ibid., 70.

21. Ibid.

Chapter Six: The Storm

1. This discussion of caste and martial races comes partly from reading a large literature in anthropology, and partly from interviews with Dorjee Lhatoo. See also Philip Mason, *A Matter of Honour: An Account of the Indian Army, Its Officers and Men* (London: Cape, 1974); David Omissi, *The Sepoy and the Raj: The Indian Army, 1860–1940* (Basingstoke, Macmillan, 1994); and Tony Gould, *Imperial Warriors: Britain and the Gurkhas* (London: Granta, 1999).

2. This quote from Aschenbrenner's diary, and the ones that follow, are from Bechtold, *Adventure*, 73–76.

3. Ang Tsering told me about the Austrians using skis to leave the Sherpas. The translator of this book into German has pointed out that there are good reasons to doubt this. The most important is that skis were much heavier back then than now. Also, by the next year, 1935, Paul Bauer was a declared enemy of Schneider and Aschenbrenner, and tried to accuse them of just about anything possible. If they had used skis, and Bauer had known it, the whole world would have heard his cry of indictment. Of course, Bauer may not have listened to Sherpas on this point. But Colonel Bruce made his own inquiry into the matter in Darjeeling. He spoke Nepali, and he never mentioned skis.

All of this suggests that maybe they did not use the skis. However, Ang Tsering was quite insistent that they did. He spoke with Pasang Picture right after they both came down the mountain. In the two years after their return from Nanga Parbat, Ang Tsering and the Sherpa survivors visited back and forth a good deal in Darjeeling. If Ang Tsering says they used skis, I am inclined to believe him.

In any case, the really important point here is not whether Schneider and Aschenbrenner used skis, but that they untied themselves and left the two Sherpas to die. About this there is no question. Whether they did this on skis or on foot is a secondary matter.

4. In a speech at a memorial meeting for the dead in Germany later that year, Schneider remembered fondly 'how our porters [fell] about in their first attempts to move off with the strange pieces of wood on their feet.' Schneider, 'Der Letzte Angriff.'

5. Aschenbrenner does not mention leaving his sleeping bag with the three Sherpas, so he probably took it with him.

6. Bechtold, *Adventure*, 77.

7. Bechtold says Kitar told him later they dug themselves a cave in the snow. This was an old Alpine trick the porters could have learned from the Germans on Nanga Parbat two years before. The principle was the same as that of an igloo, but instead of building

an ice house, Alpinists dug them. They tunneled into the ice with their axes, making an entrance just large enough for one man at a time to wriggle into. Beyond the entrance, they dug a burrow just large enough for four men, in this case, to sleep.

Done right, the thick walls of snow and ice keep out the wind and the cold. The ceiling is kept low and the entrance narrow to conserve heat. The body heat of the four men then raises the temperature inside the cave. It is still below freezing, or the cave would melt. But it is a lot warmer than sleeping outside, or even in a tent.

The difficulty is making the cave. It has to be dug into ice or hard-packed snow that is almost ice. Otherwise it will collapse. This is always difficult work in the Himalayas at altitude, taking at least as much effort as strenuous climbing, and usually taking two hours or so. For the four porters, exhausted, without food or water, it must have been doubly difficult.

Also, Bechtold says later that Ang Tsering, Gaylay, and Merkl spent a night in an ice cave. Ang Tsering says they slept on the snow. Perhaps his memory is faulty, but it is an odd thing to forget doing. And if they were using ice caves, you would expect them to have dug one that first night in the high bivouac, when the Germans and the Sherpas were together. They did not. I suspect Bechtold was trying to hide some of the suffering.

8. Bechtold, *Adventure*, 78–79.

9. Ibid., 80.

10. Ibid.

Chapter Seven: Gaylay

1. Bechtold, writing his book in 1934, said that Ang Tsering told him Dakshi died on the third night in the high bivouac, and then Ang Tsering and Gaylay left the next morning. Ang Tsering told me he was quite sure Dakshi was still alive when he left. He says that even when he finally got down to safety, he told the sahibs that Dakshi might still be alive up there. I'm inclined to believe him for two reasons. First, he is precise about

who died when and where. Second, he is unlikely to want to say that Dakshi was alive when it might reflect poorly on him to leave a living man.

. A possible reason for this confusion is that by the time the expedition was over, Bechtold clearly admired and respected Ang Tsering. One of the issues he was wrestling with in writing his book, and to some extent covering up, was the widespread feeling among both Sherpas and British climbers that some of the Germans had left Sherpas behind, while the Sherpas had stayed with German climbers. Bechtold may have wanted to gloss over this incident for Ang Tsering's sake.

It's also possible that Ang Tsering, who's now an old man, misremembers. However, I think it's unlikely.

2. This is a free translation, by Anu Sherpa of Namche and myself, of the lyrics of 'Gold Patterned Khumbu' on the cassette *Music of the Sherpa People of Nepal: Shebru Dance-Songs of Namche (Khumbu)*, recorded by Gert-Matthias Wegner (Kathmandu: Eco Himal), 1999.

3. For a man like Ang Tsering, not all mountains were gods. Nor did he invent the idea that Nanga Parbat was a god. The local people knew and must have told the Sherpas that there were demons up there, and that the mountain itself was a spirit. As Muslims, they thought of that spirit not as a god to be worshipped but as a presence to be feared.

4. Paul Bauer, *The Siege of Nanga Parbat, 1856–1953*, trans. R. W. Rickmens (London: Hart-Davis, 1956), 162.

5. Bechtold's book, based on Ang Tsering's account in 1934, says that the porters had one sleeping bag. It was so stiff with snow they could not get inside it, but one man could use it as a groundsheet. Ang Tsering let Gaylay have it. Ang Tsering says they had left all the sleeping bags the first morning they abandoned Camp 8.

There are two explanations for this discrepancy. One is that Ang Tsering was ninety-six years old when we talked and his memory was at fault. The only thing that stuck in his mind was that he had slept outside on the snow unprotected. The other possibility is that Bechtold was softening the story because he

309

was ashamed the Sherpas were made to sleep outside.

6. Müllritter, in Bechtold, *Adventure*, 81–82.

7. Bechtold says they made a snow cave for shelter. Ang Tsering says they slept out on the snow. It would have taken a fit, rested mountaineer two hours or longer to dig an ice cave, perhaps longer. Again, I suspect Bechtold is making things seem less stark than they were.

8. Tenzing Norgay, *Autobiography*, 50.

9. Bechtold, *Adventure*, 83.

Chapter Eight: Darjeeling

1. Ang Tsering identified Aiwaa for me from the photograph, but he is not absolutely sure.

2. Bechtold, *Adventure*, 85.

3. Ibid., 86–87.

4. Tenzing Norgay, *Autobiography*, 50.

5. Ang Tsering's Himalayan Club book, in his possession.

Chapter Nine: The German Siege

1. Bauer, *Siege*, 103–4.

2. Paul Bauer to von Tschammer und Osten, December 4, 1934, in Mierau, *Stiftung*, 68. All translations from Germany are by Ruard Absaroka.

3. Bauer to von Tschammer, December 10, 1934, in Mierau, *Stiftung*, 170.

4. Paul Bauer, *Himalayan Quest: The German Expeditions to Siniolchum and Nanga Parbat*, trans. E. G. Hall (London: Nicholson and Watson, 1938), 98.

5. Paul Bauer, 'Nanga Parbat, 1937,' *Himalayan Journal* 10 (1938): 145.

6. Morris, in Kenneth Mason, 'In Memoriam: The Porters Who Died on Nanga Parbat, 1937,' *Himalayan Journal* 10 (1938): 191–92.

7. Hartmann's diary, in Bauer, *Quest*, 99. This account of the 1937 Nanga Parbat expedition is based on Bauer, *Quest*, 97–150;

Martin Pfeffer and others, 'The Disaster on Nanga Parbat, 1937,' *Alpine Journal* 255 (1937): 210–27; Bauer, 'Nanga Parbat, 1937,' 145–58; Bauer, *Siege*; and Mason, 'The Porters,' 189–92.

8. Hartmann's diary, in Bauer, *Quest*, 98–99.

9. Bauer, *Quest*, 129.

10. I am assuming that Da Thundu and the others went back up with Luft. There is no mention of this, one way or the other, in the sources. But on every other occasion in a long climbing life, Da Thundu was ready and willing. It's hard to imagine that he would not have wanted to know what happened.

11. This time Bauer does specify that Da Thundu went up.

12. Bauer, *Siege*, 113.

13. Ibid., 114.

14. H. W. Tilman, *Mount Everest, 1938* (Cambridge: Cambridge University Press, 1948), 27.

15. Bauer, *Siege*, 149.

16. Ibid., 161–62, and Fritz Bechtold, preface to second edition of *Deutsche am Nanga Parbat* (Munchen: F. Bruckman, 1939), 1–7.

17. Bauer, *Siege*, 160–61.

18. The photo can be found in Mierau, *Stiftung, 136*.

19. Bauer, *Siege*, 166.

20. Ibid.

21. For the 1939 Nanga Parbat expedition, see Peter Aufschnaiter, 'Diamir Side of Nanga Parbat Reconnaissance, 1939,' *Himalayan Journal* 14 (1947): 111–15; Lutz Chicken, 'Nanga Parbat Reconnaissance, 1939,' *Himalayan Journal* 14, (1947): 53–58; and Bauer, *Siege*, 175–80.

22. Anderl Heckmair, *My Life as a Mountaineer*, trans. Geoffrey Sutton (London: Gollancz, 1975), 124.

23. Peter Aufschnaiter, 'Escape to Lhasa, 1944–5; *Himalayan Journal* 14 (1947): 116–20; Heinrich Harrar, *Seven Years in Tibet*, trans. Richard Graves (London: Flamingo, 1997, first published 1955); and Hans Kopp, *Himalaya Shuttlecock*, trans. H. C. Stevens (London: Hutchinson, 1957), 69–160.

Chapter Ten: The Sherpa Survivors

1. H. W. Tilman, *The Ascent of Nanda Devi* (Cambridge: Cambridge University Press, 1937), 63.

2. Ibid., 28.

3. Photographs – Andrew Kaufman and William Putnam, *K2: The 1939 Tragedy* (Seattle: Mountaineers, 1992), 48 ff.

4. Kaufman and Putnam, *K2*, 33–34. My account of the 1939 expedition relies mainly on Kaufman and Putnam, who had access to the unpublished and important diary of the climber Jack Durrance. Their book is wise, sympathetic, and careful in the use of evidence. I have by and large followed their judgments. See also Chappell Cranmer and Fritz Wiessner, 'The Second American Expedition to K2,' *American Alpine Journal* 4 (1940): 9–19; Eaton Cromwell, 'Obituaries, Francis Dudley Wolfe,' *American Alpine Journal* 4 (1940): 121–23; George Sheldon, 'Lost Behind the Ranges,' *Saturday Evening Post*, March 16 and 23, 1940; Fritz Wiessner, 'The K2 Expedition of 1939,' *Appalachia* 31 (1956): 60–77.

5. G. O. Dyhrenfurth, *To the Third Pole: The History of the High Himalaya*, trans. Hugh Merrick (London: Werner Lauire, 1955), 80.

6. Gonden and Dawa Thempa interviews.

7. 'In Memoriam: Pasang Kikuli, Phinsoo Sherpa and Pasang Kitar,' *Himalayan Journal* 12 (1940): 134–35.

8. Frank S. Smythe, *Kamet Conquered* (London: Gollancz, 1932), 96.

9. Frank S. Smythe, *The Valley of Flowers* (London: Hodder and Stoughton, 1938), 8–9.

10. Ibid., 113.

11. The following account of what happened on Kedarnath is based on the rather different accounts in Tenzing Norgay's *Autobiography*, 103–6; A. Lohner, Andre Roch, Alfred Sutter, and Ernst Feuz, 'The Swiss Garwhal Expedition of 1947,' *Himalayan Journal* 15 (1949): 26–28; and the account that Dorjee Lhatoo had from Andre Roch in Switzerland many years later, from Dorjee Lhatoo interviews.

12. Tenzing Norgay, *Autobiography*, 105–6.

Chapter Eleven: Tenzing Meets the Guides

1. For a delightful account of the early days of mountaineering, see Peter Hansen, 'Albert Smith, the Alpine Club, and the Invention of Mountaineering in Mid-Victorian Britain,' *Journal of British Studies* 34 (July 1995): 300–24.

2. John Morris, *Hired to Kill* (London: Hart-Davis, 1960), 145.

3. This account of Paul Petzoldt's life is based on the book by his wife, Patricia Petzoldt, *On Top of the World: My Adventures with My Mountain-Climbing Husband* (London: Collins, 1954). It's long out of print, but a joyous read, if you get the chance.

4. Ibid., 57.

5. Ibid., 79.

6. Ibid., 87.

7. Ibid., 105.

8. Ibid., 140–41.

9. Ibid., 146.

10. Maurice Herzog, *Annapurna: Conquest of the First 8,000-Metre Peak*, trans. Nea Morin and Janet Smith (London: Paladin, 1986, first published 1952), 71.

11. Ibid., 96.

12. Ibid., 137–38.

13. This account of the 1952 Swiss expeditions is based mainly on Tenzing, *Autobiography*, 182–220; and also on Galtzen interviews; Nawang Gombu interviews; Mingma Chering interview; Ang Tsering interviews; and Rene Dittert, Gabriel Chevalley, and Raymond Lambert, *Forerunners to Everest: The Story of the Two Swiss Expeditions of 1952*, trans. Malcolm Barnes (London: Allen and Unwin, 1954).

14. Tenzing, *Autobiography*, 182.

15. Ibid., 221.

16. Ibid., 184.

17. Ibid., 185.

18. The quotes that follow: Ibid., 193–201.

19. Ibid., 209–10.

Chapter Twelve: The Tribulation of a Sardar

1. For a useful and detailed account of what Sherpas were where at this point, and what expeditions they had worked on, see L. Krenek, 'Roll of Darjeeling Porters,' *Himalayan Journal* 16 (1950–51): 121–33.

2. Tenzing, *Autobiography*, 222–23.

3. Ibid., 231.

Chapter Thirteen: 1953

1. Karl Herrligkoffer, *Nanga Parbat*, trans. Eleanor Brockett and Anton Ehrenzweig (London: Elek, 1954), 97. This account of the 1953 expedition to Nanga Parbat is based on Herrligkoffer, 97–238; and Hermann Buhl, *Nanga Parbat Pilgrimage*, trans. Hugh Merrick (London: Penguin, 1982, first published 1956), 338–420. Also useful are G. J. Sutton, 'Review of *The Siege of Nanga Parbat, 1856–1953*, by Paul Bauer,' *Himalayan Journal* 20 (1957), 145–46; and G. O. Dyhrenfurth, *To the Third Pole: The History of the High Himalaya*, trans. Hugh Merrick (London: Werner Laurie, 1955), 181–83.

2. Buhl, *Pilgrimage*, 44.

3. Herrligkoffer, *Nanga Parbat*, 135.

4. Ibid., 148.

5. For the traditions of Balti and Hunza high-altitude porters, see Kenneth MacDonald and David Butz, 'Investigating Portering Relations as a Locus for Transcultural Interaction in the Karakorum Region, Northern Pakistan,' *Mountain Research and Development* 18 (1998): 333–43; and Kenneth MacDonald, 'Push and Shove: Spatial history and the construction of a portering economy in Northern Pakistan,' *Comparative Studies in Society and History* 40 (1998): 287–317.

6. Buhl, *Pilgrimage*, 380–81.

7. Ibid., 392–93.

8. The main sources for the 1953 climb are Tenzing Norgay, *Autobiography*; Edmund Hillary, *View from the Summit* (New York:

Doubleday, 1999), 1–20, 104–17; John Hunt, *The Ascent of Everest* (London: Hodder and Stoughton, 1953); Khansa interviews; Nawang Gombu interviews; Walt Unsworth, *Everest*, 1st ed. (London: Allen Lane, 1981), 314–42. See also Edmund Hillary, *High Adventure* (London: Hodder and Stoughton, 1956), 129–238; Edmund Hillary, *Nothing Venture, Nothing Win* (London: Quality Book Club, 1976), 144–62; Wilfred Noyce, *South Col: One Man's Adventure on the Ascent of Everest, 1953* (London: Heinemann, 1954); George Lowe, *Because It Is There* (London: Cassell, 1959), 20–40; and James Morris, *Coronation Everest* (London: Faber, 1958).

9. Tenzing, *Autobiography*, 235.

10. Edmund Hillary, *View*, 112.

11. Ibid., 113.

12. Ibid., 113–14.

13. Tenzing, *Autobiography*, 239.

14. Hillary, *View*, 116.

15. They also had some smaller cylinders weighing eleven and a half pounds, but as far as I can make out, they only took the larger ones up to the South Col.

16. Hillary, *View*, 3.

17. Tenzing, *Autobiography*, 252.

18. Hillary, *View*, 4–5.

Chapter Fourteen: Home

1. Hillary, *View*, 20.

2. For the Cho Oyu expedition in 1954, see Herbert Tichy, *Cho Oyu: By Favour of the Gods*, trans. Basil Creighton (London: Methuen, 1957).

3. For Tenzing's later life see the second volume of his autobiography, *After Everest: An Autobiography*, with Malcolm Barnes (New Delhi: Vikas, 1977).

4. Bauer, *Siege*, 100.

5. For Palden's life, see Nebuka, *Sherpa*, 207–31.

SOURCES AND BIBLIOGRAPHY

I have worked my way through the published sources on Sherpas and on Himalayan mountaineering. However, the bibliography here includes only the works cited in the text. Unfortunately, I have been unable to gain access to the records and climbers' diaries from the 1934 expedition to Nanga Parbat in the archives of the German climbing club in Munich. The club has so far been unable to raise enough money to sort and catalog their extensive records and so felt unable to grant access. Peter Mierau, the only historian so far given access to the records, and the author of an excellent recent history of the German Himalayan Foundation in the 1930s, assures my research assistant Ruard Absaroka that the archive is indeed not in a state to use. Moreover, all the German and Austrian veterans of 1934 are now dead.

This is unfortunate, but not as much of a handicap as it might have been, since this is primarily a book about Sherpas rather than European climbers. My main unpublished sources were interviews with Sherpa climbers, their wives, and their children.

I spent two months in Namche Bazaar in 1995, a month in 1997, and four months in 2000. During 1995 I studied the Sherpa language there with Nwang Dhoka, and in 2000 with Anu as my teacher. My command of Sherpa allowed basic conversation.

Where people spoke Sherpa, I sometimes interviewed them alone and sometimes took Anu with me as a translator. Where they spoke reasonable English, and many did, we worked in English. Where they spoke Nepali, one of their relatives or friends would translate for me.

The standard way to do oral history is to see the informant once, make a tape recording, and then a transcript of the tape. I did this a few times when working in Sherpa. But I quickly turned to more informal methods as well. I had two kinds of interviewing experience to fall back on. In 1971–73 I did anthropological field research in Afghanistan, then later worked as a counselor in health clinics in Britain for many years. In both cases, I'd found it helpful to look straight at people, listen carefully, and train myself to write up verbatim notes afterward. With practice, you can remember an enormous amount. The great advantage to this method is that it makes you a good listener. Trying to remember makes you try to really hear. It's all too easy to forget that people talk well, or badly, because of what they see, or don't see, on your face.

I'd also learned from anthropology and counseling that it helps to go back to see people over and over. This gives the person a chance to get to know me and to judge what they should tell me and what I can understand.

In this research, too, I found it useful to listen and to remember. When I forgot, I went back and asked again. During some interviews I made tapes in Nepali or Sherpa, in more I did not. In some I took notes as I went along, particularly in later interviews with Ang Tsering when he knew me well. In most cases I didn't take notes until afterward. Everyone knew I was a historian writing a book, and thus they edited what they said accordingly. They were speaking for the record. I have suppressed almost nothing of what people told me. In some cases, however, I have not given my source.

After the research was over, I realized that I could have worked only in English with translators. But I'm sure that if I'd done so, I would have missed a lot of what people were thinking and feeling. My command of the Sherpa language was basic at best.

But trying to learn it did open up for me some of the complexities of Sherpa culture.

Again, I could simply have done interviews. In ways that are probably not obvious in the book, but are still important, living in Namche for a total of seven months made an enormous difference to my understanding of what had happened in history. Particularly important was sitting in people's kitchens, watching who came and went, and also seeing how trekkers and climbers today behave with Sherpas.

List of Interviews

Ang Lhamoo, Namche, many times, in Sherpa, February to April 2000.

Major Ang Purba Sherpa, Darjeeling, several times, in English, May and December 2000.

Ang Rita Sherpa of Kunde, several times, in Kathmandu, in English, April 2000.

Ang Tashi, Khumjung, once, in English, 1997.

Ang Tsering, Darjeeling, many times, in Nepali, May and December 2000.

Anu, Namche, many times, in Sherpa and English, February to April 2000.

Chewang Nima, Thamo, once, in English, February 2000.

Dawa Thempa, Darjeeling, many times, in English, May and December 2000.

Dorjee Lhatoo, Darjeeling, several times, in English, May and December 2000.

Galtzen, Namche, twice, in Sherpa, April 2000.

Gonden, Darjeeling, once, in Nepali, December 2000.

Jamie MacGuiness, Namche, several times, in English, March 2000.

Kami Rita, Thame, twice, in English, February 2000.

Khansa, Namche, in English, January to April 2000.

Lhakpa Diki, Darjeeling, once, in Nepali, December 2000.

Lhamoo Iti, Darjeeling, once, in Nepali, December 2000.

Mingma Chering, Thame, once, in English, February 2000.
Namdu, Namche, several times, in Sherpa, March and April 2000.
Nawang Gombu, Darjeeling, twice, in English, May and December 2000.
Nwang Dhoka Sherpa, Namche, many times, in English and Sherpa, 1995, 1997, and 2000.
Pasang Digi, Thame, once, in Sherpa, February 2000.
Pasang Kami, Namche, several times, in English, March and April 2000.
Pasang Phutar, Darjeeling, twice, in Sherpa and Nepali, May and December 2000.
Pasang Phuti, Darjeeling, once, in Nepali, December 2000.
Colonel (Ms) Tshering Doma, Paul, Darjeeling, twice, in English, December 2000.
Pemba, Namche, several times, in English and Sherpa, January to April 2000.
Phu Shitta, Kunde, once, in Sherpa, April 2000.
Tawa, Kathmandu, Lukla, and Namche, many times, in English and Sherpa, January to April 2000.

Bibliography

Adams, Vincanne. *Tigers of the Snow (and Other Virtual Sherpas): An Ethnography of Himalayan Encounters*. Princeton: Princeton University Press, 1996.

Ahluwalia, H. P. S. *Faces of Everest*. New Delhi: Vikas, 1978.

Allen, W. S. *The Nazi Seizure of Power: The Experience of a Single German Town, 1930–1935*. Chicago: University of Chicago Press, 1965.

Amin, Shahid, 'Gandhi as Mahatma: Gorakhpur District, Eastern UP, 1921–2.' *Subaltern Studies* 3 (Delhi: Oxford University Press) (1984): 1–61.

———. *Event, Metaphor, Memory: Chauri Chara in 1922*. Delhi: Oxford University Press, 1995.

Aufschnaiter, Peter. 'Diamir Side of Nanga Parbat Reconnaissance, 1939.' *Himalayan Journal* 14 (1947): 111–15.

———. 'Escape to Lhasa, 1944–5.' *Himalayan Journal* 14 (1947): 116–20.

Bauer, Paul. *Himalayan Campaign: The German Attack on Kangchenjunga, the Second Highest Mountain in the World.* Trans. Summer Austin. Oxford: Basil Blackwell, 1937.

———. *Himalayan Quest: The German Expeditions to Siniolchum and Nanga Parbat.* Trans. E. G. Hall. London: Nicholson and Watson, 1938.

———. 'Nanga Parbat, 1937.' *Himalayan Journal* 10 (1938): 145–58.

———. *The Siege of Nanga Parbat, 1856–1953.* Trans. R. W. Rickmers. London: Hart-Davis, 1956.

Bechtold, Fritz. *Deutsche am Nanga Parbat.* 2nd ed. Munchen: F. Bruckman, 1939.

———. 'The German Expedition to Nanga Parbat, 1934.' *Himalayan Journal* 7 (1935): 27–37.

———. *Nanga Parbat Adventure.* Trans. H. E. G. Tyndale. London: John Murray, 1934.

Bruce, Charles Granville. *Himalayan Wanderer.* London: Maclehose, 1934.

———. *Twenty Years in the Himalayas.* London: Edwin Arnold, 1910.

Bruce, Charles Granville, et al. *The Assault on Mount Everest, 1922.* New York: Longmans Green, 1923.

Bubba, Tanka. *Dynamics of a Hill Society: The Nepalis in Darjeeling and Sikkim Himalayas.* Delhi: Mittal, 1989.

Buhl, Hermann. *Nanga Parbat Pilgrimage.* Trans. Hugh Merrick. London: Penguin, 1982, first published 1956.

Chakrabarty, Dipesh. *Rethinking Working-Class History: Bengal, 1890–1940.* Delhi: Oxford University Press, 1989.

Chicken, Lutz. 'Nanga Parbat: Reconnaissance, 1939.' *Himalayan Journal* 14 (1947): 53–58.

Collie, J. Norman. *Climbing on the Himalaya and Other Mountain Ranges.* London: David Douglas, 1902.

Cranmer, Chappell, and Fritz Wiessner. 'The Second American Expedition to K2.' *American Alpine Journal* 4 (1940); 9–19.

Crawford, C. G. 'Everest 1933: Extracts from the Everest Diary of C. G. Crawford.' *Alpine Journal* 46 (1934): 111–29.

Cromwell, Eaton. 'Obituaries, Francis Dudley Wolfe.' *American Alpine Journal* 4 (1940): 121–23.

Dash, A. J. *Darjeeling*. Alipore, Bengal: Bengal District Gazetteers, 1947.

Dittert, Rene, Gabriel Chevalley, and Raymond Lambert, *Forerunners to Everest: The Story of the Two Swiss Expeditions of 1952*. Trans. Malcolm Barnes. London: Allen and Unwin, 1954.

Dozey, E. C. *A Concise History of Darjeeling District since 1835*. Calcutta: Mukherjee, 1922.

Drexel, Alfred. 'Im Angesicht des Nanga Parbat.' *Reichsportsblatt*, 1934.

Dyhrenfurth, G. O. *To the Third Pole: The History of the High Himalaya*. Trans. Hugh Merrick. London: Werner Laurie, 1955.

Fisher, James. *Sherpas: Reflections on Change in Himalayan Nepal*. Berkeley: University of California Press, 1990.

French, Patrick. *Younghusband: The Last Great Imperial Adventurer*. New York: Harper Collins, 1995.

Fürer-Haimendorf, Christoph von. *Himalayan Traders: Life in Highland Nepal*. London: John Murray, 1975.

———. *The Sherpas of Nepal: Buddhist Highlanders*. London: John Murray, 1964.

———. *The Sherpas Transformed: Social Change in a Buddhist Society of Nepal*. New Delhi: Motilal Barnarsidas, 1984.

Gilman, Peter, and Leni Gilman. *The Wildest Dream: Mallory, His Life and Conflicting Passions*. Seattle: Mountaineers, 2000.

Gluckstein, Donny. *The Nazis, Capitalism and the Working Class*. London: Bookmarks, 1989.

'Gold Patterned Khumbu.' On the cassette *Music of the Sherpa People of Nepal: Shebru Dance-Songs of Namche (Khumbu)*. Recorded by Gert-Matthias Wegner. Kathmandu: Eco Himal, 1999.

Goldstein, Melvyn. *A Modern History of Tibet, 1913–1951: The Demise of the Lamaist State*. Berkeley: University of California Press, 1989.

Gould, Tony. *Imperial Warriors: Britain and the Gurkhas*. London: Granta, 1999.

Hansen, Peter. 'Albert Smith, the Alpine Club, and the Invention of Mountaineering in Mid-Victorian Britain.' *Journal of British Studies* 34 (July 1995): 300–324.

———. 'The Dancing Lamas of Everest: Cinema, Orientalism, and Anglo-Tibetan Relations in the 1920s.' *American Historical Review* 101, no. 3 (1996): 712–47.

Harman, Chris. *The Lost Revolution: Germany, 1918–1923.* London: Bookmarks, 1982.

Harrar, Heinrich. *Seven Years in Tibet.* Trans. Richard Graves. London: Flamingo, 1997, first published 1955.

Harris, Clare. *In the Image of Tibet: Tibetan Painting after 1959.* London: Reaktion, 1999.

Heckmair, Anderl, *My Life as a Mountaineer.* Trans. Geoffrey Sutton. London: Gollancz, 1975.

Herrligkoffer, Karl. *Nanga Parbat.* Trans. Eleanor Brockett and Anton Ehrenzweig. London: Elek, 1954.

———. *Willy Merkl: Ein Weg Zum Nanga Parbat.* Munchen: Rudolf Rother, 1937.

Herzog, Maurice. *Annapurna: Conquest of the First 8,000-Metre Peak.* Trans. Nea Morin and Janel Smith. London: Paladin, 1986, first published 1952.

Hillary, Edmund. *High Adventure.* London: Hodder and Stoughton, 1955.

———. *Nothing Venture, Nothing Win.* London: Quality Book Club, 1976.

———. *View from the Summit.* New York: Doubleday, 1999.

Holzel, Tom, and Audrey Salkeld. *The Mystery of Mallory and Irvine.* London: Cape, 1986.

Houston, Charles, *Going Higher: Oxygen, Man and Mountains.* 4th ed. Shrewsbury: Swan Hill Press, 1999.

Howard-Bury, Charles K, et al. *Mount Everest: The Reconnaissance, 1921.* London: Edwin Arnold, 1922.

Hunt, John. *The Ascent of Everest.* London: Hodder and Stoughton, 1953.

'In Memoriam: Pasang Kikuli, Phinsoo Sherpa and Pasang Kitar.' *Himalayan Journal* 12 (1940): 134–35.

Kauffman, Andrew, and William Putnam. *K2: The 1939 Tragedy.*

Seattle: Mountaineers, 1992.

Kershaw, Ian. *Hitler, 1988–1936: Hubris.* London: Allen Lane, 1999.

Knowlton, Elizabeth. *The Naked Mountain.* New York: Putnam, 1934.

Kopp, Hans. *Himalaya Shuttlecock.* Trans. H. C. Stevens. London: Hutchinson, 1957.

Krenek, L. 'Roll of Darjeeling Porters.' *Himalayan Journal* 16 (1950–51): 121–33.

Lama, Sherpa Thupten. *The Sherpas and Sharkhumbu.* Kathmandu: Eco Himal, 1999.

Lohner, A., Andre Roch, Alfred Sutter, and Ernst Feuz. 'The Swiss Garwhal Expedition of 1947.' *Himalayan Journal* 15 (1949): 18–45.

Longstaff, Tom. *This My Voyage.* London: John Murray, 1950.

Lowe, George. *Because It Is There.* London: Cassell, 1959.

MacDonald, A. W. 'The Lama and the General.' *Kailash* 1, no. 3 (1973): 225–34.

MacDonald, Kenneth. 'Push and Shove: Spatial history and the construction of a portering economy in Northern Pakistan.' *Comparative Studies in Society and History* 40 (1998): 287–317.

MacDonald, Kenneth, and David Butz. 'Investigating Portering Relations as a Locus for Transcultural Interaction in the Karakorum Region, Northern Pakistan.' *Mountain Research and Development* 18 (1998): 333–43.

Mason, Kenneth. 'In Memoriam: The Porters Who Died on Nanga Parbat, 1937.' *Himalayan Journal* 10 (1938): 189–92.

Mason, Philip. *A Matter of Honour: An Account of the Indian Army, Its Officers and Men.* London: Cape, 1974.

Mierau, Peter. *Deutsche Himalaya Stiftung: Ihre Geschichte und Ihre Expeditionen.* Munchen: Bergverlag, 1999.

Morris, James. *Coronation Everest.* London: Faber, 1958.

Morris, John. *Hired to Kill.* London: Hart-Davis, 1960.

Nebuka Makoto. *Sherpa: Death and Glory in the Himalayas.* In Japanese. Tokyo: Yama To Keikokusha, 1996.

Noel, John. *Through Tibet to Everest.* London: Edwin Arnold, 1927.

Norgay, Tenzing. *After Everest: An Autobiography.* With Malcolm Barnes. New Delhi: Vikas, 1977.

———. *Man of Everest: The Autobiography of Tenzing.* Told to James Ramsey Ullman. London: Harrap, 1955.

Norton, E. F., et al. *The Fight for Everest: 1924.* New York: Longmans Green, 1925.

Noyce, Wilfred. *South Col: One Man's Adventure on the Ascent of Everest, 1953.* London: Heinemann, 1954.

Odell, Noel. 'Reflections on Guideless Climbing.' *American Alpine Journal*, 1930, 123–24.

O'Malley, L. S. S. *Darjeeling District Gazetteer.* 1907 edition, reprinted no date.

Omissi, David. *The Sepoy and the Raj: The Indian Army, 1860–1940.* Basingstoke: Macmillan, 1994.

Ortner, Sherry. *High Religion: A Cultural and Political History of Tibetan Buddhism.* New Delhi: Motilal Barnarsidas, 1989.

———. *Life and Death on Mount Everest: Sherpas and Himalayan Mountaineering.* Princeton: Princeton University Press, 1999.

———. *Sherpas Through Their Rituals.* Cambridge: Cambridge University Press, 1978.

Petzoldt, Patricia. *On Top of the World: My Adventures with My Mountain-Climbing Husband.* London: Collins, 1954.

Pfeffer, Martin, et al. 'The Disaster on Nanga Parbat, 1937.' *Alpine Journal* 255 (1937): 210–27.

Rittenberg, Stephen. *Ethnicity, Nationalism and the Pakhtuns: The Independence Movement in India's North-West Frontier Province.* Durham, N.C.: Carolina Academic Press, 1988.

Roberts, Eric. *Welzenbach's Climbs: A Biographical Study and the Collected Writings of Willo Welzenbach.* Goring, UK: West Col, 1980.

Robertson, David. *George Mallory.* London: Faber, 1969.

Russell, Scott. 'George Finch – the Mountaineer. A Memoir.' In George Ingle Finch, *The Making of a Mountaineer.* 2nd ed. Bristol: Arrowsmith, 1988.

Sarkar, Sumit. *Modern India, 1885–1947.* 2nd ed. Basingstoke: Macmillan, 1989.

Schneider, Erwin. 'Der Letzte Angriff.' *Reichsportsblatt*, 1934.

Sen, Jahar. *Darjeeling: A Favoured Retreat.* New Delhi: Indus, 1989.

Sheldon, George. 'Lost Behind the Ranges.' *Saturday Evening Post,* March 16 and 23, 1940.

Sherpa, Ang Pinjo. *Sherpa Nepali English: A Language Guide for Beginners.* Kathmandu: Eco Himal, 1999.

Simpson, Joe. *Dark Shadows Falling.* London: Vintage, 1998, first published 1997.

———. *Touching the Void.* London: Vintage, 1997, first published 1988.

Smythe, Frank S. *Camp Six: An Account of the 1933 Mount Everest Expedition.* London: Hodder and Stoughton, 1937.

———. *Kamet Conquered.* London: Gollancz, 1932.

———. *The Kangchenjunga Adventure.* London: Gollancz, 1930.

———. *The Valley of Flowers.* London: Hodder and Stoughton, 1938.

Somervell, T. Howard. *After Everest: The Experiences of a Mountaineer and Medical Missionary.* London: Hodder and Stoughton, 1936.

Stevens, Stanley. *Claiming the High Ground: Sherpas, Subsistence, and Environmental Change in the Highest Himalaya.* New Delhi: Motilal Barnarsidas, 1996.

Sutton, G. J. 'Review of *The Siege of Nanga Parbat, 1856–1953,* by Paul Bauer.' *Himalayan Journal* 20 (1957): 145–46.

Tichy, Herbert. *Cho Oyu: By Favour of the Gods.* Trans. Basil Creighton. London: Methuen, 1957.

Tilman, H. W. *The Ascent of Nanda Devi.* Cambridge: Cambridge University Press, 1937.

———. *Mount Everest, 1938.* Cambridge: Cambridge University Press, 1948.

Unsworth, Walt. *Everest: A Mountaineering History.* 1st ed. London: Allen Lane, 1981.

Ward, Michael, James Milledge, and John West. *High Altitude Medicine and Physiology.* 2nd ed. London: Chapman Hall, 1995.

West, John. *High Life: A History of High-Altitude Physiology and Medicine.* Oxford: Oxford University Press, 1988.

Wiessner, Fritz. 'The K2 Expedition of 1939.' *Appalachia* 31 (1956): 60–77.

ACKNOWLEDGMENTS

I need to thank many people. First, Ang Tsering Sherpa of Darjeeling, a good man of great heart, without whom this would have been a far inferior book.

Nwang Dhoka of Namche was my first Sherpa-language teacher, a woman of quiet good sense, intelligence, and kindness. I am grateful to her and all her family, particularly her mother, Namdu, for being such kind hosts in Namche each time I have stayed there.

Anu was my Sherpa teacher in Namche in 2000. An experienced climber himself, he was a perceptive guide to Sherpa culture, work, love, faith, and weaknesses. He understands both his own society and the human condition, and he was constantly anxious that my research should work. I was lucky to find him.

In Darjeeling, Tenzing Loodon and Lhamoo Iti were careful hosts. Tenzing Loodon, Dawa Thempa, and Major Ang Phurba Sherpa were kind translators. Dorjee Lhatoo has been thinking about mountaineering history for many years and graciously made sense for me of many social processes I had been struggling to understand. Tshering Doma Paul and her sister gave me a lunch on Christmas Eve that was much appreciated. I am especially grateful to Ang Lhamoo of Namche, who made me so much tea and food over the months.

And of course there are the other people I interviewed. I am deeply grateful to them. In Nepal there was Khansa, Ang Lhamoo, Anu, Ang Rita, Galtzen, Jamie MacGuiness, Mingma Chering, Namdu, Nwang Dhoka, Pasang Digi, Pasang Kami, Phu Shitta, and Tawa. From Darjeeling I have to thank Ang Tsering, Major Ang Purba Sherpa, Dawa Thempa, Dorjee Lhatoo, Gonden, Lhakpa Diki, Lhamoo Iti, Nawang Gombu, Colonel Tshering Doma Paul, Pasang Phutar, and Pasang Phuti.

I am also grateful to the staff of the Baker Library at Dartmouth College in New Hampshire, the library of the School of Oriental and African Studies in London, the Geography Library at the University of Oxford, and Manor Gardens Library in Islington.

Pim Fakkeldy has been a great help with the photographs. I had careful and perceptive readers of various drafts of the manuscript, each of whom changed it in important ways: Nancy Lindisfarne, Laura Langlie, Richard Moth, Terry Neale, and Barbara Neale. Nancy was also my constant support, encouragement, and muse. I had the good fortune to have her with me twice in Nepal. She is the best field researcher I have met, and I tried to learn as much as I could from her.

Laura Langlie in New York was the ideal agent, a careful editor, demanding, gentle, clear, and very good at business. I have been a professional writer for twenty years, and to any fellow writer reading this, I can only say, if you get the chance of having Laura as your agent, jump at it.

Ruard Absaroka helped with the German sources and did all the translations from the German. I also benefited from his considerable knowledge of the period, and many insights into what the climbers might have been thinking. Ed Lindisfarne did the translation from the Japanese and I am grateful to him too.

At St Martin's Press in New York, Ezra Fitz was an excellent editor. His suggestions were thoughtful, and he stretched me as a writer, particularly in encouraging me to imagine what the Sherpa porters might have felt. Carolyn Dunkley has seen the book through to publication. At Little, Brown UK, Linda Silverman was a joy to work with on the pictures. Tim Whiting was a careful, meticulous and fun editor.

We were unable to find the copyright holders for the German photographs we have used although every effort has been made to trace them.

Finally, I have dedicated this book to my father, Terry (Walter C.) Neale. He and my mother gave me India, taking the family there for three years of my childhood, in Ludhiana, Chandigarh, and Lucknow. They were careful to live a nonexpatriate life among Indian friends and always sent us to the second-best school in town, so my friends, too, were all Indians. From both my parents I learned to listen with respect to the people who do the work of the world. Terry did pioneering work in Indian economic history, and I like to think this book follows in his footsteps. I learned my love of mountains from him on many walks. And when I was halfway through this book, I was well and truly stuck. I knew something was wrong with the manuscript, but not what. Terry read it, sat me down, and told me my trouble was looking over my shoulder at the European climbers and trying to write a mountaineering book. Forget the sahibs, he said, who cares about them? Tell me about the Sherpas. So that's what I did, and the writing flowed.

INDEX